Immigration Policy in Turmoil

Immigration Policy in Turmoil

THEODORE B. GUNDERSON

Nova Science Publishers, Inc.
New York

Senior Editors: Susan Boriotti and Donna Dennis
Coordinating Editor: Tatiana Shohov
Office Manager: Annette Hellinger
Graphics: Wanda Serrano
Book Production: Matthew Kozlowski, Jonathan Rose and Jennifer Vogt
Circulation: Cathy DeGregory, Ave Maria Gonzalez and Raheem Miller
Communications and Acquisitions: Serge P. Shohov

Library of Congress Cataloging-in-Publication Data

Immigration policy in turmoil.
    p.   cm.
ISBN 1-59033-155-9
    1. United States--Emigration and immigration--Government policy. 2. Emigration and immigration law--United States.
✓ JV6483.I5547 ᴈ00ᴈ   2002
    325.73--dc21   2001058741

Copyright © 2002 by Nova Science Publishers, Inc.
            227 Main Street, Suite 100
            Huntington, New York 11743
            Tele. 631-424-6682   Fax 631-425-5933
            e-mail: Novascience@earthlink.net
            Web Site: http://www.nexusworld.com/nova

Printed in the United States of America

CONTENTS

PREFACE

Immigration has indeed provided the lifeblood for the realization of the American dream for tremendous numbers of Americans. It has provided an ongoing source of low-cost labor, a pool of talented artisans and professions, and new citizens anxious to work hard to pursue their hopes for themselves and their families. As every coin has another side, however, so does immigration policy. Foreign countries with less than snow-white intentions have sent the United States their students to learn skills that can be used against America. Terrorists and criminals seem to enter and egress at will. The system of enforcing current laws is creaky and barely functions. This book brings into focus current policies and laws in an area which requires urgent attention.

Chapter 1

IMMIGRATION AND NATURALIZATION FUNDAMENTALS

Ruth Ellen Wasem

ABSTRACT

Congress typically considers a wide range of immigration bills, and now that the number of foreign born residents in the United States —28.4 million in 1999 is at the highest point in U.S. history, the debates over immigration policies grow in importance. As a backdrop to these debates, this chapter provides an introduction to immigration an naturalization policy, concepts, and statistical trends. It touches on a range of topics, including numerical limits, refugees and asylees, exclusion, naturalization, illegal aliens, eligibility for federal benefits, and taxation. This chapter does not track legislation.

INTRODUCTION

Four major principles underlie the U.S. policy on legal immigration: the reunification of families, the admission of immigrants with needed skills, the protection of refugees, and the diversity of admissions by the country of origin. These principles are embodied in federal law, the Immigration and Nationality Act (INA) first codified in 1952. Congress has significantly amended the INA several times since, most recently by the Illegal Immigration Reform and Immigrant Responsibility Act of 1996.[1]

An *alien* is "any person not a citizen or national of the United States" and is synonymous with *noncitizen*. It includes people who are here legally, as well as people who are here in violation of the INA. Noncitizen is generally used to describe all foreign-born persons in the United States who have not become citizens.

---

[1] Other major laws amending INA are the Immigration Amendments of 1965, the Refugee Act of 1980, the Immigration Reform and Control Act of 1986, and the Immigration Act of 1990.

The two basic types of legal aliens are *immigrants* and *nonimmigrants*. Immigrants are persons admitted as legal permanent residents (LPRs) of the United States. Nonimmigrants — such as tourists, foreign students, diplomats, temporary agricultural workers, exchange visitors, or intracompany business personnel — are admitted for a **specific purpose** and a **temporary period of time**.[2]

Nonimmigrants are required to leave the country when their visas expire, though certain classes of nonimmigrants may adjust to LPR status if they otherwise qualify. The conditions for the admission of immigrants are much more stringent than nonimmigrants, and many fewer immigrants than nonimmigrants are admitted. once admitted, however, immigrants are subject to few restrictions; for example, they may accept and change employment, and may apply for U.S. citizenship through the *naturalization* process, generally after 5 years.

NUMERICAL LIMITS AND PREFERENCE CATEGORIES

Immigration admissions are subject to a complex set of numerical limits and preference categories that give priority admission on the basis of family relationships, needed skills, and geographic diversity. These include a *flexible worldwide cap* of 675,000, not including refugees and asylees (discussed below), and a *per-country ceiling*, which changes yearly and is 25,620 for FY2001. Numbers allocated to the *three preference tracks* include a 226,000 minimum for family-based, 140,000 for employment-based, and 55,000 for diversity immigrants (*i.e.*, a formula-based visa lottery aimed at countries that have low levels of immigration to the United States). Unlike preference immigrants, the *immediate relatives of U.S. citizens* (*i.e.*, their spouses and unmarried minor children, and the parents of adult U.S. citizens) are admitted outside of the numerical limits of the per country ceilings and are the "flexible" component of the worldwide cap. The per country ceilings no longer apply to employment-based immigrants, but the worldwide limit remains in effect.

The largest number of immigrants is admitted because of family relationship to a U.S. citizen or immigrant. Of the 660,477 legal immigrants in FY1998, 72% entered on the basis of family ties.[3] *Immediate relatives of U.S. citizens* made up the single largest group of immigrants. *Family preference immigrants* — the spouses and children of immigrants, the adult children of U.S. citizens, and the siblings of adult U.S. citizens — were the second largest group. Other major immigrant groups in FY1998 were *employment-based preference immigrants*, including spouses and children, *refugees and asylees* adjusting to immigrant status, and *diversity immigrants*.

---

[2] Nonimmigrants are often referred to by the letter that denotes their section in the statute, such as H-2A agricultural workers, F-1 foreign students, J-1 cultural exchange visitors, or E-2 treaty traders.

[3] The FY1998 admission/adjustment numbers fall below the worldwide ceiling because of processing backlogs at the Immigration and Naturalization Service, not because of reduced demand for LPR visas.

Table 1. FY1998 Immigrants by Category

Total	660,477
Immediate relatives of citizens	284,270
Family preference	191,480
Employment preference	77,517
Refugee and asylee adjustment	554,709
Diversity	45,499
Other	7,002

REFUGEES AND ASYLEES

Refugee admissions are governed by different criteria and numerical limits than immigrant admissions. Refugee status requires a finding of persecution or a well-founded fear of persecution in situations of "special humanitarian concern" to the United States. The total annual number of refugee admissions and the allocation of these numbers among refugee groups are determined at the start of each fiscal year by the President after consultation with the Congress. Refugees are admitted from abroad. The INA al so provides for the granting *of asylum* on a case-by-case basis to aliens physically present in the United States who meet the statutory definition of "refugee."

EXCLUSION AND REMOVAL

All aliens must satisfy State Department consular officers abroad and INS inspectors upon entry to the U.S. that they are not ineligible for visas or admission under the so-called "grounds for inadmissibility" of the INA. These criteria categories are:

- health-related grounds;
- criminal history;
- security and terrorist concerns;
- public charge *(e.g.,* indigence);
- seeking to work without proper labor certification;
- illegal entrants and immigration law violations;
- lacking proper documents;
- ineligible for citizenship; and,
- aliens previously removed.

Some provisions may be waived or are not applicable in the case of nonimmigrants, refugees (e.g., public charge), and other aliens. All family-based immigrants entering after December 18, 1997, must have a new binding affidavit of support signed by a U.S. sponsor in order to meet the public charge requirement.

The INA also specifies the circumstances and actions that result in aliens being removed from the United States, i.e., deported. The category *of criminal alien* has been of special concern in recent years, and the Illegal Immigration Reform and Immigrant Responsibility Act of 1996 expanded and toughened the deportation consequences of criminal convictions.

STATISTICAL TRENDS

The annual number of LPRs admitted or adjusted in the United States rose gradually after World War II, as Figure 1 illustrates. However, the annual admissions never again reached the peaks of the early 20th Century. The INS data present only those admitted as LPRs or those adjusting to LPR status. The growth in immigration after 1980 is partly attributable to the total number of admissions under the basic system, consisting of immigrants entering through a preference system as well as immediate relatives of U.S. citizens, that was augmented considerably by legalized aliens.[4] In addition, the number of refugees admitted increased from 718,000 in the period 1966-1980 to 1.6 million during the period 1981-1995, after the enactment of the Refugee Act of 1980. The Immigration Act of 1990 increased the ceiling on employment-based preference immigration, with the provision that unused employment visas would be made available the following year for family preference immigration.

Figure 1. Annual Immigrant Admissions and Status Adjustments, 1900-1998

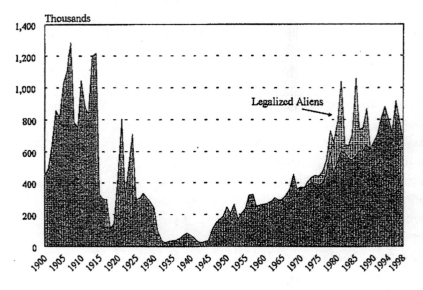

Source: CRS presentation of INS data. Aliens legalizing through the Immigration Reform and Control Act are depicted by year of arrival.

---

[4] The Immigration Reform and Control Act of 1986 legalized several million aliens residing in the United States without authorization.

There are two major statistical perspectives on trends in immigration. One uses the official INS admissions data and the other draws on Bureau of Census population surveys. The INS data present only those admitted as LPRs or those adjusting to LPR status. The census data, on the other hand, include all residents in the population counts, and the census asks people whether they were born in the United States or abroad. As a result, the census data also contain long-term temporary (nonimmigrant) residents and unauthorized residents.

The percent of the population that is foreign born, depicted in **Figure 2**, resembles the trend line of annual admissions data presented in **Figure 1**, which indicates the proportion of foreign born residents is not as large as during earlier periods. **Figure 2**, on the other hand, illustrates that the sheer number - 28.4 million in 1999 - is at the highest point in U.S. history.

Figure 2. Foreign Born Residents of the United States, 1870-1999

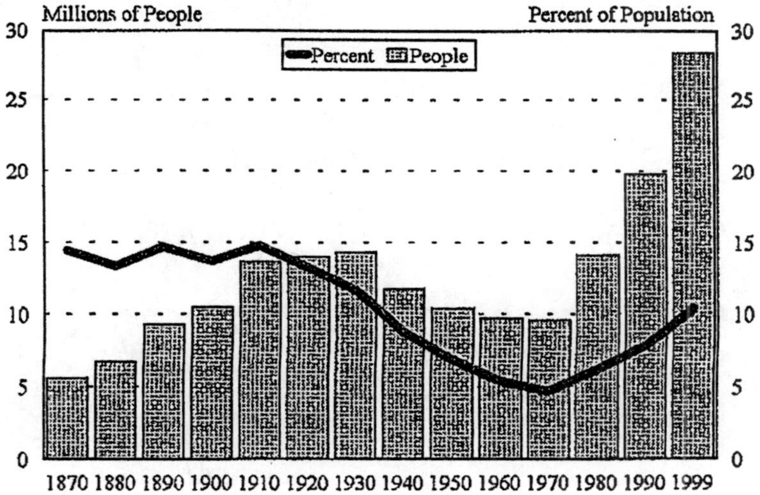

Source: CRS presentation of data from the *The Foreign-Born Population: 1994*, by K.A. Hansen & A. Bachu, U.S. Bureau of Census(1995); *The Population of the United States*, by Donald J. Bogue (1985); and the March 2000 Supplement of the CPS.

NATURALIZATION

Another tradition of immigration policy is to provide immigrants an opportunity to integrate fully into society. Under U.S. immigration law, all LPRs are potential citizens and may become so through a process known as *naturalization*. To naturalize, aliens must have continuously resided in the United States for 5 years as LPKs (3 years in the case of spouses of U.S. citizens), show that they have good moral character, demonstrate the ability to read, write, speak, and understand English, and pass an examination on U.S.

government and history. Applicants pay a fee of $225 when they file their materials and
have the option of taking a standardized civics test or of having the examiner quiz them
on civics as part of their interview.

The language requirement is waived for those who are at least 50 years old and have
lived in the United States at least 20 years or who are at least 55 years old and have lived
in the United States at least 15 years. Special consideration on the civics requirement is to
be given to aliens who are over 65 years old and have lived in the United States for at
least 20 years. Both the language and civics requirements are waived for those who are
unable to comply due to physical or developmental disabilities or mental impairment.
Certain requirements are waived for those who have served in the U.S. military.

The number of immigrants petitioning to naturalize has surged in recent years,
jumping from just over half a million applicants in FY1994 to more than 1 million in
FY1995 **(Figure 3)**. There were an unprecedented 1.6 million petitions in FY1997, but
the number fell to 460,916 petitions in FY2000.

Figure 3. Naturalization Petitions Filed and Approved, FY1990-FY2000

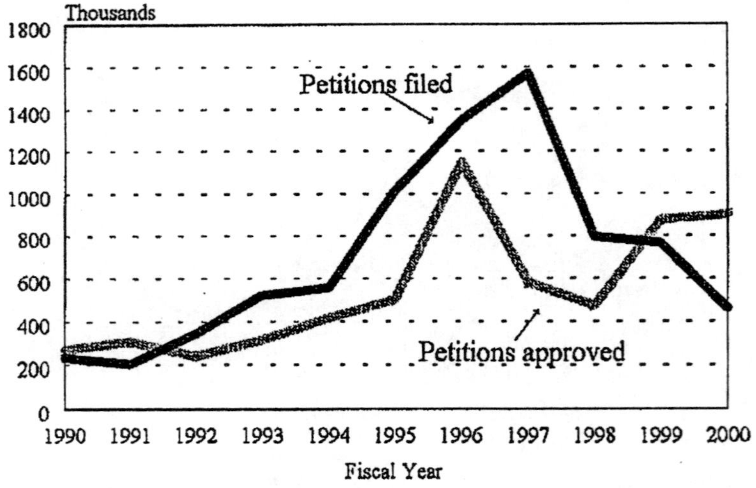

Source: INS Statistics Division
Note: As of September 30, 2000, a total of 805,562 cases were pending.

ILLEGAL ALIENS

Illegal aliens or *unauthorized aliens* are those noncitizens who either entered the
United States surreptitiously, *i.e.,* entered without inspection (referred to as EWIs), or
overstayed the term of their nonimmigrant visas, *e.g.,* tourist or student visas. Many of
these aliens have some type of document - either bogus or expired - and may have cases
pending with INS.

As the 2000 Census of the U.S. Population is being released, preliminary data analyses offer competing population totals that, in turn, imply the estimates of unauthorized residents of the United States have been understated. While the Immigration and Naturalization Service (INS) had estimated there were approximately 5.1 million unauthorized immigrants residing in the United States as of January 1997, researchers using the Current Population Survey (CPS) and the 2000 decennial census now estimate numbers as high as 9 million to I 1 million.

Using their 5.1 million estimate, the INS calculated that about 16.4% had been living in the United States for more than 10 years. About 18% of the 5.1 million unauthorized residents were estimated to have filed applications with INS that might result in receipt of legal Permanent resident status *(i.e.,* 445,600 had applications for asylum pending and 474,000 had applications for immigrant visas pending). The INS study did not estimate how many of the 5.1 million unauthorized residents had a temporary legal status, *e.g.,* Temporary Protected Status.[5]

ELIGIBILITY FOR FEDERAL BENEFITS

Noncitizens' eligibility for major federal benefit programs depends on their immigration status and whether they arrived before or after enactment of P.L. 104-193, the 1996 welfare law (as amended by P.L. 105-33 and P.L. 105-185). Refugees remain eligible for Supplemental Security Income (SSI), Medicaid, and food stamps for 7 years alter arrival, and for other restricted programs for 5 years. Most LPRs are barred from food stamps and SSI until they naturalize or meet a 10-year work requirement. LPRs receiving SSI (and SSI-related Medicaid) on August 22, 1996, the enactment date of P.L. 104-193, continue to be eligible, as do those here then whose subsequent disability makes them eligible for SSI and Medicaid. LPRs admitted by August 22, 1996, are eligible for food stamps if they were over 65, until they turn 18, and/or if they subsequently become disabled. LPRs entering after August 22, 1996, are barred from Temporary Assistance for Needy Families (TANF) and Medicaid for 5 years, after which their coverage becomes a state option. Also after the 5-year bar, the sponsor's income is deemed to be available to new immigrants in determining their financial eligibility for designated federal means-tested programs until they naturalize or meet the work requirement. Unauthorized aliens, i.e., illegal aliens, are ineligible for almost all federal benefits except, for example, emergency medical care.

---

[5] U.S. Immigration and Naturalization Service. Office of Policy and Planning. *Annual Estimates of the Unauthorized Immigrant Population Residing in the United States and Components of Change: 1987 to 1997,* by Robert Warren,, September 2000.

TAXATION

Aliens in the United States are generally subject to the same tax obligations, including Social Security (FICA) and unemployment (FUTA) as citizens of the United States, with the exception of certain nonimmigrant students and cultural exchange visitors. LPRs are treated the same as citizens for tax purposes. Other aliens, including unauthorized migrants, are held to a "substantive presence" test based upon the number of days they have been in the United States.[6] Some countries have reciprocal tax treaties with the United States that - depending on the terms of the particular treaty - exempt citizens of their country living in the United States from certain taxes in the United States.

---

[6] This "substantive presence" test is at least 31 days in the current year and 183 or more days in the two prior years, according to a formula.

Chapter 2

A BRIEF HISTORY OF U.S. IMMIGRATION POLICY

Joyce C. Vialet

ABSTRACT

The early colonists were primarily of European stock, representing the nations that claimed the "new" land. By the end of 18th century, a new society was effectively established here, taking its language and many of its customs from England. The mass migration of the 19th century was the result of a near perfect match between the needs of a new country and Europe. Europe at this time was undergoing drastic social change and economic reorganization, compounded by overpopulation. America needed immigrants for settlement, defense, and economic well-being. During the period 1820-1880, Germany, Great Britain, and Ireland accounted for the largest numbers.

In the last two decades of the 19th century, the volume of immigration continued to increase and the main sources shifted from Northern and Western to Southern and Eastern Europe. The Federal Government assumed an increasingly active role, with the first general immigration statute enacted in 1882. While the United States remained willing and able to absorb the mass migration during the end of the 19th and the beginning of the 20th centuries, the country's needs had changed. The frontier had closed, and the "new" immigrants, as they were characterized by the Dillingham Commission, fueled the industrialization and urbanization of America. However, there was growing ambivalence toward the urban immigrants by a predominantly rural country.

By the end of World War I, the era of mass migration was brought to a close by the enactment of increasingly restrictive legislation. Legislation enacted in 1917 codified existing restrictions and added new ones. During the 1920s, numerical restrictions were placed on immigration from the Eastern Hemisphere in the form of the national origins quota system. The 1917 and 1924 laws remained in effect until 1952. Immigration fell sharply during the intervening years in response to the depression of the 1930s and World War II, as well as the legislative restrictions.

Legislation in 1952 codified and carried forward the essential elements of the 1917 and 1924 Acts. Enacted over President Truman's veto, it reflected the cold war atmosphere and anti-communism of the period following World War II at the onset of the Korean War. While the national origins quota system remained in place until 1965, many refugees, immigrants, and legal and illegal temporary workers entered outside it. Reflecting a major change in public attitudes toward race and national origins, 1965 legislation repealed the national origins quota system, replacing it with a system based primarily on reunification of families and needed skills.

Since 1965, the major sources of immigration have shifted from Europe to Latin America and Asia, reversing the trend of two centuries. In the 1970s, the entry of aliens outside the restrictions of the basic law – both illegally as undocumented aliens, and legally as refugees – was increasingly the dominant pattern in immigration and the basis for the major issues confronting the Congress. A series of major laws were enacted in the 1980s through 1990, consisting of the Refugee Act of 1980, the Immigration Reform and Control Act of 1986, and the Immigration Act of 1990.

INTRODUCTION

U.S. immigration policy has been shaped not only by the perceived needs of this country, but by the needs and aspirations of the immigrants themselves. This paper reviews the major streams of immigration to the United States in the context of the country's changing views of immigration.

During the initial immigration of settlers and pioneers to the first European colonies on the North American continent, the objectives of the immigrants and their sending colonial powers were dominant – a complex blend of religious, political, and economic motives which eventually produced the new American society.

Following the establishment of the United States at the end of the 18th century, a wave of mass migration flowed from the European continent to the new nation throughout the 19th century.[1] For the immigrants, economic, religious, and political motives continued to be dominant. The United States' goals in receiving them included the need for new citizens who would participate in national economic and political growth, as well as the humanitarian desire to provide a refuge for the oppressed of other lands. During this period, there were few restrictions on the entering immigrants; our national purposes coincided with essentially unlimited immigration.

As the nation entered the 20th century, cultural conflicts resulting from the changing ethnic character of the immigrant population from Northern and Western Europe to Southern and Eastern Europe, and economic strains in the Nation began to generate domestic political opposition to unrestricted immigration. Following World War I, this political opposition led to restrictive legislation focusing predominantly on the ethnic origins of the new immigrants, and also on the size of the immigrant flow. By the 1930s this legislation, in combination with the economic disincentive of the Great Depression, had resulted in a massive reduction in the inflow of immigrants.

Following World War II and continuing through the 1950s, the pattern of immigration as we know it today began to emerge, consisting of immigrants, refugees, and temporary and/or undocumented workers. Refugees came by the hundreds of thousands, fleeing the ravages of World War II and the spread of communism. Immigrants continued to come primarily under the terms of the national origins quota system, which was extended with minor revisions in 1952, and continued in effect until

---

[1] A table prepared by the Immigration and Naturalization Service entitled, Immigration by Region and Selected Country of Last Residence, Fiscal Years 1820-1989, appears as appendix A.

1965. Agricultural workers came from Mexico, some legally as braceros and others illegally the historical predecessors of today's undocumented aliens.

The distinction between refugees and immigrants became firmly established during the period following World War II, and has continued until the present time. Defined broadly, refugees flee, generally in large groups, from political or religious persecution; immigrants come voluntarily, generally on an individual basis and in an orderly fashion. A third group, illegal or undocumented aliens, come outside the law, generally for economic reasons.

In the case of immigrants, the purposes and goals of the United States as defined in Federal immigration law are dominant in deciding who comes. The admission of refugees is also subject to Federal legislation, but it has tended to be in reaction to events beyond the control of either the receiving society or the refugees themselves.

The distinction between immigrants and refugees was unheard of during the mass migrations of the 19th century; no difference was perceived between the Irish fleeing the potato famine and the German "forty-eighters" fleeing political persecution. It developed in the wake of World War II, primarily as a means of reconciling our traditional ideal of asylum with restrictions in the immigration law.

Since the 1940s, the goals and purposes of our immigration policy have diverged regarding the admission of refugees and immigrants. In the case of refugees, humanitarian concerns and foreign policy considerations have been dominant. Domestic, as opposed to foreign, policy considerations have been paramount in the admission of immigrants. The United States' desire in the 1920s to protect and preserve what was then seen as its national ethnic heritage led to the adoption of the national origins quota system. This system was repealed in the context of the civil rights movement of the 1960s, rather than on the predominantly foreign policy grounds for change advanced in the 1950s by Presidents Truman and Eisenhower.

During the 1960s and 1970s, the flow of refugees from political turmoil in other nations continued, requiring the enactment of special legislation. The equal treatment of all nations and family reunification emerged as the primary goals of our policy for admitting immigrants. The flow of illegal or undocumented aliens, particularly from other countries in the Western Hemisphere, resulted in political pressure for more effective measures to restrict illegal immigration.

During the 1980s through 1990, Congress reviewed and revised all aspects of immigration policy in an attempt to articulate a workable approach that accommodated both our past tradition of asylum as well as the economic and political realities of the present. Legislation providing for flexibility in our response to refugees within the framework of the basic immigration law was enacted in 1980. This was followed in 1986, after lengthy and intensive debate, by legislation aimed at controlling illegal immigration. In 1990, Congress passed legislation significantly changing the regulation of legal immigration, among other things increasing the comparatively limited number of visas available for independent non-family immigration and for certain underrepresented countries. In part because of the repeal of the national origins quota system, the majority of immigrants were coming from Asia and Latin America, as opposed to Europe. Concern was expressed about the lack of accessibility for the traditional "old source" countries such as Ireland, an issue addressed by the 1990 legislation. Beyond legal immigration, the Immigration Act of 1990 represented a major revision of the Immigration and Nationality Act, which remains the basic immigration law.

EARLY IMMIGRATION

Technically speaking, U.S. immigration began with the Declaration of Independence in 1776 and the Treaty of Paris in 1783, which accorded the United States recognition as a nation. Official immigration statistics began to be kept in 1820. However, the settlers and pioneers who colonized North America before the founding of the United States were also immigrants. These early immigrants came from a variety of nations and for a variety of reasons to a new land which placed few constraints on their coming. They provided the people needed to explore and settle the continent, and to develop a new society.

The early colonists were primarily of European stock, representing the nations that laid claim to the new land. Colonists came from Great Britain, France, and the Netherlands to settle the Eastern seaboard of the continent. In the Southeast, France sent colonists to settle Louisiana. In the South and West, Spanish colonists settled in Florida, in the areas which are now Texas and New Mexico, and in California. Along with these settlers came involuntary immigrants – black men and women brought as slaves from the African continent. Colonists came for a variety of reasons: to serve as soldiers and civilian representatives of the colonizing power; to obtain religious and political freedom; to convert others to their religious views; to improve their economic status and pursue economic gain; to seek adventure; and involuntarily as slaves to provide labor for colonial agriculture and industry.

A brief listing of some of the colonial settlers suggests the diversity of motives which inspired the early immigrants as well as the kaleidoscope of nations from which they came. A combination of religious, political, and economic motives brought settlers from Great Britain to Massachusetts Bay Colony, the Quaker settlement in Pennsylvania, the Catholic settlement in Baltimore, and the colony of Georgia. Spanish settlers came to California, Florida, and Mexico to search for gold, trade with and bring Christianity to the Indians, and expand the Spanish Empire. French settlers came to Louisiana and Canada to seek land and business opportunities, convert the natives, and protect French trading interests. French Huguenots fled religious persecution after the revocation of the Edict of Nantes in 1685.

German Pietist sects, including the Mennonites and Moravians, also fled persecution in search of religious freedom, many in response to the sympathetic Quaker teachings of William Penn. A later German group, the Hessians, came to fight as mercenaries with the British in the American Revolution, and 5,000 stayed to become immigrants. Dutch and Swedes came for political freedom and economic opportunity, and the Scotch-Irish came throughout the 18th century for economic, religious, and political motives.

The first black slaves were brought to the English colonies in 1619 on a Dutch ship. The term "slave" initially was applied loosely to both white and black servants, and both were treated as indentured servants. However, conditions worsened as the slave trade became more profitable. Slaves were brought to the English, French, Portuguese, Spanish, and Dutch colonies throughout the 18th century. The numbers are now known, although they have been estimated in the millions. Slave importation was prohibited in 1808, but an illicit slave trade continued until the Civil War.

When the first census was taken in 1790, the total population was recorded at 3,227,000. English, Scots, and Scotch-Irish accounted for 75 percent; Germans made up 8 percent; other nationalities with substantial numbers included the Dutch, French, Swedish, and Spanish. The 1790 census showed a black population of approximately 750,000. By the census of 1810, the white population had increased to approximately 6 million, and the black population to approximately 1,378,000.

A new society was effectively established here by the end of the 18th century, taking its language, the basis for its law, and many of its customs from England, with major contributions from other European countries. The country's libertarian principles included a belief in the mission of America to provide asylum for the oppressed; and in the corollary right of the oppressed to seek freedom and opportunity in America. As will be seen, these ideals were remarkably appropriate to the needs of the United States and Europe during the 19th century.

At the same time, there were indications as early as the 18th century of a more negative view of immigration that was to emerge as the dominant one in the 1920s. Perhaps the best-known expression of this view was Benjamin Franklin's warning in 1753 about the Germans in Pennsylvania:

> ...those who came hither are generally the most stupid of their own nation, and as ignorance is often attended with great credulity, when knavery would mislead it, and with suspicion when honesty would set it right; and, few of the English understand the German language, and so cannot address them either from the press or pulpit, it is almost impossible to remove any prejudices they may entertain...Not being used to liberty, they know not how to made modest use of it.[2]

Franklin feared that the Germans would eventually outnumber the English, "and even our government will become precarious."

Similar fears, although not about the Germans, led to the adoption of the national origins quota system 168 years later. However, one of the largest mass migrations in recorded history preceded this step. During the century between the fall of Napoleon and World War I, from 30 to 35 million immigrants came to the United States.

19TH CENTURY IMMIGRATION

The mass migration of the 19th century was the result of a near perfect match between the needs of a new country and overcrowded Europe. Europe at this time was undergoing drastic social change and economic reorganization, severely compounded by

---

[2] Quoted by Franklin D. Scott. *The People of America: Perspectives on Immigration*. Washington, American Historical Association, AHA pamphlets 241, 1972. p. 15.

overpopulation. An extraordinary increase in population coincided with the breakup of the old agricultural order that had been in place since medieval times throughout much of Europe. Commonly held lands were broken up into individually owned farms, resulting in landless status for peasants from Ireland and Russia. At approximately the same time, the industrial revolution was underway, moving from Great Britain to Western Europe, and then to Southern and Eastern Europe. For Germany, Sweden, Russia, and Japan, the highest points of emigration coincided with the beginnings of industrialization and the ensuing general disruption of employment patterns. The artisans joined the peasants evicted from their land as immigrants to the United States. Population pressure and related economic problems, sometimes in the extreme form of famine, are generally cited as being the major causes of the mass migration of this long period, followed by religious persecution and the desire for political freedom.

America, on the other hand, had a boundless need for people to push back the frontier, to build the railways, to defend unstable boundaries, and to populate new States. The belief in America as a land of asylum for the oppressed was reinforced by the commitment to the philosophy of manifest destiny. Immigration was required for settlement, defense, and economic well-being.

The coincidence of European and American interest in mass migration during this period is well illustrated by two quotations, one from the European and one from the American point of view. The first is from a letter written home by a Frenchman, J. Hector St. John Crevecoeur, in 1792:

> There is no wonder that this country has so many charms and presents to Europeans so many temptations to remain in it. A traveler in Europe becomes a stranger as soon as he quits his own kingdom; but it is otherwise here. We know, properly speaking, no strangers; this is every person's country; the variety of our soils, situations, climates, governments, and produce, hath something which must please everybody...He does not find, as in Europe, a crowded society, where every place is over-stocked; he does not feel that perpetual collision of parties, that difficulty of beginning, that contention which oversets so many. There is room for everybody in America; has he any particular talent, or industry. He exerts it in order to procure a livelihood, and it succeeds.[3]

The second quotation is from the Republican Party platform in 1864, which Abraham Lincoln participated in writing: "Foreign immigration which in the past has added so much to the wealth, resources, and increases of power to this nation – the asylum of the oppressed of all nations – should be fostered and encouraged by a liberal and just policy."[4] The United States throughout the 19th century was in the happy position of doing well by doing good, of adding to its "wealth, resources, and increase of power" by serving as "the asylum of the oppressed of all nations."

Official, albeit imperfect, immigration statistics were recorded beginning in 1820 by the Department of State, which continued to perform this task until 1870. The immigration data collection function was subsequently transferred to the Treasury

---

[3] Crevecoeur. Letters from an American Farmer. Reprinted in *Immigration and the American Tradition*. Moses Rischin, ed. Indianapolis, Bobbs-Merrill Co., Inc., 1976. p. 29-30.
[4] Quoted by William S. Bernard. *American Immigration Policy*. New York, Harper and Bros., 1950. p. 6.

Department's Bureau of Statistics, and from there to the Bureau of Immigration, housed first in the Department of Labor and subsequently in the Department of Justice.

Data collection began in 1819 in response to a Federal law requiring ship captains arriving from abroad to submit a manifest to the customs collector showing the sex, occupation, age, and country of all passengers aboard. Initially, data was recorded only on vessels arriving at Eastern ports; Western ports were included beginning in 1850. During the Civil War, data was available only from ports under Federal control. Immigration over land borders was recorded haphazardly until around 1910.

1820-1880

The generally accepted estimate of the number of immigrants entering between the end of the Revolutionary War and 1819 is 250,000. In 1820, 8,385 entries were recorded; by 1840 annual immigration had increased tenfold, to 84,066. Germany, the United Kingdom, and Ireland accounted for 70 percent of the 750,949 entries between 1820-1840. Emigration from Ireland and England was primarily in response to economic problems. In Germany, economic problems were aggravated by liberal discontent with political developments following the Napoleonic Wars.

Immigration increased almost 600 percent, to 4,311,465, during the subsequent 20-year period, 1841-1860. Ireland, Germany, and Great Britain accounted for 87.5 percent of the total. This was the period of the potato famine, which hit hardest in Ireland but affected other parts of Europe as well.

Even with high rates of out-migration, Ireland's population had almost doubled form 1800-1840, increasing from 4.5 million to over 8 million. The increasingly impoverished peasants had become almost wholly dependent on the potato for sustenance. When the entire potato crop was wiped out in 1846 and 1847, half a million people, died, 3 million lived on charity, and hundreds of thousands fled to America. Just under 1.7 million came from Ireland between 1841-1860. Emigration from Ireland reduced rather than simply slowed population growth, and in the second half of the century significant amounts of money flowed back into the country in the form of remittances from America.

Germany sent almost 1.4 million immigrants to America during 1841-1860. Germany suffered a severe economic crisis during the 1840s, as well as political unrest culminating in the revolution of 1848. The "forty-eighters" joined those fleeing to America from the potato famine, high prices, and widespread unemployment. An additional 700,000 came from Great Britain.

By 1860, the population of the United States had increased to 31 million, from 7 million in 1810. More than 5 million immigrants had added to this increase. About half of them were from Great Britain and Ireland, followed by more than 1.5 million Germans and 50,000 Scandinavians.

Immigration to the United States was widely, although not universally, encouraged during the mid-19th century; pull factors were operative in addition to the push factors discussed above. Of major importance was the so-called "American letter." There were letters to relatives at home encouraging others to follow, and sometimes including one-way steamship tickets. Another important factor was the active recruitment of passengers by steamship companies and railroad workers by the railroads.

Following the Civil War, the development of the Union Pacific and other railways required the western movement of immigrants. The migration west of immigrants was also encouraged by western States through brochures and agents sent to New York and abroad, and by reducing the residence period required to vote. The Homestead Act of 1862 made western lands available to immigrants as well as the native-born. The Contract Labor Law passed in 1864 was intended to encourage immigration by advancing money for passage. However, it was repealed in 1868, under pressure from U.S. labor groups.

Anti-immigration, or nativist, feeling was also strong during the mid-19th century. The nativist movement of this period was inspired by a combination of anti-Catholicism, fear for American labor, the linking of immigration with crime and poverty, and concern about the political impact of immigrants. The nativist Know Nothing party showed considerable strength in the 1850s, but it ebbed by 1860.

Immigration increased to 5,127,015 during the 20-year period 1861-1880, a figure approximately equal to total previous immigration since the country had gained its independence. Germany, Great Britain, and Ireland continued to account for the largest numbers. Additionally, there were significant numbers from Sweden, Norway, and China. The high level of immigration during this period reflected, in part, the growing improvements in international communication and transportation, which resulted in widespread circulation of stories about the new land, as well as a less arduous sea voyage.

In Sweden, the winter of 1867-1868 brought a monetary crisis, followed by a crop failure and local famine. These developments, in combination with precarious agricultural conditions, the displacement of artisans by industrial development, and ideological and religious differences, resulted in mass Swedish emigration in the late 1860s. A similar pattern was repeated in Norway and throughout other countries as agrarian difficulties beset Europe during the 1880s. Eventually, the pressure was eased by the growth of industrial employment in both rural areas and the towns and a slowing population growth. Immigration from the Scandinavian countries eased off in the second decade of the 20th century.

THE 1880S THROUGH WORLD WAR I

The last two decades of the 19th century were particularly significant for immigration. The volume of immigration continued to increase, the principal sources shifted from Northern and Western Europe to Southern and Eastern Europe, and the Federal Government assumed an increasingly active role.

Federal legislation barring the entry of convicts and prostitutes was enacted on March 3, 1875. The Act of August 3, 1882, is considered the first general immigration statute. It was enacted in response to a combination of factors, including the increasing number of immigrants; the fear that criminals, paupers, and mental and physical defectives were being systematically sent to the United States; and an 1875 Supreme Court ruling that State laws regulating immigration infringed on Congress' exclusive power over foreign commerce and were unconstitutional. This latter development led to lobbying by private welfare organizations in Eastern cities for the establishment of Federal controls.

The Immigration Act of 1882 gave the Secretary of the Treasury authority over immigration, basing this jurisdiction on a newly established head tax of 50 cents per immigrant. The law also continued the bar against undesirables, including convicts, mental defectives, and paupers. This legislation marked the beginning of an active Federal role in immigration. It was enacted primarily in response to problems associated with what the Immigration Commission was to characterize in its 1911 report as the "old immigration, from Northern and Western Europe; the "new" immigration from Southern and Eastern Europe was just getting underway.

The year 1882 also saw the enactment of the first legislation basing eligibility – or ineligibility – for entry on national origin. This was the Chinese Exclusion Act of May 6, 1882, which remained in effect until its repeal in 1943. Contract labor laws, prohibiting the importation under contract of foreign labor, were also enacted in the 1880s, following the depression, strikes, and efforts of the Knights of Labor during midyears of the decade. The three elements contained in this early legislation – individual qualifications, national origin, and protection of U.S. labor –formed the basis for the restrictive policy which supplanted the policy of asylum, or essentially free immigration, after World War I. Chief in importance among these was national origin.

Immigration reached a high of 5,246,613 in 1881-1890, followed by 3,687,564 in the last decade of the 19th century. Germany, the United Kingdom, and Ireland accounted for almost half of the immigration during this period, although their numbers all declined significantly in the 1890s. Immigration from these countries continued a steady and sharp decline into the first two decades of the 20th century. This was due largely to improved economic conditions, resulting from the leveling off of population growth and the increase in industrialization which absorbed increasing numbers of workers.

In contrast, immigration from Italy and Austria-Hungary increased rapidly in the 1880s and 1890s, as it did from other countries in Southern and Eastern Europe. More than 2 million entered during the first decade of the 20th century from both Italy and Austria-Hungary, and more than 1.5 million came from Russia.

The push factors behind this immigration resembled those underlying the earlier mass migration from Northern and Western Europe. Economic difficulties beset Italy, Poland, and Greece following the collapse of the old agrarian order and the disruptive early stages in industrialization, aggravated by severe overpopulation. In Italy, the cholera epidemic of 1887 was an added impetus for migration. Again, America provided an alternative to poverty and sometimes starvation for landless peasants and unemployed artisans. Others fled because of religious and ethnic persecution. These included the Russian Jews, Russo-German Mennonites, and Armenians. Others left for predominantly political reasons, including Poles and Russians.

While the United States remained willing and able to absorb the mass migration from Southern and Eastern Europe during the end of the 19th and the beginning of the 20th centuries, the country's needs had changed. The closing of the frontier, officially announced in the 1890 census, coincided with the development of a booming industrial economy which required manpower just as settlement and the opening of the West had in a previous period. The "new" immigrants, as they were characterized by the Dillingham Commission, fueled the industrialization and urbanization of America. Quoting from the Commission's 1911 report:

> A large proportion of the southern and eastern European immigrants of the past 25 years have entered the manufacturing and mining industries of the eastern and middle western States, mostly in the capacity of unskilled laborers. There is no basic industry in which they are not largely represented and in many cases they compose more than 50 percent of the total number of persons employed in such industries. Coincident with the advent of these millions of unskilled laborers there has been an unprecedented expansion of the industries in which they have been employed. Whether this great immigration movement was caused by the industrial development or whether the fact that a practically unlimited and available supply of cheap labor existed in Europe was taken advantage of for the purpose of expanding the industries, cannot well be demonstrated. Whatever may be the truth in this regard it is certain that southern and eastern European immigrants have almost completely monopolized unskilled labor activities in many of the most important industries.[5]

The growing ambivalence toward immigration during the early 20th century is apparent in this description. Immigrants were believed by many to adversely affect the wages and working conditions of U.S. workers. They were also associated with the city by a country that was predominantly rural in its attitudes. As early as 1890, 62 percent of the foreign-born lived in urban places, compared to 26 percent of native whites born of native parents. The urban immigrant was blamed for the real and imagined evils of the city, including crime and poverty.

Immigration in the first decade of the 20th century reached 8,795,386, the highest number in the country's history to date, followed by the second highest number, 5,735,811, in 1911-1920. More than 1 million immigrants entered the United States in 1905, 1906, 1907, 1910, 1913, and 1914. By the end of World War I, the era of mass migration was brought to a close by the enactment of increasingly restrictive legislation.

Legislation enacted during World War I, the Immigration Act of February 5, 1917, codified existing restrictions on immigration and added new ones. Enacted over President Wilson's veto, the 1917 Act established the Asiatic Barred Zone, which further restricted the entry of Asians. It also prohibited the entry of aliens over age 16 who were unable to read any language, a measure specifically intended to curtail immigration from southeastern Europe. Literacy provisions had been passed previously in 1896, 1913, and 1915, and vetoed successively by Presidents Cleveland, Taft, and Wilson.

In his 1915 veto message, President Wilson charged that the literacy test marked a sharp departure from the traditional American belief in "the right of political asylum" which had heretofore characterized American immigration policy. Quoting from his message:

---

[5] U.S. Immigration Commission. Abstracts of Reports. S. Doc. 747, 61st Cong., 3d Sess., 1910-11. p. 37-38.

Hitherto we have generously kept our doors open to all who were not unfitted by reason of disease or incapacity for self support or such personal records and antecedents as were likely to make them a menace to our peace and order or to the wholesome and essential relationships of life. In this bill it is proposed to turn away from tests of character and of quality and impose tests which exclude and restrict; for the new tests here embodied are not tests of quality or of character or of personal fitness, but tests of opportunity. Those who come seeking opportunity are not to be admitted unless they have already had one of the chief of the opportunities they seek, the opportunity of education. The object of such provisions is restriction, not selection.[6]

President Wilson went on to note, "If the people of this country have made up their minds to limit the number of immigrants by arbitrary tests and so reverse the policy of all the generations of Americans that have gone before them, it is their right to do so." However, he did not believe this to be the case.

Two years later, a wartime Congress overrode a subsequent veto by President Wilson, and the literacy requirement became law. Under the combined pressure of wartime nationalism and post-war isolationism, the economics of increasing urbanization, and a concern about the large numbers of immigrants entering from southeastern Europe, the American public, as reflected by the Congress, opted to reverse the policy of providing political asylum for one of comparative restriction. Numerical limitations followed in 1921 and, in varying forms, have remained in effect ever since.

THE 1920S: NUMERICAL RESTRICTIONS

Until the 1920s, legal restrictions on immigration had essentially remained qualitative rather than quantitative. That is, there were no restrictions on the number of aliens who could enter, provided that they met the criteria set forth in the law. During the 1920s numerical restrictions were placed on immigration from the Eastern Hemisphere. Western Hemisphere immigration remained numerically unrestricted until 1968.

The temporary Quota Act of May 19, 1921, was followed by the permanent Immigration Act of May 26, 1924, which remained in force until 1952. Under the national origins quota formula which went into effect on July 1, 1929, the annual quota of any nationality was "a number which bears the same ratio to 150,000 as the number of inhabitants in the United States in 1920 having that national origin bears to the number of white inhabitants of the United States in 1920, with a minimum quota of 100 for each nationality."[7] Natives of countries in the "barred zone," encompassing most Asian countries, were generally inadmissible as immigrants with certain exceptions.

The movement toward numerical limitations initially reflected a genuine fear of being engulfed by the refugees of war-ravaged Europe, together with the growing nationalism of the United States as an emerging world power and the isolationism which

---

[6] Wilson, Woodrow. Not Tests of Quality but of Opportunity. Reprinted in *Immigration and the American Tradition.* Moses Rischin, ed. Indianapolis, Bobbs-Merrill Co., Inc., 1976. p. 285-286.

[7] U.S. Congress. House. Committee on the Judiciary. *Revising the Laws Relating to Immigration, Naturalization, and Nationality.* H.Rept. 1365, 82d Cong., 2d Sess. Feb. 14, 1952. Washington, GPO, 1952. p. 37.

characterized the country following World War I. As the 1920s progressed, the arguments in favor of numerical restrictions were buttressed and shaped by popular biological theories of the period alleging the superiority of certain races. Two statements by Dr. Harry N. Laughlin, a eugenics consultant to the House Judiciary Committee on Immigration and Naturalization in the early 1920s indicate the important role these theories played in the direction taken by immigration policy immediately after World War I:

> We in this country have been so imbued with the idea of democracy, or the equality of all men, that we have left out of consideration the matter of blood or natural born hereditary mental and moral differences. No man who breeds pedigreed plants and animals can afford to neglect this thing...
>
> The National Origins provisions of the immigration control law of 1924 marked the actual turning point from immigration control based on the asylum idea...definitely in favor of the biological basis... [8]

THE 1930S AND 1940S: REFUGEES AND BRACEROS

The history of U.S. immigration policy from the 1930s to the enactment of the Refugee Act of 1980 was characterized by a tension resulting from the attempt to accommodate our traditional ideal of providing asylum from oppression within the framework of a comparatively restrictive immigration law. This tension resulted in part from the fact that the fortunate congruence in the 19th century between our economic needs and our humanitarian desire to offer refuge to the oppressed no longer exists. We no longer have the manpower requirements that characterized the settling of the wilderness followed by the industrialization of the nation.

Immigration in the 1930s totaled 528,431, down from 4,107,209 in the 1920s, and accompanied by substantial emigration. Restrictive immigration laws combined with the Depression to slow the immigrant flow to the lowest point since the 1830s. Without question, Hitler was a major "push" factor of the period; Germany led the sending countries, and many more would have come if they had been permitted.

In a campaign speech in October 1932, Herbert Hoover said, "With the growth of democracy in foreign countries, political persecution has largely ceased. There is no longer a necessity for the United States to provide an asylum for those persecuted because of conscience."[9] Hitler came to power shortly thereafter, and proved him tragically wrong. The flight of refugees from Germany began in 1933 and continued for the rest of the decade, to be followed by an even greater exodus of displaced persons throughout Europe after World War II.

---

[8] Quoted by Abba Schwartz. *The Open Society*. New York, Simon and Schuster, 1968. p. 105-106.
[9] Quoted by Robert Divine. *American Immigration Policy, 1924-1952*. New Haven, Yale University Press, 1957. p. 92.

The United States accepted an estimated 250,000 refugees from Nazi persecution prior to our entry into the war in 1941.[10] The country was undergoing the worst depression in its history, and efforts to liberalize the immigration law were unsuccessful.

U.S. motives in the admission of refugees from the 1930s until the present time have combined humanitarian concerns with foreign policy considerations. We have, in effect, traded the wilderness for the world. Our sense of our role as the leader of the Western alliance was a major factor in the passage of special legislation allowing for the admission of displaced persons and refugees in the wake of World War II.

The Displaced Persons Act of 1948 was the first refugee legislation enacted in the Nation's history. Together with its subsequent amendments, it provided for the admission of more than 400,000 displaced persons through the end of 1951, by mortgaging future immigration quotas. Poles accounted for one-third of the admissions, followed by German ethnics.[11]

Total immigrant admissions doubled during the 1940s compared to the 1930s, going from 528,431 to 1,035,039. This was still the lowest 10-year figure since the 1830s, exclusive of the preceding decade. Of this number, 354,804 entered from the Western Hemisphere.

The total number of permanent entries from the Western Hemisphere during the 1940s and 1950s was far exceeded by the number of admissions for temporary employment from the Western Hemisphere countries, led overwhelmingly by Mexico. The Mexican bracero program lasted from 1942 until 1964, and authorized the entry of between 4 and 5 million temporary agricultural workers. Significant, although much smaller numbers also entered from the Bahamas, Jamaica, Barbados, British Honduras, Canada, and Newfoundland.

THE IMMIGRATION AND NATIONALITY ACT OF 1952

The Immigration and Nationality Act enacted on June 27, 1952, was a major re-codification and revision of existing immigration and nationality law. It codified and carried forward, with modifications, the essential elements of both the 1917 and 1924 Acts discussed above, as well as those provisions of the Internal Security Act of September 23, 1950, relating to the exclusion of Communists.

The 1952 legislation reflected the cold war atmosphere and anti-communism of the period, following World War II and at the onset of the Korean War. The law was, Robert Divine asserted, "in essence an act of conservatism rather than of intolerance."[12] The Difference between the climate of opinion in the 1920s and the early 1950s is apparent in the following statement in the 1950 report of the Senate Judiciary Committee, "Without giving credence to any theory of Nordic superiority, the subcommittee believes that the

---

[10] Ibid., p. 104.

[11] A table prepared by the Immigration and Naturalization Service entitled, Refugees and Asylees Granted Lawful Permanent Residents Status by Region and Selected Country of Birth, Fiscal Years 1946-89, appears as appendix B.

[12] Divine, *American Immigration Policy*, p. 190.

adoption of the national origins quota formula was a rational and logical method of numerically restricting immigration in such a manner as to best preserve the sociological and cultural balance of the United States."[13] In contrast to the 1920s, the case for the national origins quota system in the 1950s was not generally argued on the grounds of racial superiority, but on sociological theories of the time relating to cultural assimilation. The provisions effectively prohibiting entry from most Asian countries were also slightly relaxed by the 1952 Act.

However, the legislation was characterized by supporters and opponents alike as a restrictionist measure, and was a severe disappointment to those who had hoped for a liberalization of the immigration law. In particular, the continuation of the national origins quota system was viewed by critics of the legislation as being inappropriate to the needs of U.S. foreign policy. Foremost among these critics was President Truman, whose veto was overridden by a vote of 278 to 113 in the House, and 57 to 26 in the Senate. Quoting from his veto message:

> Today, we are "protecting" ourselves as we were in 1924, against being flooded by immigrants from Eastern Europe. This is fantastic. The countries of Eastern Europe have fallen under the Communist yoke – they are silenced, fenced off by barbed wire and minefields – no one passes their borders but at the risk of his life. We do not need to be protected against immigrants from these countries – on the contrary we want to stretch out a helping hand, to save those who have managed to flee into Western Europe, to succor those who are brave enough to escape from barbarism, to welcome and restore them against the day when their countries will, as we hope, be free again…These are only a few examples of the absurdity, the cruelty of carrying over into this year of 1952 the isolationist limitations of our 1924 law.
>
> In no other realm of our national life are we so hampered and stultified by the dead hand of the past, as we are in this field of immigration.[14]

In addition to continuing the national origins quota system for the Eastern Hemisphere, the 1952 Act also established a four-category selection system. Fifty percent of each national quota was allocated for first preference distribution to aliens with high education or exceptional abilities, and the remaining three preference categories were divided among specified relatives of U.S. citizens and permanent resident aliens. This four-point selection system was the antecedent of our current preference system, which places higher priority on family reunification than on needed skills. However, under the 1952 law national origins remained the determining factor in immigrant admissions, and Northern and Western Europe were heavily favored. As in the past, the Western Hemisphere was not subject to numerical limitations.

Immigration during the decade 1951-1960 totaled 2,515,479, the highest since the 1920s. This was not surprising, since the two intervening decades included the depression of the 1930s and World War II. The gap between Eastern and Western Hemisphere

---

[13] U.S. Congress. Senate. Committee on the Judiciary. *The Immigration and Naturalization Systems of the United States.* S.Rept. 1515, 81st Cong., 2d Sess. Washington, GPO, 1950. p. 455.

[14] U.S. Congress. House. Message from the President of the United States. H. Doc. 520, 82d Cong., 2d Sess. June 25, 1952. p. 5.

immigration also narrowed: of the 2.5 million entries, almost a million entered from the Western Hemisphere.

Less than half of the immigrants who entered during the 1950s were admitted under the quota system. While many came under special temporary laws enacted to permit the admission of refugees and family members outside the quotas, many others entered as non-quota immigrants (e.g., from the Western Hemisphere) under the basic law. The gradual recognition that the national origins quota system was not functioning effectively as a means of regulating immigration was an important factor leading to the major policy revision that came in 1965.

REFUGEE ADMISSIONS IN THE 1950S AND 1960S

Major refugee admissions occurred outside the national origins quota system during the 1950s. The Refugee Relief Act of August 7, 1953, and the August 31, 1954 amendments authorized the admission of 214,000 refugees from war-torn Europe and escapees from Communist-dominated countries. Thirty percent of the admissions during the life of the Act were Italians, followed by Germans, Yugoslavs, and Greeks.

The Refugee Relief Act originated as an Administration bill, and combined humanitarian concerns for the refugees and escapees with "international political considerations." Quoting from President Eisenhower's letter which accompanied the draft legislation:

> These refugees, escapees, and distressed peoples now constitute an economic and political threat of constantly growing magnitude. They look to traditional American humanitarian concern for the oppressed. International political considerations are also factors that are involved. We should take reasonable steps to help these people to the extent that we share the obligation of the free world.[15]

In particular, the inclusion of the category of "escapees" from Communist domination in this and subsequent refugee legislation reflected the preoccupations of this Cold War period. This concern was also a major factor in the admission of refugees from the unsuccessful Hungarian revolution of October 1956. A total of 38,000 Hungarian refugees were eventually admitted to the United States, 6,130 with Refugee Relief Act visas and the remainder under the parole provision of the Immigration and Nationality Act.

The Act of September 11, 1957, sometimes referred to as the "Refugee-Escapee Act," provided for the admission of certain aliens who were eligible under the terms of the Refugee Relief Act, as well as "refugee-escapees," defined as persons fleeing persecution in Communist countries or countries in the Middle East. This was the basis for the definition of "refugee" incorporated in the Immigration and Nationality Act from

---

[15] U.S. Congress. Senate. Final Report of the Administrator of the Refugee Relief Act of 1953, As Amended. *Refugee Relief Act of 1953, As Amended.* Committee Print, 85th Cong., 1st Sess. Nov. 15, 1957. Washington, GPO, 1958. p. 1.

1965 until 1980. A total of 29,000 entered under the temporary 1957 refugee provisions, led by Hungarians, Koreans, Yugoslavs, and Chinese. Many entered with visas authorized by, but unused under, the expired Refugee Relief Act. In addition, the 1957 legislation repealed the quota deductions required by the Displaced Persons Act.

During the 1960s, refugees from persecution in communist dominated countries in the Eastern Hemisphere and from countries in the Middle East continued to be admitted, first under the Fair Share Law, enacted July 14, 1960, and subsequently under the Immigration and Nationality Act. Approximately 19,700 refugees entered under the 1960 legislation. Its primary purpose was to enable the United States to participate in an international effort to close the refugee camps which had been in operation in Europe since the end of World War II. U.S. participation was limited to one-fourth of the total number resettled.

Cuban refugees began entering the United States with the fall of the Batista government in 1959, and continued throughout the 1960s and, in smaller numbers, the 1970s. Approximately 700,000 Cuban refugees had entered the United States prior to new influx that began in April 1980. In the past, the United States has accepted the Cubans as refugees from communism through a variety of legal means.

THE IMMIGRATION AND NATIONALITY ACT AMENDMENTS OF 1965 AND THEIR AFTERMATH

The 1965 amendments to the 1952 Act repealed the national origins quota system and, according to one authority, "represented the most far-reaching revision of immigration policy in the United States since the First Quota Act of 1921."[16] In place of nationality and ethnic considerations, the Immigration and Nationality Act amendments of October 3, 1965 (P.L. 89-236; 79 Stat. 911) substituted a system based primarily on reunification of families and needed skills.

The circumstances that led to this major shift in policy in 1965 were a complex combination of changing public perceptions and values, politics, and legislative compromise. Public support for the repeal of the national origins quota system reflected changes in public attitudes toward race and national origins. It can be argued that the 1965 immigration legislation was as much a product of the mid-1960s and the heavily Democratic 89th Congress which also produced major civil rights legislation, as the 1952 Act had been a product of the Cold War period of the early 1950s.

The 1965 amendments replaced the national origins quota system as the primary control of Eastern Hemisphere immigration with an annual ceiling on Eastern Hemisphere immigration of 170,000 and a 20,000 per country limit. Within these restrictions, immigrant visas were distributed according to a seven-category preference system placing priority, in order, on family reunification, attracting needed skills, and refugees. The 1965 law also provided that effectively July 1, 1968, Western Hemisphere

---

[16] Harper, Elizabeth J. *Immigration Laws of the United States.* 3d ed. Indianapolis, Bobbs-Merrill Co., Inc., 1975. p. 38.

immigration would be limited by an annual ceiling of 120,000, without per-country limits or a preference system.

The Immigration and Nationality Act Amendments of 1976 (P.L. 94-571; 90 Stat. 2703) extended the 20,000 per-country limit and a slightly modified version of the seven-category preference system equally to the Western Hemisphere. The preference system and the per-country limits were applied to the two hemispheres under the separate ceilings of 170,000 for the Eastern Hemisphere, and 120,000 for the Western Hemisphere. Legislation enacted in 1978 (P.L. 95-412; 92 Stat. 907) combined the separate ceilings into a single worldwide ceiling of 290,000 with a single preference system. The Refugee Act of 1980 (P.L. 96-212; 94 Stat. 102) eliminated refugees as a category of the preference system, and set the worldwide ceiling of 270,000, exclusive of refugees.

The major source of immigration to the United States has shifted since 1965 from Europe to Latin American and Asia, reversing the trend of nearly two centuries. According to the *1988 Statistical Yearbook of the Immigration and Naturalization Service* (p. xvii-xviii), Europe accounted for 50 percent of U.S. immigration during the decade fiscal years 1955-64, followed by North America (defined by the Immigration and Naturalization Service to include Mexico, the Caribbean, and Central America) at 36 percent, and Asia at 8 percent. In fiscal year 1988, Asia was highest at 41 percent, followed by North America at 39 percent, and Europe at 10 percent. In order, the countries exceeding 20,000 immigrants in fiscal year 1988 were Mexico, the Philippines, Haiti, Korea, India, Mainland China, the Dominican Republic, Vietnam, and Jamaica.

These figures reflect a shift in both accessibility and demand by the sending countries. For example, Asian immigration was severely limited prior to the 1965 amendments, and has subsequently been augmented by the large number of Indochinese refugees adjusting to immigrant status outside the numerical limits. On the other hand, Irish immigration fell from 6,307 in fiscal year 1964 to 1,839 in fiscal year 1986, with 734 entering under the preference system and the majority entering as the immediate relatives of U.S. citizens. Ireland had been heavily favored under the national origins quota system. It has been commonly assumed that many Irish would like to immigrate to the United Sates, but lacked the necessary family relationships or skills to qualify under the preference system prior to the 1990 amendments.

THE 1970S THROUGH 1990: IMMIGRATION ISSUES, REVIEW, AND REVISION

The patterns of immigration and the policy considerations relating to it in the 1970s resembled in some respects those of the 1950s after the enactment of the Immigration and Nationality Act. In both decades, the entry of aliens outside the qualitative and quantitative restrictions of the basic law – both illegally as undocumented aliens, and legally as refugees – was increasingly the dominant pattern in immigration and the basis for the major issues confronting the Congress. Legislative response to the issue of refugees in 1980 and undocumented aliens in 1986 was followed in 1987 by a shift in congressional attention to legal immigration.

The 1981 report of the Select Commission on Immigration and Refugee Policy has contributed to the recent and ongoing congressional review of immigration issues. The 16-member Select Commission was created by legislation enacted in 1978 (P.L. 95-412; 92 Stat. 907) to conduct a study and evaluation of immigration and refugee laws, policies, and procedures. Its basic conclusion was that controlled immigration had been and continued to be in the national interest, and this underlay many of its recommendations. The Commission's recommendations were summed up as follows by Chairman Theodore Hesburgh in his introduction:

> We recommend closing the back door to undocumented/illegal migration, opening the front door a little more to accommodate legal migration in the interests of this country, defining our immigration goals clearly and providing a structure to implement them effectively, and setting forth procedures which will lead to fair and efficient adjudication and administration of U.S. immigration laws.[17]

Refugees and the Refugee Act of 1980

During the 5-year period, 1975-1980, refugees and refugee-related issues dominated congressional concern with immigration more than they had since the years following World War II. Beginning with the fall of Vietnam and Cambodia in April 1975, this period saw the admission of more than 400,000 Indochinese refugees, the enactment of major amendments to the Immigration and Nationality Act in the form of the Refugee Act of 1980, and the exodus from Mariel Harbor, Cuba to southern Florida.

The 1980 refugee legislation was enacted in part in response to Congress' increasing frustration with the difficulty of dealing with the ongoing large-scale Indochinese refugee flow under the existing ad hoc refugee admission and resettlement mechanisms. By the end of the 1970s, a consensus had been reached that a more coherent and equitable approach to refugee admission and resettlement was needed. The result was the amendments to the Immigration and Nationality Act contained in the Refugee Act of 1980, enacted on March 17, 1980 (P.L. 96-212; 94 Stat. 102).

The Refugee Act repealed the ideological and geographic limitations which had previously favored refugees fleeing communism or from countries in the Middle East and redefined "refugee" to conform with the definition used in the United Nations Protocol and Convention Relating to the Status of Refugees. The term "refugee" is now defined by the Immigration and Nationality Act as a person who is unwilling or unable to return to his country of nationality or habitual residence because of persecution or a well-founded fear of persecution on account of race, religion, nationality, membership in a particular social group, or political opinion. The 1980 amendments made provision for both a regular flow and the emergency admission of refugees, following legislatively prescribed

---

[17] Ibid., p. 3.

consultation with the Congress. In addition, the law authorized Federal assistance for the resettlement of refugees.

Shortly after the enactment of the Refugee Act of 1980, large numbers of Cubans entered the United States through southern Florida, totaling an estimated 125,000, along with continuing smaller numbers of Haitians. The Carter Administration was unwilling to classify either group as refugees, and no action was taken on the special legislation sought by the Administration. Beginning in 1984, the Reagan Administration adjusted the majority of the Cubans to lawful permanent resident status under P.L. 89-732, 1966 legislation enacted in response to the Cuban refugee situation in the 1960s. However, the status of the Cuban/Haitian entrants was not resolved finally until enactment of the Immigration Reform and Control Act of 1986, which included special legalization provisions.

Illegal Immigration and the Immigration Reform and Control Act of 1986

Immigration legislation focusing on illegal immigration was considered and passed by the 99th Congress, and enacted as P.L. 99-603 (Act of November 6, 1986; Stat. 3359), the Immigration Reform and Control Act of 1986. P.L. 99-603 consists primarily of amendments to the basic immigration law, the Immigration and Nationality Act of 1952, as amended (8 U.S.C. 1101 *et seq.*).

Reform of the law relating to the control of illegal immigration had been under consideration for 15 years, since the early 1970s. The 1986 legislation marked the culmination of bipartisan efforts both by Congress and the executive branch under four Presidents. As an indication of the growing magnitude of the problem, the annual apprehension of undocumented aliens by the Department of Justice's Immigration and Naturalization Service increased from 505,949 in 1972, the first year legislation aimed at controlling illegal immigration received House action, to 1,767,400 in 1986. Immigration and Naturalization Service apprehensions dropped to 1,190,488 in fiscal year 1987.

The prospect of employment at U.S. wages generally has been agreed to be the economic magnet that draws aliens here illegally. The principal legislative remedy proposed in the past and included in the new law is employer sanctions, or penalties for employers who knowingly hire aliens unauthorized to work in the United States. The other major provisions of the new law directly relate to employer sanctions. First, in an attempt to deal humanely with aliens who established roots here before the change in policy represented by the new Act, a legalization program was established that provides legal status for otherwise eligible aliens who had been here illegally since prior to 1982. Second, the legislation sought to respond to the apparent heavy dependence of seasonal agriculture on illegal workers by creating a 7-year special agricultural worker program, and by streamlining the previously existing "H-2" temporary worker program to expedite availability of alien workers and to provide statutory protections for U.S. and alien labor.

Legal Immigration and the Immigration Act of 1990

Following the enactment in 1986 of major legislation relating to illegal immigration, congressional legislative attention shifted to legal immigration, including the numerical limits on permanent immigration. This was an issue for a number of reasons. The numerical limits and preference system regulating the admission of legal immigrants originated in 1965, with some subsequent amendments. Since that time, and particularly in recent years, concern arose over the greater number of immigrants admitted on the basis of family reunification compared to the number of "dependent" non-family immigrants, and over the limited number of visas available under the preference system to certain countries. There was also concern about the backlogs under the existing preference system and, by some, about the admission of immediate relatives of U.S. citizens outside the numerical limits. Major legislation addressing these concerns passed the Senate and was introduced in the House in the 100th Congress (1987-1988). However, only temporary legislation addressing limited concerns passed both; leaving further consideration of a full-scale revision of legal immigration to the 101st Congress.

Major omnibus immigration legislation, the Immigration Act of 1990, was signed into law as P.L. 101-649 by President Bush on November 29, 1990. The Act represented a major revision of the Immigration and Nationality Act, which remained the basic immigration law. A primary focus of P.L. 101-649 was the numerical limits and preference system regulating permanent legal immigration. Beyond legal immigration, the eight-title Act dealt with many other aspects of immigration law, ranging from non-immigrants to criminal aliens to naturalization.

Major changes relating to legal immigration included an increase in total immigration under an overall flexible cap, an increase in annual employment-based immigration from 54,000 to 140,000, and a permanent provision for the admission of "diversity immigrants" from underrepresented countries. P.L. 101-649 provided for a permanent annual level of at least 675,000 immigrants beginning in fiscal year 1995, preceded by an annual level of approximately 700,000 during fiscal years 1992 through 1994. Refugees were the only major group of aliens not included. The Act established a three-track preference system for family-sponsored, employment-based, and diversity immigrants. Additionally, the Act significantly amended the work-related nonimmigrant categories for temporary admission.

P.L. 101-649 addressed a series of other issues pending before the Congress. It provided undocumented Salvadorans with temporary protected status for a limited period of time, and amended the Immigration and Nationality Act to authorize the Attorney General to grant temporary protected status to nationals of designated countries subject to armed conflict or natural disasters. It authorized a temporary stay of deportation and work authorization for legalized aliens' eligible immediate family members, and made 55,000 additional numbers available for them annually during fiscal years 1992-1994. In response to criticism of employer sanctions, it expanded the anti-discrimination provisions of the Immigration Reform and Control Act, and increased the penalties for unlawful discrimination. As part of a revision of all the grounds for exclusion and deportation, it significantly rewrote the political and ideological grounds that had been controversial since their enactment in 1952.

REFERENCES

Bennett, Marion T. *American immigration policies: a history*. Washington, Public Affairs Press, 1963. 362 p.

Bernard, William S., ed. *Immigration policy – a reappraisal*. New York, Harper & Brothers, 1950. 341 p.

Divine, Robert A. *American immigration policy, 1924-1952*. New Haven, Yale University Press, 1957. 220 p.

Gordon, Charles, and Harry N. Rosenfield. *Immigration law and procedure*. Rev. ed., New York, Matthew Bender, 1980. 6 v.

Handlin, Oscar. *The Americans*. Boston, Little, Brown and Co., 1963. 434 p.

---, ed. *Immigration as a factor in American history*. Englewood Cliffs, Prentice-Hall, Inc., 1959. 206 p.

--- *The Uprooted*. 2d ed. Boston, Little, Brown and Co., 1973. 333 p.

Harper, Elizabeth J. *Immigration laws of the United States*. 3d ed. Indianapolis, Bobbs-Merrill Co., Inc., 1975. 756 p.

Higham, John. *Send these to me*. New York, Atheneum, 1975. 259 p.

--- *Strangers in the land, patterns of American nativism, 1860-1925*. New Brunswick, Rutgers University Press, 1955. 431 p.

Immigration. Law and contemporary problems, *Duke University School of Law, v. 21*, Spring 1956: 211-426.

Jones, Maldwyn Allen. *American immigration*. Chicago, University of Chicago Press, 358 p.

Rischin, Moses, ed. *Immigration and the American tradition*. Indianapolis, Bobbs-Merrill Co., Inc., 1976. 456 p.

Schwartz, Abba P. *The Open society*. New York, William Morrow & Co., Inc., 1968. 241 p.

Scott, Franklin D. *The peopling of America: perspectives on immigration*. Washington, American Historical Association, 1972. 75 p. (AHA pamphlets 241).

Taylor, Philip. *The Distant magnet, European emigration to the U.S.A.* New York, Harper & Row, 1971. 326 p.

U.S. Congress. Senate. Committee on the Judiciary. The immigration and Naturalization systems of the United States. Washington, GPO, 1950. 925 p. (81st Congress, 2d session. Senate. *Report No. 1515*).

U.S. Department of Justice. Immigration and Naturalization Service. *1987 Statistical Yearbook*. Washington, GPO, 1988. 146 p.

U.S. Immigration Commission. Brief statement of the investigations of the Immigration Commission, with conclusions and recommendations and views of the majority. *U.S. Senate Doc. 747*, 61st Congress, 3d session. Washington, GPO, 1910-1911.

U.S. Interagency Task Force on Immigration Policy. Staff report. [Washington] Departments of Justice, Labor, and State, March 1979. 540 p.

U.S. Library of Congress. Congressional Research Service. Immigration Act of 1990 (P.L. 101-649), by Joyce Vialet and Larry Eig. [Washington] Dec. 14, 1990. 27 p. (*CRS Report for Congress No. 90-601 EPW*)

--- U.S. immigration law and policy: 1952-1986; report prepared for the Subcommittee on Immigration and Refugee Affairs, Committee on the Judiciary, U.S. Senate. Dec. 1987. Washington, GPO, 1988. 138 p. (100th Congress, 1st session. *Committee Print. S. Prt. 100-100*).

U.S. President's Commission on Immigration and Naturalization. *Whom we shall Welcome; report.* Washington, GPO [1953] 319 p.

U.S. Select Commission on Immigration and Refugee Policy. *Final report: U.S. Immigration policy and the national interest.* Mar. 1, 1981. Washington, GPO, 1981. 453 p.

White, Jerry C. A Statistical history of immigration. *I and N Reporter, v. 25,* summer 1976: 1-9.

APPENDIX A. IMMIGRATION BY REGION AND SELECTED COUNTRY OF LAST RESIDENCE - FISCAL YEARS 1820-1989

Region and country of last residence[1]	1820	1821 - 30	1831 - 40	1841 - 50	1851 - 60	1861 - 70	1871 - 80	1881 - 90
All countries	8,385	143,439	599,125	1,713,251	2,598,214	2,314,824	2,812,191	5,246,613
Europe	7,690	98,797	495,681	1,597,442	2,452,577	2,065,141	2,271,925	4,735,484
Austria-Hungary	(¹)	(¹)	(¹)	(¹)	(¹)	7,800	72,969	353,719
Austria	(¹)	(¹)	(¹)	(¹)	(¹)	[9] 7,124	63,009	226,038
Hungary	(¹)	(¹)	(¹)	(¹)	(¹)	[5] 484	9,960	127,681
Belgium	1	27	22	5,074	4,738	6,734	7,221	20,177
Czechoslovakia	(¹)	(¹)	(¹)	(¹)	(¹)	(¹)	(¹)	(¹)
Denmark	20	169	1,063	539	3,749	17,094	31,771	88,132
France	371	8,497	45,575	77,262	76,358	35,986	72,206	50,464
Germany	968	6,761	152,454	434,626	951,667	787,468	718,182	1,452,970
Greece	-	20	49	16	31	72	210	2,308
Ireland[6]	3,614	50,724	207,381	780,719	914,119	435,778	436,871	655,482
Italy	30	409	2,253	1,870	9,231	11,725	55,759	307,309
Netherlands	49	1,078	1,412	8,251	10,789	9,102	16,541	53,701
Norway-Sweden	3	91	1,201	13,903	20,931	109,298	211,245	568,362
Norway	(¹)	(¹)	(¹)	(¹)	(¹)	(¹)	95,323	176,586
Sweden	(¹)	(¹)	(¹)	(¹)	(¹)	(¹)	115,922	391,776
Poland	5	16	369	105	1,164	2,027	12,970	51,806
Portugal	35	145	829	550	1,055	2,658	14,082	16,978
Romania	(¹)	(¹)	(¹)	(¹)	(¹)	(¹)	[7] 11	6,348
Soviet Union	14	75	277	551	457	2,512	39,284	213,282
Spain	139	2,477	2,125	2,209	9,298	6,697	5,266	4,419
Switzerland	31	3,226	4,821	4,644	25,011	23,286	28,293	81,988
United Kingdom[4][5]	2,410	25,079	75,810	267,044	423,974	606,896	548,043	807,357
Yugoslavia	(¹)	(¹)	(¹)	(¹)	(¹)	(¹)	(¹)	(¹)
Other Europe	-	3	40	79	5	8	1,001	682
Asia	6	30	55	141	41,538	64,759	124,160	69,942
China[16]	1	2	8	35	41,397	64,301	123,201	61,711
Hong Kong	(¹¹)	(¹¹)	(¹¹)	(¹¹)	(¹¹)	(¹¹)	(¹¹)	(¹¹)
India	1	8	39	36	43	69	163	269
Iran	(¹³)	(¹³)	(¹³)	(¹³)	(¹³)	(¹³)	(¹³)	(¹³)
Israel	(¹³)	(¹³)	(¹³)	(¹³)	(¹³)	(¹³)	(¹³)	(¹³)
Japan	(¹³)	(¹³)	(¹³)	(¹³)	(¹³)	186	149	2,270
Korea	(¹³)	(¹³)	(¹³)	(¹³)	(¹³)	(¹¹)	(¹¹)	(¹¹)
Philippines	(¹³)	(¹³)	(¹³)	(¹³)	(¹³)	(¹¹)	(¹¹)	(¹¹)
Turkey	1	20	7	59	83	131	404	3,782
Vietnam	(¹¹)	(¹¹)	(¹¹)	(¹¹)	(¹¹)	(¹¹)	(¹¹)	(¹¹)
Other Asia	3	-	1	11	15	72	243	1,910
America	387	11,564	33,424	62,469	74,720	166,607	404,044	426,967
Canada & Newfoundland[17][18]	209	2,277	13,624	41,723	59,309	153,878	383,640	393,304
Mexico[19]	1	4,817	6,599	3,271	3,078	2,191	5,162	[19] 1,913
Caribbean	164	3,834	12,301	13,528	10,660	9,046	13,957	29,042
Cuba	(¹)	(¹)	(¹)	(¹)	(¹)	(¹)	(¹)	(¹)
Dominican Republic	(¹)	(¹)	(¹)	(¹)	(¹)	(¹)	(¹)	(¹)
Haiti	(¹)	(¹)	(¹)	(¹)	(¹)	(¹)	(¹)	(¹)
Jamaica	(¹)	(¹)	(¹)	(¹)	(¹)	(¹)	(¹)	(¹)
Other Caribbean	164	3,834	12,301	13,528	10,660	9,046	13,957	29,042
Central America	2	105	44	368	449	95	157	404
El Salvador	(¹)	(¹)	(¹)	(¹)	(¹)	(¹)	(¹)	(¹)
Other Central America	2	105	44	368	449	95	157	404
South America	11	531	856	3,579	1,224	1,397	1,128	2,304
Argentina	(¹)	(¹)	(¹)	(¹)	(¹)	(¹)	(¹)	(¹)
Colombia	(¹)	(¹)	(¹)	(¹)	(¹)	(¹)	(¹)	(¹)
Ecuador	(¹)	(¹)	(¹)	(¹)	(¹)	(¹)	(¹)	(¹)
Other South America	11	531	856	3,579	1,224	1,397	1,128	2,304
Other America	(¹)	(¹)	(¹)	(¹)	(¹)	(¹)	(¹)	(¹)
Africa	1	16	54	55	210	312	358	857
Oceania	1	2	9	29	158	214	10,914	12,574
Not specified[22]	300	33,030	69,902	53,115	29,011	17,791	790	789

See footnotes at end of table.

Appendix A – Continued

Region and country of last residence[1]	1891 - 1900	1901 - 10	1911 - 20	1921 - 30	1931 - 40	1941 - 50	1951 - 60	1961 - 70
All countries	3,687,564	8,795,386	5,735,811	4,107,209	528,431	1,035,039	2,515,479	3,321,677
Europe	3,555,352	8,056,040	4,321,887	2,463,194	347,566	621,147	1,325,727	1,123,492
Austria-Hungary	[23] 592,707	[23] 2,145,266	[23] 896,342	63,548	11,424	28,329	103,743	26,022
Austria	[3] 234,081	[3] 668,209	453,649	32,868	[24] 3,563	[24] 24,860	67,106	20,621
Hungary	[3] 181,288	[3] 808,511	442,693	30,680	7,861	3,469	36,637	5,401
Belgium	18,167	41,635	33,746	15,846	4,817	12,189	18,575	9,192
Czechoslovakia	(*)	(*)	3,426	102,194	14,393	8,347	918	3,273
Denmark	50,231	65,285	41,983	32,430	2,559	5,393	10,984	9,201
France	30,770	73,379	61,897	49,610	12,623	38,809	51,121	45,237
Germany	[25] 505,152	[25] 341,498	[25] 143,945	412,202	[34] 114,058	[25] 226,578	477,765	190,796
Greece	15,979	167,519	184,201	51,084	9,119	8,973	47,608	85,969
Ireland[4]	388,416	339,065	146,181	211,234	10,973	19,789	48,362	32,966
Italy	651,893	2,045,877	1,109,524	455,315	68,028	57,661	185,491	214,111
Netherlands	26,758	48,262	43,718	26,948	7,150	14,860	52,277	30,606
Norway-Sweden	321,281	440,039	161,469	165,780	8,700	20,765	44,632	32,600
Norway	95,015	190,505	66,395	68,531	4,740	10,100	22,935	15,484
Sweden	226,266	249,534	95,074	97,249	3,960	10,665	21,697	17,116
Poland	[25] 96,720	(*)	[25] 4,613	227,734	17,026	7,571	9,985	53,539
Portugal	27,508	69,149	89,732	29,994	3,329	7,423	19,588	76,065
Romania	12,750	53,008	13,311	67,646	3,871	1,076	1,039	2,531
Soviet Union	[25] 505,290	[25] 1,597,306	[25] 921,201	61,742	1,370	571	671	2,465
Spain	8,731	27,935	68,611	28,958	3,258	2,898	7,894	44,659
Switzerland	31,179	34,922	23,091	29,676	5,512	10,547	17,675	18,453
United Kingdom[5] [6]	271,538	525,950	341,408	339,570	31,572	139,306	202,824	213,822
Yugoslavia	(*)	(*)	[5] 1,888	49,064	5,835	1,576	8,225	20,381
Other Europe	282	39,945	31,400	42,619	11,949	8,486	16,350	11,604
Asia	74,862	323,543	247,236	112,059	16,595	37,028	153,249	427,642
China[16]	14,799	20,605	21,278	29,907	4,928	16,709	9,657	34,764
Hong Kong	(*)	(*)	(*)	(*)	(*)	(*)	[11] 15,541	75,007
India	68	4,713	2,082	1,886	496	1,761	1,973	27,189
Iran	(*)	(*)	(*)	[12] 241	195	1,380	3,388	10,339
Israel	(*)	(*)	(*)	(*)	(*)	[13] 476	25,476	29,602
Japan	25,942	129,797	83,837	33,462	1,948	1,555	46,250	39,988
Korea	(*)	(*)	(*)	(*)	(*)	[14] 107	6,231	34,526
Philippines	(*)	(*)	(*)	(*)	[16] 528	4,691	19,307	98,376
Turkey	30,425	157,369	134,066	33,824	1,065	798	3,519	10,142
Vietnam	(*)	(*)	(*)	(*)	(*)	(*)	[17] 335	4,340
Other Asia	3,628	11,059	5,973	12,739	7,435	9,551	21,572	63,369
America	38,972	361,888	1,143,671	1,516,716	160,037	354,804	996,944	1,716,374
Canada & Newfoundland[17] [18]	3,311	179,226	742,185	924,515	108,527	171,718	377,952	413,310
Mexico[19]	[19] 971	49,642	219,004	459,287	22,319	60,589	299,811	453,937
Caribbean	33,066	107,548	123,424	74,899	15,502	49,725	123,091	470,213
Cuba	(*)	(*)	(*)	[12] 15,901	9,571	26,313	78,948	208,536
Dominican Republic	(*)	(*)	(*)	(*)	[25] 1,150	5,627	9,897	93,292
Haiti	(*)	(*)	(*)	(*)	[35] 191	911	4,442	34,499
Jamaica	(*)	(*)	(*)	(*)	(*)	(*)	[25] 8,869	74,906
Other Caribbean	33,066	107,548	123,424	58,996	4,590	16,874	[25] 20,935	58,980
Central America	549	8,192	17,159	15,769	5,861	21,665	44,751	101,330
El Salvador	(*)	(*)	(*)	(*)	[35] 673	5,132	5,895	14,992
Other Central America	549	8,192	17,159	15,769	5,168	16,533	38,856	86,338
South America	1,075	17,280	41,899	42,215	7,803	21,831	91,628	257,954
Argentina	(*)	(*)	(*)	(*)	[35] 1,349	3,338	19,486	49,721
Colombia	(*)	(*)	(*)	(*)	[35] 1,223	3,858	18,048	72,028
Ecuador	(*)	(*)	(*)	(*)	[35] 337	2,417	9,841	36,780
Other South America	1,075	17,280	41,899	42,215	4,894	12,218	44,253	99,425
Other America	(*)	(*)	(*)	[35] 31	25	29,276	59,711	19,530
Africa	350	7,368	8,443	6,286	1,750	7,367	14,092	28,954
Oceania	3,965	13,024	13,427	8,726	2,483	14,551	12,976	25,122
Not specified[22]	14,063	[22] 33,523	1,147	228	-	142	12,491	93

See footnotes at end of table.

Appendix A – Continued

Region and country of last residence[1]	1971 - 80	1981 - 89	1984	1985	1986	1987	1988	1989	Total 170 years 1820 - 1989
All countries	4,493,314	5,801,579	543,903	570,009	601,708	601,516	643,025	1,090,924	55,457,531
Europe	800,368	637,524	69,879	69,526	69,224	67,967	71,854	94,338	36,977,034
Austria-Hungary	16,028	20,152	2,846	2,521	2,604	2,401	3,200	3,586	4,338,049
Austria	9,478	14,566	2,351	1,930	2,039	1,769	2,493	2,845	[3] 1,825,172
Hungary	6,550	5,586	495	591	565	632	707	741	[3] 1,666,801
Belgium	5,329	6,239	787	775	843	859	706	705	209,729
Czechoslovakia	6,023	6,649	693	684	588	715	744	526	145,223
Denmark	4,439	4,696	512	465	544	515	561	617	369,738
France	25,069	28,068	3,335	3,530	3,876	3,809	3,637	4,101	783,322
Germany	74,414	79,809	9,375	10,028	9,853	9,823	9,748	10,419	7,071,313
Greece	92,369	34,490	3,311	3,487	3,497	4,067	4,590	4,588	700,017
Ireland[4]	11,490	22,229	1,096	1,288	1,757	3,032	5,121	6,983	4,715,393
Italy	129,368	51,008	6,328	6,351	5,711	4,666	5,332	11,069	5,356,862
Netherlands	10,492	10,723	1,313	1,235	1,263	1,303	1,152	1,253	372,717
Norway-Sweden	10,472	13,252	1,455	1,557	1,564	1,540	1,669	1,809	2,144,024
Norway	3,941	3,612	403	386	367	372	446	556	[5] 800,672
Sweden	6,531	9,640	1,052	1,171	1,197	1,168	1,223	1,253	[5] 1,283,097
Poland	37,234	64,888	7,229	7,409	6,540	5,818	7,298	13,279	587,972
Portugal	101,710	36,365	3,800	3,811	3,804	4,009	3,290	3,861	497,195
Romania	12,393	27,361	2,956	3,764	3,809	2,741	2,915	3,535	201,345
Soviet Union	38,961	42,898	3,349	1,532	1,001	1,139	1,408	4,570	3,428,927
Spain	39,141	17,689	2,188	2,278	2,232	2,056	1,972	2,179	282,404
Switzerland	8,235	7,561	795	960	923	964	920	1,072	358,151
United Kingdom[6] [8]	137,374	140,119	16,516	15,591	16,129	15,889	14,667	16,961	5,100,096
Yugoslavia	30,540	15,984	1,404	1,521	1,915	1,793	2,039	2,464	133,493
Other Europe	9,287	7,324	611	719	771	708	785	741	181,064
Asia	1,588,178	2,416,276	247,775	255,164	258,546	248,293	254,745	296,420	5,897,301
China[10]	124,326	306,108	29,109	33,095	32,389	32,669	34,300	39,284	873,737
Hong Kong	113,467	83,848	12,290	10,795	9,930	8,785	11,817	15,257	[11] 287,863
India	164,134	221,977	23,617	24,536	24,808	26,394	25,312	28,599	426,907
Iran	45,136	101,267	11,131	12,327	12,031	10,323	9,846	13,027	[12] 161,946
Israel	37,713	38,367	4,136	4,279	5,124	4,753	4,444	5,494	[13] 131,634
Japan	49,775	40,654	4,517	4,552	4,444	4,711	5,085	5,454	[14] 455,813
Korea	267,638	302,782	32,537	34,791	35,164	35,397	34,151	33,016	[15] 611,284
Philippines	354,987	477,485	46,985	53,137	61,492	58,315	61,017	66,119	[16] 955,374
Turkey	13,399	20,028	1,652	1,690	1,975	2,080	2,200	2,538	409,122
Vietnam	172,820	266,027	25,803	20,367	15,010	13,073	12,856	13,174	[17] 443,522
Other Asia	244,783	557,735	55,998	55,595	56,179	51,793	53,717	74,458	940,099
America	1,982,735	2,564,698	208,111	225,519	254,078	265,026	294,906	672,639	12,017,021
Canada & Newfoundland[17] [18]	169,939	132,296	15,659	16,354	16,060	16,741	15,821	18,294	4,270,943
Mexico[18]	640,294	975,657	57,820	61,290	66,753	72,511	95,170	405,660	3,208,543
Caribbean	741,126	759,416	68,368	79,374	98,527	100,615	110,949	87,597	2,590,542
Cuba	264,863	135,142	5,699	17,115	30,787	27,363	16,610	9,523	[12] 739,274
Dominican Republic	148,135	209,899	23,207	23,861	26,216	24,947	27,195	26,744	[18] 468,000
Haiti	56,335	118,510	9,554	9,872	12,356	14,643	34,858	13,341	[18] 214,888
Jamaica	137,577	184,481	18,997	18,277	18,916	22,430	20,474	23,572	[21] 405,833
Other Caribbean	134,216	111,384	10,911	10,249	10,252	11,232	11,812	14,417	762,547
Central America	134,640	321,845	27,626	28,447	30,086	30,366	31,311	101,273	673,385
El Salvador	34,436	133,938	8,753	10,093	10,881	10,627	12,043	57,628	[20] 195,066
Other Central America	100,204	187,907	18,873	18,354	19,205	19,739	19,268	43,645	478,319
South America	295,741	375,026	38,536	40,052	42,650	44,782	41,846	59,812	1,163,482
Argentina	29,897	21,374	2,287	1,925	2,318	2,192	2,556	3,766	[20] 125,165
Colombia	77,347	99,066	10,897	11,802	11,213	11,482	10,153	14,918	[20] 271,570
Ecuador	50,077	43,841	4,244	4,601	4,518	4,656	4,736	7,587	[20] 143,293
Other South America	138,420	210,745	21,208	21,724	24,601	26,452	24,201	33,541	623,454
Other America	995	458	2	2	2	11	9	3	110,126
Africa	80,779	144,096	13,594	15,236	15,500	15,730	17,124	22,485	301,348
Oceania	41,242	38,401	4,249	4,552	4,352	4,437	4,324	4,956	197,818
Not specified[22]	12	582	295	12	8	63	72	86	267,009

See footnotes at end of table.

Appendix A – Continued

1. Data for years prior to 1906 relate to country whence alien came; data from 1906-79 and 1984 89 are for country of last permanent residence; and data for 1980-83 refer to country of birth. Because of changes in lists of countries, and lack of data for specified countries for various periods, data for certain countries, especially for the total period 1820-1989, are not comparable throughout. Data for specified countries are included with countries to which they belonged prior to World War I.

2. Data for Austria and Hungary not reported until 1861.

3. Data for Austria and Hungary not reported separately for all years during the period.

4. No data available for Czechoslovakia until 1920.

5. Prior to 1926, data for Northern Ireland included in Ireland.

6. Data for Norway and Sweden not reported separately until 1871.

7. No data available for Romania until 1880.

8. Since 1925, data for United Kingdom refer to England, Scotland, Wales, and Northern Ireland.

9. In 1920, a separate enumeration was made for the Kingdom of Serbs, Croats, and Slovenes. Since 1922, the Serb, Croat, and Slovene Kingdom recorded as Yugoslavia.

10. Beginning in 1957, China includes Taiwan.

11. Data not reported separately until 1952.

12. Data not reported separately until 1925.

13. Data not reported separately until 1949.

14. No data available for Japan until 1861.

15. Data not reported separately until 1948.

16. Prior to 1934, Philippines recorded as insular travel.

17. Prior to 1920, Canada and Newfoundland recorded as British North America. From 1820-98, figures include all British North America possessions.

18. Land arrivals not completely enumerated until 1906.

19. No data available for Mexico until 1888-93.

20. Data not reported separately until 1932.

21. Data for Jamaica not collected until 1953. In prior years, consolidated under British West Indies, which is included in "Other Countries."

22. Included in countries "Not specified" until 1925.

23. From 1899-1919, data for Poland included in Austria-Hungary, Germany, and the Soviet Union.

24. From 1938-45, data for Austria included in Germany.

25. Includes 32,897 persons returning in 1906 to their homes in the United States.

* Represents zero.

Note: From 1820-67, figures represent alien passengers arrived at seaports form 1866-91 and 1895-97, immigrant aliens arrived; from 1892-94 and 1989-1989, immigrant aliens admitted for permanent residence. From 1892-1903, aliens entering by cabin class were not counted as immigrants. Land arrivals were not completely enumerated until 1908.

See Glossary for fiscal year definitions. For this table, fiscal year 1843 covers 9 months ending September 1843; fiscal years 1832 and 1850 cover 15 months ending December 31 of the respective years; and fiscal year 1868 covers 6 months ending June 30, 1888.

Source: Immigration and Naturalization Service, 1989 Statistical Yearbook, p. 2-5.

APPENDIX B. REFUGEES AND ASYLEES GRANTED LAWFUL PERMANENT RESIDENT STATUS BY REGION AND SELECTED COUNTRY OF BIRTH - FISCAL YEARS 1946-89

Region and country of birth	Total	1946-50	1951-60	1961-70	1971-80	1981-89
All countries	2,374,264	213,347	492,371	212,843	539,447	916,256
Europe	917,623	211,983	456,146	55,235	71,858	122,401
Albania	4,074	29	1,409	1,952	395	289
Austria	17,046	4,801	11,487	233	185	340
Bulgaria	5,333	139	1,138	1,799	1,238	1,019
Czechoslovakia	35,844	8,449	10,719	5,709	3,646	7,321
Estonia	11,284	7,143	4,103	16	2	20
Germany[1]	100,998	36,633	62,860	665	143	697
Greece	30,849	124	28,568	586	478	1,093
Hungary	74,302	6,086	55,740	4,044	4,358	4,074
Italy	63,151	642	60,657	1,198	346	308
Latvia	38,312	21,422	16,783	49	16	42
Lithuania	27,384	18,694	8,569	72	23	26
Netherlands	17,617	129	14,336	3,134	8	10
Poland	198,917	78,529	81,323	3,197	5,882	29,986
Portugal	5,063	12	3,650	1,361	21	19
Romania	56,819	4,180	12,057	7,158	6,812	26,612
Soviet Union	125,431	14,072	30,059	871	31,309	49,120
Spain	10,330	1	246	4,114	5,317	652
Yugoslavia	84,468	9,816	44,755	18,299	11,297	301
Other Europe	10,401	1,082	7,687	778	382	472
Asia	925,331	1,106	33,422	19,895	210,683	660,225
Afghanistan	21,345	-	1	-	542	20,802
Cambodia	117,084	-	-	-	7,739	109,345
China[2]	38,990	319	12,008	5,308	13,760	7,595
Hong Kong	8,558	-	1,076	2,128	3,468	1,886
Indonesia	17,490	-	8,253	7,658	222	1,357
Iran	38,856	118	192	58	364	38,124
Iraq	14,499	-	130	119	6,851	7,399
Japan	4,525	3	3,803	554	56	109
Korea	4,615	-	3,116	1,316	65	118
Laos	154,830	-	-	-	21,690	133,140
Syria	3,594	4	119	383	1,336	1,752
Thailand	27,451	-	15	13	1,241	26,182
Turkey	6,332	603	1,427	1,489	1,193	1,620
Vietnam	454,191	-	2	7	150,266	303,916
Other Asia	12,971	59	3,280	862	1,890	6,880
Africa	30,202	20	1,768	5,486	2,991	19,937
Egypt	8,588	8	1,354	5,396	1,473	357
Ethiopia	18,230	-	61	2	1,307	16,860
Other Africa	3,384	12	353	88	211	2,720
Oceania	162	7	75	21	37	22
North America	497,625	163	831	132,068	252,633	111,930
Cuba	488,779	3	6	131,557	251,514	105,699
El Salvador	1,184	-	-	1	45	1,138
Nicaragua	3,937	1	1	3	36	3,896
Other North America	3,725	159	824	507	1,038	1,197
South America	3,185	32	74	123	1,244	1,712
Chile	940	-	5	4	420	511
Other South America	2,245	32	69	119	624	1,201
Unknown or not reported	136	36	55	15	1	29

[1] Includes East and West Germany.
[2] Includes Mainland China and Taiwan.
- Represents zero.
NOTE: See Glossary for fiscal year definitions. Data for fiscal years 1987-88 have been adjusted. The data no longer include aliens granted permanent resident status under the Cuban/Haitian entrant provisions of the Immigration Reform and Control Act of 1986.

Source: Immigration and Naturalization Service, 1989 Statistical Yearbook, p. 65.

[1]   Includes East and West Germany.
[2]   Includes Mainland China and Taiwan.
- Represents zero.

Note: See Glossary for fiscal year definitions. Data for fiscal years 1987-88 have been adjusted. The data no longer include aliens granted permanent resident status under the Cuban/Haitian entrant provisions of the Immigration Reform and Control Act of 1986.

Source: Immigration and Naturalization Service, 1989 Statistical Yearbook, p. 65.

Chapter 3

IMMIGRATION: S VISAS FOR CRIMINAL AND TERRORIST INFORMANTS

Karma Ester

ABSTRACT

In response to the terrorist acts of September 11, 2001, Congress passed legislation making permanent a provision that allows aliens with critical information on criminal or terrorist organizations to come into the United Sates in order to provide information to law enforcement officials. This legislation (S. 1424) became P.L. 107-45 on October 1, 2001. The law amends the Immigration and Nationality Act to provide permanent authority for the administration of the "S" visa. Up to 200 criminal informants and 50 terrorist informants may be admitted annually. Since FY1995, almost 700 informants and their accompanying family members have entered on S visas.

BACKGROUND

Following the 1993 bombing of the World Trade Center in New York City, Congress amended the Immigration and Nationality Act (INA) to establish the new "S" nonimmigrant visa category for alien witnesses and informants as part of the Violent Crime Control Act of 1994.[1] Nonimmigrants are admitted for specific purpose and a temporary period of time. Nonimmigrants – such as B-2 tourists, F-1 foreign students, A-1 diplomats, H-2A temporary agricultural workers, J-1 exchange visitors, or L intra-company business personnel – are typically referred to by the letter denoting the subsection of the INA that provides the authority for their admission; hence "S visas" is the abbreviated reference to §101(a)(15)(S) of the INA.

The provision establishing the S visa in the INA was originally due to expire on September 13, 1999, but Congress had extended it until September 13, 2001.[2] Aliens

---

[1] 8 U.S.C. §1101(a)(15)(S).
[2] 8 U.S.C. §1184(k)(2); INA §214(k)(2).

The provision establishing the S visa in the INA was originally due to expire on September 13, 1999, but Congress had extended it until September 13, 2001.[2] Aliens admitted through the S visa categories are designated as S-5 and S-6 nonimmigrants.[3] Request for these visas must be filed by a state or federal law enforcement agency, and the filing agency must assume responsibility for the alien from their time of entry until their departure, or until they adjust status. Under this law, the Attorney General has the discretion to waive any ground of exclusion for an "S" nonimmigrant, except for those regarding Nazi persecution and genocide.[4] The length of stay for an S-5 or S-6 nonimmigrant is limited to 3 years, and no extension of stay is permitted, but adjustment to legal permanent residence (LPR) is possible. As **Table 1** indicates, 409 informants have been admitted from FY1995 through June FY2001.

CRIMINAL INFORMANTS (S-5)

The S-5 classification may be granted to a foreign national who has been determined by the Attorney General to possess critical, reliable information concerning a criminal organization or enterprise. The alien must be willing to supply or have supplied this information to federal or state law enforcement authorities, or to a federal or state court. The Attorney General must also determine that the alien's presence in the United States is essential to the success of an authorized criminal investigation or to the successful prosecution of an individual involved in a criminal organization or enterprise. The number of witnesses or informants granted S-5 status in a fiscal year may not exceed 200.[5]

TERRORIST INFORMANTS (S-6)

The S-6 category of classification may be granted to an alien who the Attorney General and Secretary of State have determined possesses critical, reliable information concerning a terrorist organization, operation, or enterprise, and who is willing to supply or has supplied information to federal law enforcement authorities or to a federal court. The Attorney General and Secretary must also determine that the alien has been or will be placed in danger as a result of providing information, and is eligible to receive a cash reward under §36(a) of the State Department Basic Authorities Act of 1956.[6] The number of informants admitted under this classification may not exceed 50 in any fiscal year.

---

[2] 8 U.S.C. §1184(k)(2); INA §214(k)(2).
[3] Due to prior use of S-1 and S-2 classification codes, the S informants are designated as S-5 and S-6 even though the statutory cites are 101(a)(15)(S)(i) and (ii) of INA.
[4] 8 U.S.C. §1182(a)(3)(E); INA §212(a)(3)(E).
[5] 8 U.S.C. §1184(j)(1); INA §214(j)(1).
[6] 8 U.S.C. §1255(j)(2).

ACCOMPANYING FAMILY MEMBERS (S-7)

The law allows the informant's accompanying family members – including spouses, married or unmarried children, and parents – to receive S nonimmigrant visas. These accompanying family members are referred to as S-7 nonimmigrants. As detailed in **Table 1**, 245 family members of informants have been admitted from FY1995 through June FY2001.

Table 1. Nonimmigrants Admitted Under S-Visa Category, FY1995-FY2001

Fiscal year	Informants admitted	Family members admitted
1995	59	77
1996	98	21
1997	35	19
1998	90	56
1999	50	33
2000	21	17
2001[a]	56	22
Total	409	245

Source: CRS presentation of data from the Immigration and Naturalization Service.
[a] FY2001 data are current through June 2001.

ADJUSTMENT OF STATUS

The Attorney General may adjust the status of S-5 nonimmigrants and their family members to that of aliens lawfully admitted for permanent residence (LPRs) if the aliens have supplied information as agreed, and the information has contributed substantially to a successful criminal investigation. The Attorney General likewise may adjust the status of S-6 nonimmigrants and their accompanying family members to LPR status if the aliens have – in the sole discretion of the Attorney General – substantially contributed information that led to:

- the prevention or frustration of an act of terrorism against the United States, or
- a successful investigation or prosecution of an individual in such an act of terrorism.

The informants also must have received a reward under §36(a) of the State Department Basic Authorization Act of 1956.[7]

In order for an "S" nonimmigrant to adjust status, a Form I-854 must be filed on the alien's behalf by the federal or state law enforcement agency that originally requested the visa. This application must be approved by the Assistance Attorney General in charge of

---

[7] 8 U.S.C. §1255(j); INA §245(j).

the Criminal Division of the Department of Justice, and the INS Commissioner, before the alien can file the Form I-854. These LPR adjustments are then counted under the country ceilings of the numerically limited legal immigration system. Upon adjusting status, the nonimmigrant will remain deportable, if convicted of a crime involving moral turpitude, for 10 years after the date of adjustment.

OTHER CONDITIONS AND REQUIREMENTS

Aliens admitted under the S-5 and S-6 categories are required to report quarterly to the Attorney General. If an alien fails to meet the reporting requirements, INS may institute deportation proceedings. The alien will lose lawful nonimmigrant status if convicted of any criminal offense punishable by one year or more of imprisonment after the date of admission. The alien must waive the right to contest (other than on the basis of an application for withholding of deportation) any action of deportation instituted before that alien obtains lawful permanent residence status. The alien must also abide by any other limitations, restrictions, or conditions imposed by the Attorney General.[8]

LEGISLATIVE ACTIVITY

Senator Edward Kennedy, chairman of the Senate Committee on the Judiciary's Subcommittee on Immigration, introduced legislation (S. 1424) providing permanent authority for the S visa on September 13, 2001, two days after the terrorist attacks in New York and Washington, D.C. The Senate passed S. 1424 by unanimous consent that same day. The House likewise passed S. 1424 by unanimous consent on September 15, 2001, and the legislation was cleared for the White House the same day. Members of Congress stated that it was very important to pass this legislation to aid federal, state, and local law enforcement agencies in their investigation of the terrorist attacks of September 11, 2001. On October 1, 2001, President Bush signed P.L. 107-45, providing permanent authority for admission under the S visa.

---

[8] 8 U.S.C. §1184(k)(4); INA §214(k).

Chapter 4

IMMIGRATION AND INFORMATION TECHNOLOGY JOBS: THE ISSUE OF TEMPORARY FOREIGN WORKERS

Ruth Ellen Wasem

ABSTRACT

A congressional debate is occurring about whether a shortage of information technology (IT) workers exists and whether, in response, the annual cap on admission of nonimmigrant (temporary) H-1B specialty workers should be raised. H-1B visas are issued for periods up to 3 years to foreign nationals who are professionals in specialty occupations. The current statutory limit for H-1B visas issued is 65,000 annually. Some are arguing that the cap should be removed entirely so that there are no limits on H-1B visas. Others favor a temporary raising of the ceiling as a quick response to a perceived heightened need for IT workers over the next few years. Many who favor raising the ceiling maintain that it should only be done as part of a package of reforms to the H-1B program as well as in conjunction with incentives to educate and retrain U.S. workers. Others oppose any changes to the H-1B provision.

The demand for H-1B workers is increasing, as attestations filed by employers – often for more than one job opening – have grown from 53,485 in FY1992 to 180,739 in FY1997. The U.S. Department of Labor (DOL) certified 398,324 job openings in FY1997. In FY1996 computer-related occupations became the largest category of DOL-approved job openings, having risen from 25.6% in FY1995. It continued to lead in openings approved for H-1Bs in FY1997 at 44.4% of the total. Many more job openings are approved by DOL than are actually filled by an alien admitted by the Immigration and Naturalization Service. For the first time, the 65,000 numerical limit on H-1B visas was reached prior to the end of FY1997, with visa numbers running out by September. The ceiling for FY1998 was reached in May of this year.

The increased use of the H-1B provision to obtain IT workers is perceived by some observers as one of a number of sings that there is an inadequate supply of U.S. workers to fill IT jobs. There does not appear to be a consensus at the present time, however, about the existence of an IT worker shortage. As often happens, each set of arguments is supported by a host of well-selected anecdotes; and some of their points are more valid than others. Some who do not believe a shortage exists might acknowledge that, at least for some IT jobs, the labor market is tight. They would disagree, however, that importing foreign workers should be the first means turned to in order to increase the supply of labor.

Some policymakers view H-1B visas as an opportunity for U.S. employers to try out the "best and brightest" from around the world, promoting a cross fertilization that improves the competitiveness of U.S. firms. Yet, others question whether the current language defining H-1B specialty occupations is a high enough threshold to target the "best and brightest" since having a baccalaureate degree or the requisite work experience remains sufficient to meet the H-1B qualifications. These observers consider H-1B a rather blunt instrument if the objective is to draw on the most promising and talented foreign nationals or to recruit IT workers to fill a shortage. That the H-1B visa is often the conduit for foreign students to become legal permanent residents is labeled a misuse of immigration laws by some and a positive chain of events by others.

After simmering for a year or so, interest in "the information technology (IT) worker shortage" boiled over in 1998 when the Senate Judiciary Committee and the House Judiciary Subcommittee on Immigration and Claims held hearings. These committees have jurisdiction because the issue initially was framed in terms of lessening the perceived problem by raising the annual cap on nonimmigrant H-1B specialty workers.[1] In FY1997, the 65,000 visa limit for skilled temporary workers had been reached by September, and in FY1998, all of the visas were claimed by May.

This report will first provide a brief description of the H-1B program, including how many of the temporary workers have been approved to come into the United States to fill IT jobs. It then will present the arguments that have been made, pro and con, about the existence of a spot labor shortage and suggest why no consensus on this point has yet been reached. A variety of possible remedies for a tight labor market are described and the extent to which the H-1B visa targets IT workers is examined before the report closes with a discussion of the nexus between foreign students, the H-1B program, and employment-based immigration.

THE H-1B PROGRAM

The major nonimmigrant category for temporary workers is the H visas.[2] The largest classification of H visas is the H-1B workers in specialty occupations. "Specialty occupation" is defined in law and regulation as requiring theoretical and practical application of a body of highly specialized knowledge in fields of human endeavor including, but not limited to, architecture, engineering, mathematics, physical sciences,

---

[1] Some legislative proposals and Administration initiatives include provisions to address the IT worker issue not only through raising the H-1B cap but also through incentives for education and training of U.S. students and workers. For information on the content and status of legislation, see: CRS Report 96-333, *Immigration: Nonimmigrant H-1B Specialty Worker Facts and Issues*, by Ruth Ellen Wasem.

[2] A nonimmigrant is an alien legally in the United States for a **specific purpose** and a **temporary period of time**. There are over 20 major nonimmigrant visas categories specified in the Immigration and Nationality Act (INA), and they are commonly referred to by the letter that denotes their subcategory in that section of the statute (hence, H-1B).

social sciences, medicine and health, education, law, accounting, business specialties, theology and the arts, and requiring the attainment of at least a bachelor's degree or its equivalent.[3] Fashion models (who are prominent) are also admitted on H-1B visas. H-1B nonimmigrants are admitted for periods up to 3 years and may stay for a maximum of 6 years. The statutory limit for H-1B visas issued is 65,000 annually.

Requirements for H-1B Employers

Any employer wishing to bring an H-1B nonimmigrant into the United States must attest in an application to the U.S. Department of Labor (DOL) that: the employer will pay the nonimmigrant the greater of the actual wages paid other employees in the same job or the prevailing wage for that occupation; the employer will provide working conditions for the nonimmigrant that do not cause the working conditions of the other employees to be adversely affected; and, there is no strike or lockout. The employer also must post at the workplace the application to hire nonimmigrants. The prospective H-1B nonimmigrant must demonstrate that they have the requisite education and work experience for the posted positions.

DOL initially reviews the application for completeness and obvious inaccuracies, but does not conduct inquiries into the facts presented on the attestation. Only if a complaint subsequently is raised challenging the employer's application can DOL conduct an investigation. If DOL then finds the employer failed to comply, the employer may be fined, denied the right to apply for additional H-1Bs, and may be subject to other penalties. While DOL is responsible for certifying the attestations, the Immigration and Naturalization Service (INS) actually admits the nonimmigrants. Petitions are approved for periods up to 3 years, and an alien can stay a maximum of 6 years on an H-1B visa.

Trends in H-1B Approvals

As Figure 1 depicts, demand for H-1B workers has been increasing over the past 5 years. Both the number of attestations that firms have filed – often for more than one job opening – and the number of positions approved is growing, with the exception of a downturn in openings approved in FY1996. Since it is not uncommon for some firms to obtain approval to employ more nonimmigrants than they actually hire, the DOL data greatly overstates prospective H-1B admissions. In addition to these "anticipatory" filings, firms usually file attestations for each work site the H-1B may be assigned to, especially if these work sites are in different labor markets. Such multiple attestations are reportedly common for firms that are subcontractors – referred to by some as "outsourcers" and by others as "body shops."

---

[3] Section 101(a)(15)(H)(1)(B) of INA.

Figure 1. Trends in H-1B Attestations and Approvals

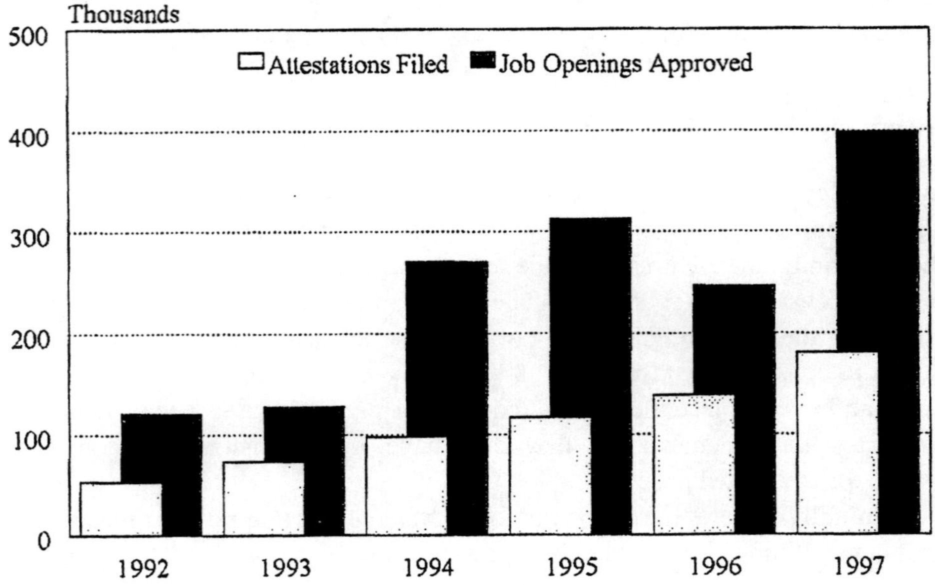

Source: CRS presentation of DOL data.
Note: Attestations often include multiple job openings.

In addition to the multiple counts of potential H-1Bs in the DOL data, DOL data are not linked to the INS admissions data so we do not know which of the 389,324 job openings in FY1997 were filled by H-1B nonimmigrants. Nor does INS issue reports of the occupations and employers of the H-1Bs nonimmigrants that it admits.[4] Despite the multiple counts in the DOL attestation data and the inadequacies of the INS nonimmigrant data, it is evident that H-1B visa demand is pressing against the statutory ceiling. For the first time, the INS reached the 65,000 numerical limit on H-1B visas prior to the end of FY1997, with visa numbers running out by September 1997. The ceiling for FY1998 was reached in May of this year.

In FY1996 computer-related occupations became the largest category and continue to lead in job openings approved for H-1Bs, going from 25.6% in FY1995, to 41.5% in FY1996, to 44.4% of the openings approved in FY1997. Therapists – mostly physical therapists, but also some occupational therapists, speech therapists and related occupations – fell from over half (53.5%) of those approved in FY1995 to one-quarter (25.9%) in FY1997. The other notable occupational categories in FY1997 were electrical

[4] INS admissions data for H-1B also pose problems of multiple counts, but for different reasons. Its data do not distinguish newly arriving H-1Bs from those H-1B visa holders who happen to be coming back from a trip abroad.

engineers (3.1%), auditors and accountants (2.4%), university faculty (2.0%), and physicians and surgeons (1.8%). Since these jobs may be approved for periods up to 3 years, employers of H-1Bs approved in FY1995 may be seeking to renew them in FY1998.

COMPETING "FINDINGS"

Assertions about the impact on the economy of an alleged shortage of information technology (IT) workers has prompted some policymakers to propose raising the admissions cap on H-1B workers. A set of "findings" has emerged to support this viewpoint, namely, that:

- Employment in "core" IT occupations (i.e., computer engineers and scientists, systems analysts, and computer programmers) has been, and is projected to continue, expanding rapidly through the early years of the next century.[5]
- Hundreds of thousands of IT job vacancies[6] and low unemployment rates for IT workers[7] exist despite substantial increases in occupational wages,[8] which taken together purportedly demonstrate the existence of a spot labor shortage; and
- Through the mid-1990s, the number of graduates from 4-year colleges in the United States with computer science, math, and engineering degrees diminished and is insufficient to meet current demand. Moreover, many of the students with these majors are foreign nationals who could be lost to U.S. firms upon

---

[5] U.S. Department of Commerce (DOC). Office of Technology Policy. *America's New Deficit: The Shortage of Information Technology Workers.* Washington 1997. For updated employment projections by the U.S. Bureau of Labor Statistics (the source of the job growth data in the DOC report), see: Silvestri, George T. Occupational Employment Projections to 2006. *Monthly Labor Review*, November 1997. For related information see: Luker Jr., William and Donald Lyons. Employment Shifts in High-Technology Industries, 1988-96. *Monthly Labor Review*, June 1997.

[6] There could be 190,000 unfilled IT jobs (broadly defined) at large and mid-sized firms nationwide, according to the Information Technology Association of America (ITAA). *Help-Wanted: the IT Workforce Gap at the Dawn of a New Century, 1997.* There could be 346,000 vacant positions in the core IT occupations at small to large companies nationwide, according to the Virginia Polytechnic Institute and State University and the ITAA. *Help Wanted: A Call for Collaborate Action for the New Millennium, 1998.*

[7] The unemployment rate in 1997 for computer systems analysts and scientists was 1.1% and for electrical and electronic engineers, it was 0.9%. The rate for the broader group of all workers in professional occupations was considerably higher, at 2.1%. In 1997, the unemployment rate was 1.6% for computer programmers. It was half-again as much, 2.4%, for the broader group of all workers in technical and related occupations. (Source: U.S. Bureau of Labor Statistics, unpublished data.)

[8] An annual compensation survey conducted by William M. Mercer for the ITAA found average hourly compensation increases ranging from 12%-20% in a variety of IT jobs between 1995 and 1996. (Source: ITAA, *Help-Wanted: the IT Workforce Gap at the Dawn of a New Century.*) Another survey reported that salaries for computer network professionals rose 7.4%, on average, in the 1996-1997 period. A third estimated that the average salary increase for systems analysts was 15%, programmer/analysts 11%, and directors of systems development 10% from 1996 to 1997. (Source: DOC, *American's New Deficit.*)

graduation if not for the H-1B program. They would instead return to their home countries and staff the competitors of U.S. firms.[9]

- Without an increase in the supply of skilled/trained workers "at the right price" to fill employer demand, both IT and non-IT firms will expand less rapidly than they have been and thereby slow down the rate of economic growth in the United States. Rather than forego expansion, these firms will be spurred to export IT jobs to foreign countries through outsourcing or relocation of facilities.[10]

However, other "findings" refute those presented above. They include:

- Rapid job growth in the past few years and in the coming years does not properly characterize all IT occupations (e.g., computer programmers). While projections of above-average employment gains may prove true over the long run for some IT occupations, at least one – engineers – has been prone to a boom-bust cycle in the short run due to unanticipated events.[11]
- Vacancies are not necessarily indicative of a labor shortage, and a larger than average share of unfilled positions would be expected at firms with relatively high employee turnover and growth rates.[12] Some also assert surveying employers about vacancies could result in some double counting – particularly in the Washington, D.C. metropolitan area where multiple companies vying for the same federal government or private sector contracts may each have claimed as vacant, job slots which were contingent on future awards.[13]
- While some studies have found evidence of large wage increases in IT jobs, other surveys have found considerably smaller gains.[14]

---

[9] American Electronics Association. *American's High-Tech Workforce: Supply of workers Not Satisfying Industry Demand,* 1998; Friedman, Thomas L. Foreign Affairs: Help Wanted. *New York Times,* April 14, 1998; see U.S. Congress. House. Committee on the Judiciary. Subcommittee on Immigration and Claims. *Immigration and America's Workforce for the 21st Century.* Washington, April 21, 1998. (Hereafter cited as House Subcommittee on Immigration, *Immigration and America's Workforce*)

[10] ITAA, *Help-Wanted: the IT Workforce Gap at the Dawn of a New Century.*

[11] Testimony by Dr. Robert I. Lerman, Urban Institute and American University; and by John R. Reinert, Institute of Electrical and Electronics Engineers – USA. See: U.S. Congress. Senate. Committee on the Judiciary. *The High Tech Worker Shortage and U.S. Immigration.* Washington, February 25, 1998. (Hereafter cited as Senate Committee on the Judiciary, *High Tech Worker Shortage*)

[12] Ibid.

[13] This point was made by analysts at George Mason University who, based on their survey of high-technology firms in Northern Virginia, reported 19,000 job vacancies. Peter, Behr. Tech Industry's Data Crunch. *Washington Post,* April 20, 1998.

[14] In his testimony, John R. Fraser, Deputy Wage and Hour Administrator at the U.S. Department of Labor noted that "the wage growth record for the IT industry is mixed. Though BLS wage trends for broad computer-related categories show only average wage growth between 1988 and 1997 for all categories, it only shows above-average wage growth in 1996 and 1997 and only in the lower-skill computer-related categories, particularly programmers. At the same time, a variety of **industry** wage surveys show larger wage increases in 1996 and 1997 in specialized high-skill occupations." [Note: It has been suggested that the recent increase in demand for programmers is associated with the Year 200 problem. It true, the wage acceleration shown by BLS data for programmers could be short lived.] See, House Subcommittee on Immigration, *Immigration and America's Workforce.*

- Because graduates of bachelor's degree programs in computer and information science are not the only source of labor for IT jobs, their small number relative to vacancy estimates does not prove that a shortage exists. Since the mid-1990s there appears to have been an increase in college students enrolling in computer science, computer engineering, and information management programs, which suggests that the labor market already has begun to adjust to increased demand.[15]

- There are certain benefits that arise from a tight labor market. Employers typically raise wages, improve working conditions, and provide more training in the short-supply occupation. In response to increased employer demand, education/training institutions expand their relevant programs and students as well as workers have a greater incentive to enroll in them. If the cap on H-1B workers were raised to increase the supply of labor to IT jobs, it would well delay or prevent these labor market adjustments.[16]

As often happens, each set of arguments is supported by a host of well selected anecdotes; and some of their points are more valid than others. These statements, however, raise as many questions as they appear to answer. For example, what exactly is an IT job and how many are there? Has demand increased at unusually high rates, compared to historical standards, for all or just some IT jobs and are relatively rapid gains likely to continue in the near term? What are the requisite qualifications of the rapidly expanding IT jobs and how many of them are vacant? How long have they been vacant and by how much have their wages risen? Is there an economically or socially acceptable limit to how high wages should go to attract additional U.S. workers to high-demand jobs before the labor market adjustment process[17] is supplemented by measures like importing temporary workers? It there a bias toward hiring younger workers in this field? Why do math, engineering, and computer/information science majors attract the numbers of foreign compared to U.S. students that they do? Is the U.S. educational (K-12 and post-secondary) or economic system in some way dissuading domestic students from choosing their majors? With the globalization of individual countries' markets for goods and services, should the United States continue to largely confine U.S.-based firms' choice of workers to the domestic labor force?

---

[15] Testimony by John R. Reinert, Senate Committee on the Judiciary, *The High Tech Worker Shortage*; and testimony by Dr. Norman Matloff, University of California at Davis, House Subcommittee on Immigration, *Immigration and America's Workforce*.

[16] U.S. Department of Labor (DOL). Testimony by Raymond J. Uhalde, Acting Assistance Secretary of Labor, Employment and Training Administration, Senate Committee on the Judiciary, *The High Tech Worker Shortage*.

[17] According to economic theory, there is a market-clearing or equilibrium wage at which supply equals demand. If this balance is disturbed because, for example, employers demand more workers than are willing to provide their services at the current market-clearing wage, firms will have to bid up wages to entice workers to increase their supply of services (e.g., switch from other occupations or undertake qualifying coursework). This labor market adjustment, which could take some time when a lengthy education period is a job requirement, continues until supply and demand attain a new balance at a higher market-clearing wage.

IS THERE A CONSENSUS ON A SHORTAGE?

There does not appear to be a consensus at the present time about the existence of an IT worker shortage. Some who do not believe a shortage exists might acknowledge that, at least for some IT jobs, the labor market is tight. They would disagree, however, that importing foreign workers should be the first means utilized to increase the supply of labor.

The Supply of and Demand for IT Workers

There are no direct measures of occupational labor supply and demand imbalances.[18] Although demand-side variables are available, they do not reflect differences within occupations in employer needs by education or experience level (e.g., demand conditions for 45-year-old workers with bachelor's degrees in computer science who have 15 years of experience versus demand conditions for recent college graduates who majored in computer science or closely related fields for entry-level IT jobs).[19] The supply-side is even more problematic.

It is very difficult to estimate the supply of labor to particular occupations and whether shortages exist because, among other things, there rarely is just one source of workers for a given job. Although individuals with bachelor's degrees in engineering, math, and computer science might be expected to be the major source of labor for IT jobs, they are substantially augmented by workers with bachelor's degrees in other disciplines as well as graduates from masters and doctoral programs. For example, of students who graduated with bachelor's degrees in 1992-93 and were employed in computer-related occupations in 1994, 55% had *not* been computer science or engineering majors.[20] In addition to 4-year colleges and universities, community colleges and private vocational institutions can prepare students for IT jobs as can company training programs. Individuals also can acquire IT skills through training provided while they were members of the Armed Forces.[21]

Because of these multiple sources, it is not only difficult to determine the supply of labor by occupation but it also makes the occupational unemployment rate a tenuous measure of shortages due to the potential mobility of workers from different occupations

---

[18] For more information on the complexities involved in estimating supply-demand imbalances, see: Cohen, Malcolm S. *Labor Shortages as America Approaches the Twenty-first Century*. Ann Arbor, University of Michigan Press, 1995.

[19] A subtext of the IT worker debate is whether all workers or just young workers are in short supply. It has been suggested, based largely on anecdotal evidence, that IT firms are demanding recent college graduates to whom they can pay entry-level wages rather than drawing from the available pool of mid-career IT workers whose skills might or might not need upgrading and who would be relatively more expensive to employ.

[20] Lerman, Robert I. It There A Labor Shortage in the Information Technology Industry? *Issues in Science and Technology*, spring 1998.

[21] The failure of the DOC report to balance demand projections against contributions to the IT labor supply from these multiple sources was one of the report's weaknesses, according to the U.S. General Accounting

and from outside the labor force into IT jobs. The unemployment rate for a given occupation reflects the number of workers in the labor force who report that their last job was in that occupation. Thus, the unemployment rate for systems analysts neither picks up workers with a computer science degree who have not yet gotten a job or who are employed in other fields, nor workers with degrees in related fields who are potentially qualified to work as system analysts but are not otherwise employed. It also does not take into account qualified workers, who are not in the labor force but might reenter under the right circumstances (e.g., retirees from IT companies).

The occupational unemployment rate alone is a faulty indicator of labor scarcity for yet another reason. Rather than reflecting a shortage, a below-average unemployment rate might mean a balance in supply-demand conditions if the frictional component of unemployment typically is small because workers and firms have good information and are quickly able to make suitable matches. The level of an occupation's unemployment rate over time, and its historical relationship to the broader group in which it falls (e.g., all professional or all technical workers), would provide more insight than the snapshot of an occupation's unemployment rate in one period and in isolation.

The number of vacancies also in an inadequate measure of labor scarcity. Are the 190,000-346,000 job vacancies estimated by the ITAA and Virginia Polytechnic Institute and State University consistent with past vacancy levels for IT jobs? Are vacancies remaining unfilled for longer periods than in the past? A certain number of vacancies for one period does not in itself provide much insight into how atypical, or not, the current situation is. And, what are the salary levels associated with these vacancies? It is possible that some jobs remain unfilled because employers are not offering wages sufficiently high to attract available workers. Moreover, the vacancy estimates are themselves suspect because, according to the General Accounting Office, the response rates of the two surveys which produced them are below the level commonly accepted to enable generalizations from the respondent firms to the entire survey population.[22] The low response rate could account for discrepancy between the Virginia's Polytechnic Institute's estimate (3.4 million) and the Census Bureau's estimates (1.5 million in 1996 according to employers and 2 million in 1997 according to households) of employment in core IT occupations.[23]

Remedies for a Tight Labor Market

There are several ways to address an occupational scarcity of workers. Firms can increase and broaden their recruitment efforts, rely more on overtime or labor-saving technologies, lower the job's minimum qualifications, reorganize its duties to use workers in other positions, provide training to upgrade the skills of new hires or current employees, and improve wage and benefit packages as well as working conditions.

Office (GAO). *Information Technology: Assessment of the Department of Commerce's Report on Workforce Demand and Supply.* GAO/HEHS-98-106R.

[22] Ibid.

[23] Testimony by Robert I. Lerman, Senate Committee on the Judiciary, *The High Tech Worker Shortage.*

Individuals, in reaction to rising wages and expanding job opportunities, could be spurred to undertake education/training to acquire the requisite skills. Firms could bring workers into the United States – either on a temporary or permanent basis – to fill the jobs, or they could export the jobs to other countries. Depending on the situation at hand, some of these strategies may be more feasible or costly than others.

For occupations in short supply that requires a fairly long preparation period (e.g., completion of a 4-year college education), it could be argued that importing workers or exporting jobs would be a quicker fix than allowing the domestic labor market to adjust. However, a short-term fix has the potential to develop into a long-term dependence because individual choice among educational and training options (e.g., majoring in engineering versus medicine) is partially based on their expectations about the relative wage and employment prospects of different occupations. If people perceive that the wage of computer engineers is being held down compared to the wage of doctors due to the importation of labor or the exportation of jobs, their incentive to invest in an engineering degree is likely to diminish. Provisions in bills that propose raising the H-1B cap which would encourage U.S. students to major in math and science might help offset this disincentive and reflect the desire to avoid long-term dependence on the H-1B program as a source of IT workers.

Some policy makers question whether H-1B visas were intended as a response to specific shortages in the labor market. Congress provided for temporary employment of foreign workers to alleviate labor shortages when it enacted the Immigration and Nationality Act of 1952, but as Congress revised the law governing the H visas at various times over the past few decades it did not link the H-1B subcategory to labor shortages. Many in the business community are reluctant to link H-1B visas to labor shortages because it would likely lead to labor market tests that they view as time consuming and burdensome.

AVENUE OF "THE BEST AND THE BRIGHTEST?"

Some policymakers view H-1B visas as an opportunity for U.S. employers to try out the "best and the brightest" from around the world, promoting a cross fertilization that improves the competitiveness of U.S. firms. At one time, the H-1B nonimmigrants were described as aliens of "distinguished merit and ability," but Congress replaced that definition with the "specialty occupation" language several years ago. This change reportedly was prompted by court interpretations of "distinguished merit and ability" that enabled anyone with a baccalaureate degree to qualify and was considered by many as a refinement of the law that clarified, perhaps even raised, the standards.

Some question whether the H-1B specialty occupation language is a high enough threshold to target the "best and the brightest" since having a baccalaureate degree or the requisite work experience remains sufficient to meet the H-1B qualifications.[24] These

---

[24] DOL underscores its views that H-1B are not always the "best and the brightest" by citing data that 80% of H-1B jobs pay less than $50,000 a year. Senate Committee on the Judiciary, *The High Tech Worker Shortage*.

observers consider H-1B a rather blunt instrument if the objective to draw on the most promising and talented foreign nationals or to recruit IT workers to fill a shortage. As data presented earlier in **Figure 2** reveal, jobs certified for H-1Bs extend well beyond IT occupations. Since international trade agreements make it difficult to raise the qualifications for H-1B visa holders, some advocates for the "best and the brightest" favor another subcategory of H temporary visas targeted to this potential migrant.[25]

Just as there are a complex set of issues surrounding the adequacy of the IT workforce, there are other concerns revolving around the H-1B visas. For several years, some Members of Congress have been seeking to revise the H-1B provisions, with possible changes ranging from relaxing requirements for employers to tightening protections for U.S. workers. This debate to increase the 65,000 ceiling offers an opportunity to make other revisions in the H-1B provisions.[26]

Figure 2. Top Five Occupations for Approved H-1B Openings

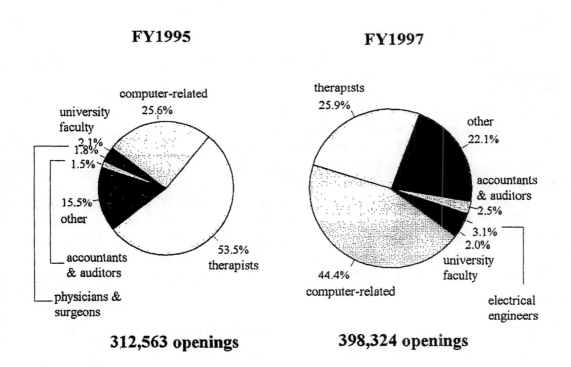

FY1995

computer-related 25.6%

university faculty
2.1%
1.8%
1.5%

15.5% other

53.5% therapists

accountants & auditors

physicians & surgeons

312,563 openings

FY1997

therapists 25.9%

other 22.1%

accountants & auditors
2.5%

3.1%
2.0%
university faculty

44.4% computer-related

electrical engineers

398,324 openings

Source: CRS presentation of DOL data.

---

[25] General Agreement on Trade in Services (GATS), Uruguay Round Trade Agreements, Schedule of Specific Commitments. For legal analysis see: CRS Congressional Distribution Memorandum, *U.S. Immigration –Related obligations under the WTO General Agreement on Trade in Services* by Jeanne J. Grimmett. May 12, 1998.

[26] For analysis of this ongoing debate, see: CRS Report 96-333, *Immigration: Nonimmigrant H-1B Specialty Worker Facts and Issues*, by Ruth Ellen Wasem.

PATHWAY TO PERMANENT RESIDENCE?

In practically terms, the H-1B visa links the foreign student (F-1 visa) to legal permanent residence (LPR).[27] Anecdotal accounts tell of foreign students who are hired by U.S. firms as they are completing their programs. The employers obtain H-1B visas for the recent graduates, and if the employees meet expectations, the employers may also petition for the nonimmigrants to become legal permanent residents through one of the employment-based immigration categories.[28] Some policymakers consider this a natural and positive chain of events, arguing that it would be foolish to educate these talented young people only to make them leave to work for foreign competitors. Others consider the "F-1 to H-1B to LPR" pathway an abuse of the temporary element of nonimmigrant status and a way to circumvent the laws and procedures that protect U.S. workers from being displaced by immigrants.[29] A brief overview of foreign students and employment-based immigration follows.

Foreign Students[30]

The most common visa for foreign students is the F-1 visa. It is tailored for international students pursuing a full-time academic education, and there are no numerical limits. The F-1 student is generally admitted as a nonimmigrant for the period of the program of study, referred to as the duration of status. The law requires that the student have a foreign residence that they do not intend to abandon. Once in the United States on an F visa, the nonimmigrants are generally barred from off-campus employment. An alien on an F visa who otherwise accepts employment violates the terms of the visa and is subject to removal and other penalties.

Generally, foreign students are likely to major in business, engineering, and the sciences, often obtaining degrees that are well suited for IT careers. Data from the National Council Survey of Earned Doctorates reveal the dominance of foreign students in science and engineering. During 1995 there were more foreign Ph.D. recipients in engineering than U.S. citizen recipients – 2,523 and 2,382 respectively. In 1970,

---

[27] In 1970, Congress removed the "double temporary" requirement that both the H-1B's stay *and the job* be temporary.

[28] DOL reports that nearly half the permanent employment-based immigrants converted from H-1B status. House Subcommittee on Immigration, *Immigration and America's Workforce*.

[29] During the 104th Congress and earlier, some observers maintained that many foreign students violate the intent of the provision that requires they have a foreign residence that they do not intend to abandon. Specifically, the practice of a foreign student petitioning to change status to nonimmigrant H-1B professional and specialty workers raised concerns. Fears that foreign students, as well as H-1Bs, were "leap frogging" the laws that protect U.S. workers from being displaced by immigrants prompted some to suggest that all foreign students and foreign temporary workers return home for 2 years to establish residency if they wish to return to the United States. This proposal circulated in the Senate, but it met with strong and varied opposition from the educational community and business interests. Many argued it would just lead to abuses and increase incentives to manipulate the nonimmigrant visa process.

[30] For further background and analysis, see: CRS Report 97-576, *Immigration: Foreign Students in the United States*, by Ruth Ellen Wasem.

however, there were 2,514 U.S. citizens and only 471 foreign students who received PhD's in engineering.

It is quite possible that the swelling demand for H-1B workers in IT occupations is in part a reflection of the prevalence of foreign students studying science and engineering at U.S. colleges and universities. Employers do not have to go abroad to recruit foreign workers with the requisite skills in IT. Some label this a result of the U.S. being home to world-class universities, while others see this as a result of U.S. students being less likely to major in science and engineering because other fields offer more profitable futures.[31]

Permanent Employment-Based Immigration

If an employer wishes to hire an alien to work on a permanent basis in the United States, the alien may petition to immigrate to the United States through one of the employment-based categories. The employer petitions for the prospective immigrant, and if the petition is successful, the alien becomes a legal permanent resident.[32] Many H-1B nonimmigrants may have education, skills, and experience that are similar to the requirements for three of the five preference categories for employment-based immigration: priority workers – i.e., persons of extraordinary ability in the arts, sciences, education, business, or athletics, outstanding professors and researchers, and certain multinational executives and managers (first preference); members of the professions holding advanced degrees or persons of exceptional ability (second preference); and skilled workers with at least 2 years training and professionals with baccalaureate degrees (third preference).[33]

Employment-based immigrants applying through the second and third preferences must have job offers for positions in which the employers have obtained labor certification. The labor certification is intended to demonstrate that immigrants are not taking jobs away from qualified U.S. workers, and many consider the labor certification process far more arduous than the attestation process used for H-1B nonimmigrants.[34] More specifically, the employer who seeks to hire a prospective immigrant worker petitions with the INS and DOL on behalf of the alien. The prospective immigrant must demonstrate that he or she meets the qualifications for the particular job as well as the preference category. If the DOL determines that a labor shortage exists in the occupation for which the petition is filed, labor certification will be issued.[35] If there is not a labor

---

[31] U.S. Congress. Senate. Committee on the Judiciary. *Examining Nonimmigrant Immigration Issues*. S. Hearing 104-814, Serial No. J-104-48. Washington, September 28, 1995.

[32] There are also per-country numerical limits. For more information, see: CRS Report 94-146, *Numerical Limits on Permanent Admissions*, by Joyce C. Vialet and Molly Forman.

[33] Third preference also includes 10,000 "other workers," i.e., unskilled workers in occupations in which U.S. workers are in short supply.

[34] Certain second preference immigrants whose admittance is deemed to be "in the national interest" are exempt from labor certification.

[35] Through regulation, DOL has established the "Schedule A" listing of occupations for which shortages have already been determined. These occupations are physical therapists, professional nurses, and those of exceptional ability in the sciences or the arts. "Schedule B" conversely lists the occupations for which

shortage in the given occupation, the employer must submit evidence of extensive recruitment efforts in order to obtain certification.

While the demand for H-1B workers has been exceeding the limit, the number of immigrants who were admitted or adjusted under one of the employment-based preferences – 117,499 – was considerably fewer than the statutory limit of 140,000 in FY1996. The first and second preferences fell far short of the almost 40,040 available to each category, with 27,501 and 18,462 respectively. The third preference drew on some of the unused numbers of the first and second preferences to exceed the admissions numbers allocated to it, reaching 62,756 in FY1996.

Currently, prospective immigrants in first preference do not have to wait for a visa, except for immigrants from China. However, those H-1B workers seeking to adjust status who are from India (reportedly a significant portion of H-1B visa holders) and from China face a backlog of several years if they petition for a second or third preference visa. Some speculate that firms would bring in more workers through employment-based preference if the numerical limits for these countries were lifted.

---

shortages do not exist and for which the hiring of immigrants would adversely affect U.S. workers. These 49 occupations range from assembler to yard workers.

Chapter 5

IMMIGRATION LEGALIZATION AND STATUS ADJUSTMENT LEGISLATION

Ruth Ellen Wasem

ABSTRACT

Although President George Bush has said he opposes broad legalization for unauthorized migrants, there have been reports that the President will recommend legislation to legalize an estimated 3 million Mexicans working in the United States without legal authorization. President Bush and Mexican President Vicente Fox have established a Cabinet-level working group to develop "an orderly framework for migration that ensures humane treatment [and] legal security, and dignifies labor conditions." Initial speculation that the President would unveil a legalization proposal in early September has been tempered by recent reports that he will recommend a more gradual series of proposals.

On August 2, Congressional Democrats announced a set of principles that will guide broad immigration legislation they intend to propose, and among those principles is a plan for "earned legalization." Their proposal would not be limited to nationals of any one country and would focus on "longtime, hard-working residents of good moral character, with no criminal problems ... who are otherwise eligible to become U.S. citizens."

While supporters characterize legalization provisions as fair treatment of aliens who have been living and working here for years as good neighbors and dedicated employees, opponents describe the such proposals as an unfair reward to illegal aliens who violated the law to get into the United States.

During the 106th Congress, Democratic Members, with support from the Clinton Administration, unsuccessfully tried to enact a set of immigration legalization and status adjustment provisions known as the "Latino and Immigrant Fairness Act" (S. 3095). Congress ultimately enacted a set of provisions (**P.L. 106-553** and **P.L. 106-554**) known as the "Legal Immigration Family Equity Act" (LIFE). LIFE establishes a new nonimmigrant "V" visa for certain immediate relatives of legal permanent residents (LPRs), expands the use of the "K" nonimmigrant visa to include immediate relatives of citizens with petitions pending, allowing aliens in the "late amnesty" class action court cases to adjust to LPR status, and — most notably — temporarily reinstated §245(i) of the Immigration and Nationality Act (INA) enabling unauthorized aliens to adjust to LPR status if they are otherwise eligible for visas.

President Bush expressed support for an extension of §245(i), which expired April 30, 2001. A variety of bills to extend §245(i) of INA have been introduced, and H.R. 1885, a 245(i) extension bill introduced by House Judiciary Immigration Subcommittee Chairman George Gekas, passed the House of Representatives May 21. The Senate Judiciary Committee reported S. 778 with amendments on July 26.

Data from the 2000 decennial census, meanwhile, are adding further complexity to the debate. Recent estimates of unauthorized aliens based upon the 2000 census range from 7.5 to 9 million, with some suggesting that unauthorized aliens in the United States may be more than twice the 5.1 million total INS estimated previously.

BACKGROUND

Legalization

The issue of whether aliens residing in the United States without legal authorization may be permitted to become legal permanent residents (LPRs) has been debated periodically, and at various times Congress has enacted legalization programs. In 1929, for example, Congress enacted a law that some consider a precursor to legalization because it permitted certain aliens arriving prior to 1921 "in whose case there is no record of admission for permanent residence" to register with INS's predecessor agency so that they could become LPRs. In 1952, Congress included a registry provision when it codified the Immigration and Nationality Act (INA) and this provision evolved into an avenue for unauthorized aliens to legalize their status.[1] When Congress passed the Immigration Reform and Control Act (IRCA) in 1986, it included provisions that enabled several million aliens illegally residing in the United States to become LPRs. Generally, legislation such as IRCA is referred to as an "amnesty" or a legalization program because it provides LPR status to aliens who are otherwise residing illegally in the United States.[2] Although legalization is considered distinct from adjustment of status, most legalization provisions are codified under the adjustment or change of status chapter of INA.

Adjustment of Status

In addition to laws such as IRCA that have permitted aliens residing illegally in the United States to legalize their status, Congress has enacted statutes that enable certain aliens I the United States on a recognized – but non-permanent – basis to adjust their

---

[1] For background and analysis, see: CRS Report RL30578, *Immigration: Registry as Means of Obtaining Lawful Permanent Residence*, by Andorra Bruno.

[2] Some consider the Nicaraguan Adjustment and Central American Relief Act (NACARA) of 1997 a legalization program because the primary beneficiaries were Nicaraguans and Cubans who had come to the United States by December 1, 1995, but who had not been given any recognized legal status typically afforded to humanitarian migrants such as Temporary Protected Status, Extended Voluntary Departure, or Deferred Enforced Departure. Others view the Nicaraguans as having a quasi-legal status because the creation of the Nicaraguan Review Program in 1987 by then-Attorney General Edwin Meese gave special attention to the Nicaraguans who had been denied asylum.

status to legal permanent residence when they are not otherwise eligible for an immigrant visa. Since the codification of the INA in 1952, there have been at least 16 Acts of Congress that enable aliens in the United States in some type of temporary legal status to adjust to LPR status. Most of these adjustments of status laws focused on humanitarian cases, *e.g.*, parolees or aliens from specific countries given blanket relief from removal such as temporary protected status (TPS), deferred enforced departure (DED), or extended voluntary departure (EVD).[3]

Estimates of Unauthorized Residents

While the Immigration and Naturalization Service (INS) had estimated there were approximately 5.1 million unauthorized immigrants residing in the United States as of January 1997, recent estimates of unauthorized aliens based upon the 2000 census range from 7.5 to 9 million. Using their 5.1 million estimate, the INS calculates that about 16.4% have been living in the United States for more than 10 years. About 18% of the 5.1 million unauthorized residents are estimated to have filed applications with INS that might result in receipt of legal permanent resident status (*i.e.,* 445,600 have applications for asylum pending and 474,000 have applications for immigrant visas pending). The INS study does not estimate how many of the 5.1 million unauthorized residents have a temporary legal status, *e.g.* TPS.[4]

As the 2000 Census of the U.S. Population is being released, preliminary data analyses offer competing population totals that, in turn, imply that illegal migration soared in the late 1990s and that estimates of unauthorized residents of the United States have been understated. Demographer Robert Warren of the INS now estimates that there were about 7.5 million unauthorized aliens living in the United States. In testimony before the House Committee on the Judiciary Subcommittee on Immigration and Claims, Jeffrey Passel, a demographic researcher at the Urban Institute, offered an estimate of 8 to 9 million unauthorized residents. Economists at Northeastern University drew on employment data reported by business establishments as well as 2000 census totals to infer that unauthorized migration may range about 11 million.[5]

---

[3] For background on blanket forms of relief and the nationals who have received it, see: CRS Report RS20844, *Temporary Protected Status: Current Immigration Policy and Issues,* by Ruth Ellen Wasem and Shirin Kaleel.

[4] "Annual Estimates of the Unauthorized Immigrant Population Residing in the United States and Components of Change: 1987 to 1997" by Robert Warren, Office of Policy and Planning, U.S. Immigration and Naturalization Service, September 2000.

[5] U.S. House of Representatives, Committee on the Judiciary Subcommittee on Immigration and Claims, *Hearing on the U.S. Population and Immigration,* August 2, 2001.

ISSUES OF DEBATE IN 106TH CONGRESS

"Late Amnesty"

"Late amnesty" is shorthand for aliens involved in litigation resulting from the sweeping legalization program enacted in 1986 by IRCA. That time-limited legalization program, codified at §245A of the INA, enabled certain illegal aliens who entered the United States before January 1, 1982, to become LPRs. Several class action lawsuits challenged various regulations adopted by INS to implement the legalization program as being improperly restrictive. As part of the Illegal Immigration Reform and Immigrant Responsibility Act (IIRIRA) of 1996, Congress placed jurisdictional limitations on challenges to the legalization program[6] in an effort, according to the conference report on the IIRIRA bill, "to put an end to litigation seeking to extend the amnesty provisions of [IRCA]."[7] A Senate Judiciary Committee press release dated October 21, 2000, estimates that 400,000 aliens were involved in this litigation.

Legalization through Registry

Registry is a provision of immigration law (§249) that enables certain unauthorized aliens in the United States to acquire lawful permanent resident status. It grants the Attorney General the discretionary authority to create a record of lawful admission for permanent residence for an alien who lacks such a record, has continuously resided in the United States since before January 1, 1972, and meets other specified requirements. The INS estimates that 500,000 aliens would be eligible to legalize to LPR status if the registry date would be advanced to 1986.[8] Supporters of advancing it argue it is once again time to move up the date since it was set at 1972 in 1986, and now the registry date should be advanced to 1986. Opponents to advancing the registry date argue that it is not meant to be a "rolling date" and that such a legalization program would serve as a magnet for further illegal migration.

Reunification of LPR Relatives and Pending Cases

The spouses and minor children of LPRs (who do not accompany them when they initially immigrate to the United States) are eligible to become LPRs through the second preference category that governs admission of immigrants. Due to the numerical limits on the admission of immigrants – both country and worldwide ceilings – as well as the percentage allocation of immigrant visas across preference categories, more than one

---

[6] IIRIRA is Division C of P.L. 104-208, September 30, 1996; 110 Stat. 3009, The IIRIRA provision limiting litigation (§ 377) is at 110 Stat. 3009-649.

[7] U.S. Congress. Conference Committees. *Illegal Immigration Reform and Immigrant Responsibility Act of 1996*, conference report to accompany H.R. 2202, 140th Cong., 2nd Sess., H.Rept. 104-828. p. 230.

[8] For background and analysis, see: CRS Report RL30578, *Immigration: Registry and Means of Obtaining Lawful Permanent Residence*, by Andorra Bruno.

million people are waiting for a second preference visa. The estimated wait for some of these immediate relatives of LPRs may be as long as 6 years. INA make these aliens ineligible for visitors' visas because they have petitions for legal permanent residence pending. Some maintain that special provisions should be made to reunite these family members because the separation poses an undue hardship on the families. Others point out that million of other people are also waiting for immigrant visas, including relatives of U.S. citizens, and that long wait lists are a regrettable, but inherent, element of the contemporary immigration experience.

"NACARA Parity"

Hundreds of thousands of Nicaraguans, Salvadorans, and Guatemalans fled civil conflicts in their native countries throughout the 1980s. Many of these Central Americans entered without proper documents; most were denied asylum and placed in deportation proceedings. Yet, policy decisions – notably the creation of the Nicaraguan Review Office in 1987, legislation giving TPS to Salvadorans in 1990, and an out-of-court settlement for Salvadorans and Guatemalans of the *American Baptist Churches v. Thornburgh* case in 1990 – permitted these aliens to remain in the United States with employment authorizations.

The Nicaraguan Adjustment and Central American Relief Act (NACARA), part of the District of Columbia Appropriations Act for FY1998 (P.L. 105-100), enabled Nicaraguans and Cubans who had come to the United States by December 1, 1995, to become LPRs. NACARA also allows Salvadorans, Guatemalans, and unsuccessful asylum seekers from former Soviet Union and Eastern Bloc countries[9] to seek legal permanent residency under the more generous standards of hardship relief in place prior to the tightening of immigration laws in 1996. Subsequently, Congress enacted the Haitian Refugee Immigration Fairness Act (HRIFA) of 1998, which allows certain specified Haitians to adjust to LPR status, as part of the FY1999 omnibus appropriations act (P.L. 105-277). Many, including former President Clinton, have been critical of the differential treatment afforded the Nicaraguans and Cubans in contrast to the Salvadorans, Guatemalans and Eastern Europeans. Some are now arguing for the Hondurans, Salvadorans, Guatemalans, and Haitians not covered by HRIFA, and Eastern Europeans to be eligible for the same benefits as the Nicaraguans and Cubans, *i.e.*, "NACARA parity." Others are criticizing NACARA and any effort to broaden it as a legalization program that backslides from the reforms made by the 1996 immigration

---

[9] The language specifies nationals of the Soviet Union, Russia, any republic of the former Soviet Union, Latvia, Estonia, Lithuania, Poland, Czechoslovakia, Romania, Hungary, Bulgaria, Albania, East Germany, Yugoslavia, or any state of the former Yugoslavia.

act.[10] The INS estimates that about 680,000 Central Americans and Haitians (excluding derivative family members) would be eligible to adjust under "NACARA parity."[11]

Adjustment of Status for Liberians

Approximately 10,000 Liberians in the United States were given DED after their TPS expired September 29, 1999. These Liberians have had protections for the longest period, of those who currently have TPS or other forms of blanket relief from deportation, having received TPS in March 1991. The Attorney General had indicated that she did not wish to keep extending TPS or DED for Liberians. Some assert that it is now safe for the Liberians to return home and that they should do so. Others maintain that those Liberians who have lived in the United States for almost a decade have firm roots in the community and should be permitted to adjust to LPR status.

Adjustment of Status under §245(i)

Section 245 of the INA permits an alien who is legally but temporarily in the United States to adjust to permanent resident status if the alien becomes eligible on the basis of a family relationship or job skills, without having to go abroad to obtain an immigrant visa. Section 245 was limited to aliens who were here legally until 1994, when Congress enacted a 3-year trial provision (§245(i)) allowing aliens here illegally to adjust status once they become eligible for permanent residence, provided they paid a large fee. This provision was effectively repealed by the FY1998 CJS appropriations act (P.L. 105-119), which provided that only aliens who were beneficiaries of an immigration petition or a labor certification application filed on or before January 14, 1998, would be eligible for adjustment under §245(i).[12] Supporters point out that the beneficiaries of §245(i) are aliens eligible for immigrant visas even if they currently lack legal status, while opponents observe that it flied in the face of other immigration provisions designed to stymie illegal immigration.

---

[10] See CRS Report 98-270, *Immigration: Haitian Relief Issues and Legislation*, by Ruth Ellen Wasem and CRS Report 97-810, *Central American Asylum Seekers: Impact of 1996 Immigration Law*, by Ruth Ellen Wasem.

[11] This estimate of 680,000 includes many aliens who would also be able to adjust if the registry date would be advanced to 1986, so the two estimates are not cumulative.

[12] See CRS Report 97-946, *Immigration: Adjustment to Permanent Residence Status under Section 245(i)*, by Larry Eig and William Krouse.

LEGISLATION IN 106TH CONGRESS

A variety of legalization and status adjustment proposals were put forward in the 106th Congress.[13] These proposals covered a range of immigration issues, such as "NACARA parity," advancing the registry date to 1986, "late amnesty," and creating a V nonimmigrant visa for certain immediate relatives of LPRs. A table that summarizes the main features of the two competing proposals – H.R. 4942, the "Legal Immigration Family Equity Act" (LIFE), and S. 3095, the "Latino and Immigration Fairness Act" (LIFA) – as well as the compromise language amending LIFE in H.R. 4577, follows. President Clinton signed P.L. 106-553 (H.R. 4942) and P.L. 106-554 (H.R. 4577), the legislation containing LIFE and amendments to it, on December 21, 2000.

LIFA

"NACARA parity," Liberian adjustment, advancement of the registry date, and reinstatement of §245(i) were included in the "Latino and Immigrant Fairness Act" (LIFA) that was introduced as S. 3095. Estimates of aliens and their derivative relatives who would have benefited from this bill were as high as 2 million. This bill was comparable to language that the Senate Democrats tried unsuccessfully to bring up as an amendment during the floor consideration of S. 2045 (the H-1B legislation) on September 27. The sponsors of LIFA did not include provisions for "late amnesty" because those individuals would have been able to legalize through the advancement of the registry date, a main feature of S. 3095. In an October 26 letter to congressional leaders, President Clinton led his list of reasons he would veto the CJS appropriations bill with failure to include LIFA.

LIFE

Senate Judiciary Committee Chair Orrin Hatch, along with Congressmen Henry Bonilla and Lamar Smith, offered an alternative proposal called the "Legal Immigration Family Equity Act" (LIFE) that focused on the "late amnesty" cases and the immediate relatives of legal permanent residents (LPRs) who have second preference petitions pending. Those aliens who are part of the "late amnesty" litigation are permitted to legalize under the terms of §245A originally established by IRCA. According to the sponsors, about 600,000 aliens would benefit from a new temporary "V" visa for spouses and children of LPRs. This language was added to the CJS appropriations bill (H.R. 4690) that, in turn, was folded into the District of Columbia appropriations conference agreement (H.R. 4942, H.Rept. 106-1005), which became P.L. 106-553. After intense negotiations, amendments to LIFE were included in the Labor, Health and Human Services, Education FY2001 appropriations conference agreement (H.R. 4577, H. Rpt.

---

[13] For further discussion of immigration legislation, see: CRS Report RS20836, *Immigration Legislation in the 106th Congress*, by Ruth Ellen Wasem.

106-1033), which became P.L. 106-554. The amendments to LIFE include a temporary reinstatement of §245(i) through April 30, 2001 and a modification of the "late amnesty" provisions to cover those aliens who unsuccessfully sought to legalize through IRCA and were part of the *Zambrano v. INS* class action suit.

**Comparison of Leading Proposals to Legalize or Adjust
Certain Unauthorized Immigrants in 106th Congress**

Major Features	Legal Immigrant Family Equity Act (P.L. 106-553)	Amendments to LIFE (P.L. 106-554)	Latino and Immigrant Fairness Act (S. 3095)
"Late amnesty"	Makes IRCA §245A provisions applicable to those in "late amnesty" class action cases, enabling them to legalize	Adds aliens from the "Zambrano v. INS" class action case.	*[presumed to be covered by advancing the registry date]*
Registry date			Would amend INA to advance it to 1986 and create mechanism for a rolling registry date up to 1991.
Family reunification	Amends INA to provide nonimmigrant "V" visa for certain immediate relatives of LPRs with cases pending for 3 years or more; would also modify the K nonimmigrant visa to include spouses of U.S. citizens who marry abroad and the spouses' minor children.	Clarifies that spouses and minor children of beneficiaries are eligible for the "family unity" provisions of the Immigration Act of 1990	
"NACARA parity"		Makes technical corrections to NACARA and HRIFA that waives certain grounds of inadmissibility.	Would enable aliens from El Salvador, Guatemala, Haiti, Honduras, the former Soviet Union, and Eastern Bloc countries who meet certain conditions to become LPRs.
Liberians			Would adjust status to LPR.
§245(i)	*[conferees dropped from CJS bill]*	Reinstates through April 30, 2001.	Would amend INA to reinstate it.

"Late Amnesty" and Registry

Prior o LIFE and LIFA, a variety of bills addressed "late amnesty" and the registry. H.R. 2125 would have amended the INA to repeal the judicial review limitation on denial of adjustment for certain applicants for legalization IRCA. S. 1552, H.R. 3149, and H.R. 4966 had the same "late amnesty" provisions and also would have extended the admission registry date for permanent residence. Other bills proposing to change the registry date included H.R. 4172 (introduced on behalf of the Clinton Administration), S. 2047, S. 2668, and S. 2912. These four bills and H.R. 4966 would have moved the registry date to January 1, 1986. In addition, S. 2407 and S. 2668 contained "rolling registry date" provisions to advance the registry date 1 year annually, 2002-2006.

"NACARA Parity" and Liberian Adjustment

On behalf of the Clinton Administration, a bipartisan group of Members originally introduced a "NACARA parity" bill (H.R. 2722) and a comparable bill (S. 1592) in the Senate. Similar provisions were included in H.R. 4200, S. 2912, S. 2668, and H.R. 4966. Separate bills before Congress (H.R. 919, S. 656) would have provided for the adjustment of status of certain Liberians in the United States to lawful permanent resident status. Liberian adjustment provisions also were included in S. 2668 and H.R. 4966.

Reinstating §245(i)

A stand-alone bill (H.R. 1841) to restore §245(i) to its pre-1997 status was introduced, and similar provisions also were included in S. 2668, H.R. 4966, and S. 2912. In addition, the Senate-reported version of the FY2001 CJS appropriations act (H.R. 4690) also included such a provision, but it was dropped from the District of Columbia conference agreement (H.R. 4942) that included the CJS bill. It was folded back into the LIFE amendments in H.R. 4577, but only temporarily reinstated through April 30, 2001.

Temporary Agricultural Workers

Legislation to modify or supplement the H-2A temporary agricultural program was before Congress. S. 1814/H.R. 4056 would have established a time-limited amnesty program for aliens who have worked here illegally in seasonal agriculture and who continued to do so for a specified time. Although media reports indicated that a new temporary agricultural worker program with a legalization provision would also be included in the LIFE amendments, it was not in the final agreements.[14]

---

[14] For analysis and discussion of the temporary agricultural worker proposals, see: CRS Report RL30852, *Immigration of Agricultural Guest Workers: Policy, Trends, and Legislative Issues*, by Ruth Ellen Wasem and Geoffrey K. Collver.

ISSUES AND LEGISLATION IN THE 107TH CONGRESS

The resolution of the "late amnesty" cases, the enactment of the V visa for the immediate relatives of LPRs who have second preference petitions pending, and the temporary reinstatement of §245(i) addressed some, but not all of the immigration issues pertaining to legalization and status adjustment of aliens.

Legalization

Although President George Bush has said he opposes broad legalization for unauthorized migrants, there have been reports that the President will recommend legislation to legalize an estimated 3 million Mexicans living in the United States without legal authorization. President Bush and Mexican President Vincente Fox have established a Cabinet-level working group to develop "an orderly framework for migration that ensures humane treatment [and] legal security, and dignifies labor conditions." U.S. Secretary of State Colin Powell, Mexican Foreign Minister Jorge Castaneda, U.S. Attorney General John Ashcroft, and Mexican Interior Secretary Santiago Creelto are leading the bi-national group.

President Vincente Fox of Mexico is encouraging the United States to "regularize" the immigration status of Mexicans living and working in the United States without authorization. The term "regularize" is not an immigration term, but its current usage in this debate implies a legalization of status that may be only temporary and not necessarily a pathway to permanent residence. Initial speculation that President Bush would unveil a major immigration proposal in early September that includes a legalization program has been tempered by more recent reports that he will recommend a more gradual set of proposals.

On August 2, Congressional Democrats announced a set of principles that will guide broad immigration legislation they intend to propose, and among those principles is a plan for "earned legalization." Their proposal would not be limited to nationals of any one country and would focus on "longtime, hard-working residents of good moral character, with no criminal problems...who are otherwise eligible to become U.S. citizens." The Democrat's stated principles also included a family reunification element and an "enhanced" temporary worker program.

Proponents of legalization are awaiting the introduction of broad legislation, characterizing legalization provisions as fair treatment of aliens who have been living and working here for years as good neighbors and dedicated employees. They argue that the unauthorized aliens are already residing here, benefiting the United States. Supporters assert it is not feasible or humane to round up millions of people and deport them.

Opponents, on the other hand, describe legalization as an unfair reward to illegal aliens who violated the law to get into the United States. They state that such migrants jumped the line ahead of millions of family members of U.S. residents and potential employees of U.S. businesses who wait their turn to enter the United States legally. They maintain that – rather than solving the problem of illegal migration – amnesty provisions fuel further illegal migration, pointing to the rise in unauthorized migration over the decade following the implementation of IRCA.

§245(i)

President Bush announced that he would support legislation to extend §245(i). On May 17, House Committee on the Judiciary Immigration Subcommittee Chairman George Gekas, introduced H.R. 1885, which passed the House May 21. H.R. 1885 would reinstate §245(i) for 120 days after enactment, with the stipulations that the applicants were physically present by December 21, 2000 [when the LIFE Act was signed] and that the familial or employment relationships qualifying the applicant for the visa existed prior to April 30, 2001 [when the §245(i) provision of LIFE expired]. Representatives Charles Rangel (H.R. 1195) and Sheila Jackson-Lee (H.R. 1615) and Senator Chuck Hagel (S. 778) all have introduced legislation to extend INA §245(i) for 1 year. These bills would expand the number of aliens eligible to become LPRs if their immigrant petitions and labor certifications are filed by April 30, 2002. Representative Peter King's bill (H.R. 1242) would extend the §245(i) through October 31, 2001.

The Senate Judiciary Committee reported S. 778 with amendments on July 26. As amended by the Judiciary Committee, S. 778 would now require that the familial or employment relationships qualifying the applicant for the visa existed on or before the date of enactment. The Senate Appropriations Committee included a permanent reinstatement of §245(i) in its version of the 2002 Commerce-Justice-State (CJS) appropriations act (S. 1214) that was reported July 20.

NACARA Parity

Two bills have been introduced in the House that would expand to other Central American nationals the immigration relief provided by NACARA to Nicaraguans and Cubans. Both H.R. 348 (Representative Luis Gutierrez) and H.R. 707 (Representative Chris Smith) would allow certain Guatemalans, Haitians, Hondurans and Salvadorans to adjust the LPR status under terms comparable to the 1997 NACARA law.

Liberian Adjustment

Legislation has been introduced to adjust to LPR status Liberians who had been given blanket relief from removal from the United States. Representative Patrick Kennedy is sponsoring the House bill (H.R. 357), and Senator Jack Reed is sponsoring the Senate bill (S. 656).

Andean Adjustment

Representative Lincoln Diaz-Balart has introduced legislation (H.R. 945) to enable Peruvians and Colombians in the United States by December 1995 to adjust to LPR status under specified conditions.

Registry

Among other provisions, H.R. 500 (Representative Luis Gutierrez) would advance the registry date from January 1, 1972, to February 6, 1996, and would establish a "rolling registry date" that would advance the registry date annually until it reaches February 6, 2001, in 2007. Upon enactment, unauthorized migrants living in the United States as of February 6, 1996, would be eligible to adjust to LPR status if they met the conditions of INA §249. In 2003, those residing there as of February 6, 1997, would be eligible to adjust, and accordingly each year through 2007 when those residing here as of February 6, 2001, would be eligible to adjust.

Temporary Agricultural Workers

Several H-2A reform bills that include provisions for status adjustment have been introduced thus far in the 107th Congress. Senator Ted Kennedy, chairman of the Senate Committee on the Judiciary Subcommittee on Immigration, and Representative Howard Berman have introduced the "H-2A Reform and Agricultural Worker Adjustment Act of 2001" (S. 1313/H.R. 2736), which includes provisions that would allow unauthorized foreign agricultural workers to become legal temporary residents if they have worked in agriculture for at least 90 days in the 18-month period prior to July 2001 and are otherwise admissible as an immigrant. S. 1313/H.R. 2736 would enable these temporary residents subsequently to adjust to LPR status after certain other requirements are met. The "Agricultural Job Opportunity, Benefits, and Security (AgJOBS) Act of 2001," (S.1161) introduced by Senator Larry Craig, includes provisions that would allow H-2A workers to apply for LPR status if they worked 150 days in any consecutive 12-month period during the 18 months prior to July 2001.

Chapter 6

IMMIGRATION: VISA ENTRY/ EXIT CONTROL SYSTEM

William J. Krouse and Ruth Ellen Wasem

ABSTRACT

Section 110 of the Illegal Immigration Reform and Immigrant Responsibility Act of 1996 (IIRIRA; Division C of P.L. 104-208) mandates the development of an automated entry/exit control system to create a record for every alien departing from the United States and match it with the record for the alien arriving to the United States. Section 110 also requires that this system identify nonimmigrants who overstay the terms of their admission through online computer searching. The FY1999 Omnibus Consolidated and Emergency Supplemental Appropriations Act (P.L. 105-277) amends Section 100 to extend the original implementation deadline of September 30, 1998 to March 31, 2001 for land border and seaports of entry, but leaves the end of FY1998 deadline in place for airports of entry. Further, P.L. 105-277 includes directing that the entry/exit control system must "not significantly disrupt trade, tourism, or other legitimate cross-border traffic at land border ports of entry."

This extension occurred because implementing Section 110 has proven more difficult at land border and seaports of entry than at airports of entry, because the capacity to record alien arrivals and departures at land border and seaports is not as fully developed. The Administration had proposed eliminating the FY1998 deadline altogether for land border and seaports of entry, citing the need to conduct feasibility and cost/benefit studies. Opponents of Section 100 cited concerns about reciprocity, trade, tourism, and border congestion. Supporters of Section 110 and its implementation at all ports of entry (air, land, and sea) asserted that the need for an automated entry/exit control system had been widely recognized years before the passage of IIRIRA. They maintained further that such a system is essential to ensure the integrity of all nonimmigrants admissions and to maintain control of U.S. borders. The 105th Congress acted upon several pieces of legislation, which would have taken varying approaches to Section 110 by either extending or eliminating deadlines for certain types of ports of entry, or repealing Section 110 altogether.

P.L. 105-277 also amends another provision of IIRIRA that some observers view as instrumental in implementing Section 110 at southern land border ports of entry. This provision, Section 104, mandates the replacement of all Border Crossing Cards – the most common document presented by Mexican nationals seeking to cross the border temporarily – by September 30, 1999. The Administration and groups representing Transborder communities, however, maintained that the FY1999 deadline was unfeasible for the replacement of an estimated 5.5 million Border Crossing Cards in circulation, and that forcing such a timetable would cause needless hardship and inconvenience for legitimate border crossers. Therefore, P.L. 105-277 amends Section 104 to extend this provision's deadline to September 30, 2001. It also limits the fee to recover the cost of manufacturing the documents to $13 for minors under 15 years of age.

Finally, report language accompanying the FY1999 INS appropriation (also included in P.L. 105-277) earmarks an increase of $20 million to continue the development of a Section 110 system.

INTRODUCTION

The Department of Justice's Immigration and Naturalization Service (INS) Inspections program and the Department of the Treasury's U.S. Customs Service share jurisdiction over international ports of entry. The Customs Service is responsible for clearing the entry of goods and merchandise into the country; INS is responsible for managing the admission of both citizens and foreign nationals. At many ports of entry, INS and Customs inspectors are cross designated to enforce one another's respective areas of the law.[1] Therefore, both INS and Customs inspectors clear persons for entry into the United States. In FY1997, these agencies conducted approximately one-half billion inspections. As illustrated in **Figure 1**, more than 416 million inspections are conducted at land border ports.

Section 110 of the Illegal Immigration Reform and Immigrant Responsibility Act (Division C of P.L. 104-208; IIRIRA) requires the Attorney General to develop an automated entry/exit control system to create a record for every alien departing from the United States and match it with the alien's record of arrival. Section 110 also requires that this system identify nonimmigrants who overstay the terms of their admission through online computer searching. The goal of Section 110 is greater immigration enforcement and border security through better record keeping of the arrival and departure of non-citizens. Section 110, as originally included in IIRIRA, required further that this system be established at all international ports of entry by September 30, 1998. Implementing Section 110, however, has proven more difficult at land border and seaports of entry than at airports of entry, because the capacity to record alien arrivals and departures at land border and seaports is not as fully developed.

Consequently, the FY1999 Omnibus Consolidated and Emergency Supplemental Appropriations Act (P.L. 105-277) amends Section 110 to extend the September 30, 1998 deadline to March 31, 2001 for land border and sea ports of entry, but leaves the end of FY1998 deadline in place for air ports of entry (now October 15, 1998).

---

[1] This is the case generally at most land border and sea ports of entry; however, at most major air ports of entry, INS and Customs inspections are conducted separately.

Figure 1. FY1997 INS Inspections Land, Air & Sea Ports of Entry

(499 million inspections)

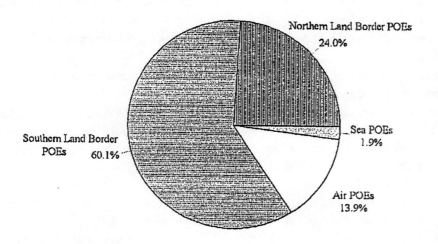

CRS presentation of data provided by INS.

Implementing Section 110 has proven difficult because INS has not tracked arrivals and departures for immigrants (non-citizens admitted for permanent residence) and has had only limited success in tracking arrivals and departures for nonimmigrants (non-citizens admitted on a temporary basis). An automated entry/exit control system, when fully developed and implemented, would provide a method by which to identify nonimmigrant overstays (those who violate the period of their temporary admission). It would also provide an objective criterion by which to extend visa waivers to other countries under the Visa Waiver Pilot Program.[2] In addition, Section 110 requires that the system capture the arrival and departure of all aliens, including those admitted for permanent residence (immigrants). Such information could be used to determine whether immigrants have abandoned their U.S. residence. In some cases, those immigrants who have not maintained their U.S. residency may be in jeopardy of losing their permanent resident alien card. Such a system, if effectively linked to law enforcement databases, would also serve as a means of screening aliens who may be subjected to removal or exclusion from the United States.

In November 1997, before the Senate Judiciary's Immigration Subcommittee, INS outlined five strategic considerations that the agency viewed as essential to the development of an automated entry/exit control.

---

[2] The Visa Waiver Program (VWPP) authorizes the Attorney General to waive the visa documentary requirements for aliens traveling from certain designated countries as temporary visitors for business or pleasure (tourists). Nationals from participating countries simply complete an admission form before their arrival and are admitted for up to 90 days. For further information, see CRS Report 97-309, *Immigration: Visa Waiver Pilot Program.*

- One, the system should be operational in all settings and would record alien arrivals and departures into an online database (such a database does currently exist).
- Two, the system should not unduly increase the amount of time a person spends in the inspection process.
- Three, INS must take full advantage of modern information management technologies.
- Four, to minimize costs, the system should be grafted upon already existent procedures and systems.
- And five, because many parties, both public and private, have an interest in facilitating international travel, stakeholder involvement is essential in crafting a system that would provide "equal or better" service to "the traveling public, trade and transportation interests, and the American people."

The agency cited as a particular concern, "the logistics and costs of modifying and rebuilding land and seaports of entry to accommodate an automated departure management system." For these reasons, INS also conveyed the Administration's proposal that the FY1998 deadline for an automated entry/exit control system at land border and seaports of entry be eliminated. In July 1998, these concerns were reiterated by INS in a hearing before the House Judiciary's Immigration and Claims Subcommittee.[3]

ARRIVAL/DEPARTURE MANAGEMENT AND NONIMMIGRANT OVERSTAYS

A Principal focus of Section 110 is the enumeration and identification of nonimmigrant overstays, i.e., those persons who are admitted legally to the United States on a temporary basis and subsequently overstay the terms of their admission. In February 1997, INS estimated the resident illegal alien population at 5 million persons as of October 1996. that population was roughly divided between illegal aliens who had entered without inspection (59%) and those who had overstayed the terms of their temporary admission (41%). As illustrated in **Figure 2**, over half of the estimated 2.1 million nonimmigrant overstays are from this hemisphere. Some observers have been critical of INS enforcement efforts for being too heavily weighted towards stopping illegal aliens who enter without inspection over those who overstay the terms of their nonimmigrant admission.

INS currently tracks nonimmigrant arrivals and departures through the Form I-94, the Arrival/Departure Record: the arrival portion of Form I-94 is collected upon entry and the departure portion is collected upon exit. Arrivals and departures are then keyed manually into the Nonimmigrant Information System – the current system for managing approximately 25 million nonimmigrant files. For matched I-94s, INS assumes the nonimmigrant departed; for unmatched I-94s, the agency assumes they did not. Although nearly all nonimmigrants entering the United States at airports and seaports (other than alien crewmembers) are required to fill out I-94s, nonimmigrants entering the United States at land border ports are required to fill out I-94s much less frequently. There have also been difficulties in collecting departure forms from departing aliens. INS has been criticized, moreover, for not producing timely and accurate data on nonimmigrant overstays from what data it does collect.

Figure 2. Estimated Nonimmigrant Overstay Population
(2.1 million as of October 1996)

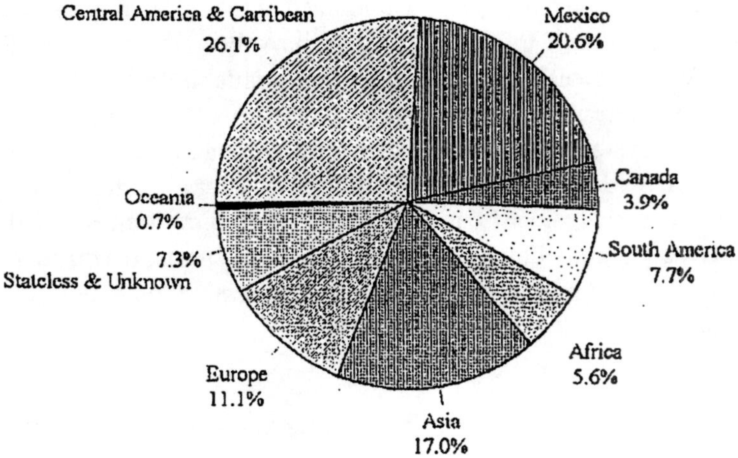

CRS presentation of estimated provided by INS Office of Policy and Planning.

As a remedy, Section 110 requires an annual report to Congress that is to include (1) the number of departure records collected, including the nationalities of the departing aliens; (2) the number of departure records successfully matched with prior arrival records, including the aliens' nationalities and immigrant or nonimmigrants classifications; and (3) the number, nationalities, and dates of arrival of nonimmigrants who arrived in the United States under the Visa Waiver Pilot Program, for whom no corresponding departure record has been entered into the system and matched with a corresponding arrival record, indicating that they have overstayed the terms of their admission. Furthermore, Section 110 requires that nonimmigrant overstay information gained through this system be incorporated into INS and State Department immigration-related databases. INS currently captures the greatest amount of arrival/departure data for nonimmigrants at airports.

---

[3] The subject of this hearing was alternative technologies for the implementation of Section

ARRIVAL/DEPARTURE MANAGEMENT AT AIRPORTS

There are nearly 133 international airports of entry and 15 pre-inspection stations on foreign territory. In FY1997, INS and USCS inspectors conducted nearly 69 million inspections (almost 14% of total inspections, as Figure 1 illustrates) at airports of entry. At airports of entry, inspectors enter the names of all persons, citizen and non-citizen, into the InterAgnecy Border Inspection System (IBIS)[4] to clear them for entry into the United States. In addition, air carriers are required by law to present properly completed I-94s to an immigration officer for all nonimmigrants arriving and departing the country.

For nonimmigrants, INS has recently conducted a pilot program with USAirways on the Munich, Germany to Philadelphia, Pennsylvania flight in which I-94 arrival/departure records were captured electronically and uploaded into the Nonimmigrant Information System. So far, the results of this pilot program have been favorable. INS testified that based on the Philadelphia pilot program and other available technologies, a preliminary entry/exit control system could be established at major airports of entry by the end of FY1998, but such a system would still be in a developmental stage. According to INS, entry/exit records would be captured by scanning machine-readable passports, reentry permits, legal permanent resident cards, and other immigration-related documentation. Indeed, machine readable documents, whether I-94s, passports, permanent resident cards (green cards), or border crossing cards, are an integral component of an automated entry/exit control system.

ARRIVAL/DEPARTURE MANAGEMENT AT SEAPORTS

In FY1997, INS and Customs inspectors conducted approximately 10 million inspections at 70 seaports of entry (2% of total FY1997 inspections), but this number does not accurately reflect the total number of non-citizens entering the United States on an annual basis through seaports of entry. For example, alien crewmembers are often only inspected once every 90 days under current law as their vessels travel along coastlines or criss-cross international waterways. Passengers on cruise lines, moreover, may debark and embark many times into U.S. territory, but generally are only inspected at the outset and end of a cruise. Whether alien crewmembers and cruise line passengers make up a large enough component of the undocumented immigrant population to warrant the additional inspections and an entry/exit control system at seaports remains a question.

---

[4] IBIS is a multi-agency centralized lookout database that is linked to a number of immigration and law enforcement databases.

ARRIVAL/DEPARTURE MANAGEMENT AT LAND BORDER PORTS

Many people who cross the land border frequently reside in the region. Therefore, in the past, documenting inspections at land border ports have not been conducted with the same level of intensity as at airports. At land border ports, inspectors visually screen applicants for admission in the primary inspection lanes. As the vehicle approaches the inspections booth, the inspector usually enters the automobile license plate number into IBIS to check whether there is a lookout record on it. If there is a record, the vehicle is detoured into secondary inspection for further examination. In addition, the inspector queries the vehicle's occupants for documentation, intended destination, and length of stay. If in the inspector's judgment no further examination is warranted, the vehicle and its occupants are waved through.

In FY1997, INS and Customs inspectors conducted nearly 416 million land border inspections: 297 million inspections on our southern land border and nearly 119 million on our northern land border (see **Figure 1**). There are 107 land border ports of entry on the 4,780 mile long border between Canada and the lower 48 states. There are 37 land border ports of entry on the 1,952 mile long border between Mexico and the United States. On both borders, the ratio of citizens to non-citizens inspected is estimated at roughly 1:2.

Northern Land Border

The Canadian government has expressed strong opposition to the implementation of Section 110 on the northern land border, as have some northern border congressional delegations. Canadians who enter the United States through land border ports are not required to present a passport, and are often not required to obtain a visa.[5] In addition, Canadian citizens and British subjects residing in Canada are generally not required to obtain an I-94 form, if they are entering the United States temporarily for business or pleasure. Canadians entering the United States for purposes other than business or pleasure, e.g., employment, trade, and diplomatic activities, etc., are issued an I-94. Upon departure, the Canadian government collects I-94 departure records for the INS. Canadians, however, are not exempted from Section 110. Legislation has been introduced that would exempt Canadians from the requirements of Section 110. Nevertheless, even if Canadian nationals were exempted, this would not obviate the need for an entry/exit control system for non-Canadian nationals entering the United States through northern land border ports.

---

[5] Section 212(d)(4)(B) of the INA gives the Secretary of State and the Attorney General the discretionary authority to waive documentary requirements for admission. And, these requirements are often waived on a basis of reciprocity.

Southern Land Border

The Mexican government has long complained about the difference in treatment of its nationals at the border as compared to Canadian nationals. Mexican nationals applying for admission to the United States as visitors are required to obtain a visa or hold a Border Crossing Card, either of which can be inconvenient to obtain. Border Crossing Cards are issued to Mexican nationals who are frequent border crossers and who can demonstrate that they are unlikely to abandon their Mexican residence. If they intend to go 25 miles or further inland and/or stay longer than 72 hours, they are also required to obtain an I-94.[6] Upon departure, I-94s are to be deposited into boxes at ports of entry, however, this act is completely voluntary. Some Members of Congress have also questioned this difference in treatment.

However, current policy on the southern land border has been justified primarily because inadmissible applicants for admission are interdicted at ports of entry in greater frequency on the southern land border than on the northern land border. For example, in FY1997, for every one inadmissible alien interdicted on the northern border, 28 were interdicted on the southern border.[7] In addition, in recent years, the Border Patrol has apprehended over a million Mexican nationals annually attempting to enter the United States without inspection between ports of entry. Moreover, federal law enforcement agencies have estimated that a very large percentage of illegal narcotics entering the United States are smuggled across the southern land border, both between and through ports of entry. On the other hand, as it does on the northern land border, a very large volume of legitimate commercial and private traffic flows across the southern land border.

A related provision of the Illegal Immigration Reform and Immigrant Responsibility Act, Section 104, requires that a biometric identifier be developed and incorporated into all new Border Crossing Cards by April 1, 1998; and that only the new card will be accepted after September 30, 1999. Section 104 requires further that aliens presenting the new document not be allowed to cross the border unless that biometric identifier matches the alien document holder's characteristics. The Border Crossing Card is by far the most common document presented by Mexican nationals seeking to enter the United States temporarily at land border ports.[8] As such, some observers view the replacement of the Border Crossing Card with a more secure/machine readable document as instrumental in implementing Section 110 on the southern land border.

The document required by Section 104 has been designated by INS and the Department of State as the "laser visa." On April 1, 1998, the Department of State began replacing the Border Crossing Cards with the "laser visa," which combines the functions of the Border Crossing Card with the B-1/B-2 nonimmigrant temporary visa for business or pleasure. Unlike in the past, however, the Administration decided that INS will not

---

[6] Prior to April 1997, Mexican nationals with Border Crossing Cards were issued I-444s, instead of I-94s.

[7] Inadmissible aliens interdicted include those aliens reported by INS as having either presented fraudulent documents, made false claims to U.S. citizenship, or made other false claims to inspectors at ports of entry.

[8] Border Crossing Cards are also issued to Canadians, but much less frequently, and INS intends to phase their use out for Canadians in the near future.

process claims for "laser visas" as they did for Border Crossing Cards at ports of entry; rather, the Department of State will be entirely responsible for adjudicating all such claims at the U.S. Embassy in Mexico City and at U.S. consulates within Mexico. Moreover, there is a $45 fee attached to the "laser visa;" whereas, the Border Crossing Card only costs $26. Critics point out that attaining a "laser visa" is more inconvenient and costly today than attaining a Border Crossing Card was previously. To facilitate the replacement of the estimated 5.5 million Border Crossing Cards currently in circulation, the Department of State has approached the Mexican government about opening several temporary offices in Mexican border cities.

The FY1990 Omnibus Appropriations Act (P.L. 105-277) included a provision that amends Section 104 to extend the deadline for the replacement of the old Border Crossing Cards with "laser visas" from September 30, 1999 to September 30, 2001. Additionally, P.L. 105-277 limits the fee for minors under 15 years of age to $13 so as to recover the cost of manufacturing the documents. This provision also requires the Secretary of State to process such claims in the Mexican border cities of Nogales, Nuevo Laredo, Ciudad Acuna, Piedras Negras, Agua Prieta, and Reynosa through the end of FY2001.

Land Border Automated Entry/Exit Control System

At land border ports of entry, there is currently no procedure or system in place upon which to build an automated entry/exit control system. INS is likely to build upon recent technological initiatives, like dedicated commuter lanes and other expedited inspection processes (based upon machine readable documents, biometrics, and radio frequency tags), but there is currently no comprehensive technological solution that will allow the agency to rapidly implement Section 110 at land border ports. It is also probable that intensifying the inspections process at land border ports will necessitate more inspection lanes, booths, and staff. Furthermore, capturing departure records essentially means that INS will create some sort of departure process to collect information where none exists today. This may mean duplicating, at least to some degree, the inspections process for returning traffic. Where possible, this may also require segmenting vehicular traffic; for example, commercial trucks would be inspected in designated lanes, as would citizens, frequent border crossers, and all others.

Meanwhile, many content that if Section 110 is implemented without a clear assessment of system requirements, it will cause gridlock at land border ports, disrupting trade, commerce, tourism, and other legitimate cross-border traffic. Others argue further that there is no need for the creation of a record of arrival and departure for all aliens every time they cross the border; i.e., the costs of Section 110 will outweigh its benefits. Some have proposed that a risk analysis approach would be more efficient, that by increasing inspections staff and the number of random inspections, border security could be increased with greater efficiency and less cost. Such arguments lead others to propose postponing the Section 110 deadline indefinitely until feasibility and cost/benefit studies can be conducted.

Proponents of Section 110 maintain that they have lost patience with INS, asserting that the need for an automated entry/exit control system was recognized long before the passage of the Illegal Immigration Reform and Immigrant Responsibility Act. They argue that such a system is essential to ensure the integrity of nonimmigrant admissions as well as the control of U.S. borders. Some further assert that an entry/exit control system would eliminate or reduce the practice of profiling persons of "foreign appearance or accent," and, as a benefit, U.S. citizens and legal permanent residents who might fit these "foreign" profiles would not be subjected to secondary inspections as frequently.

LEGISLATION RELATED TO SECTION 110 ACTED ON IN THE 105TH CONGRESS

The Omnibus Consolidated and Emergency Supplemental Appropriations Act for FY1999 (P.L. 105-277) amends Section 110 to extend the deadline for the implementation of an entry/exit control system for land border and sea ports of entry from September 30, 1998 to March 31, 2001, but leaves the end of FY1998 deadline in place for airports of entry (now October 15, 1998). This amendment also includes a clause directing that the entry/exit control system must "not significantly disrupt trade, tourism, or other legitimate cross-border traffic at land border ports of entry." The Section 110 amendment included in P.L. 105-277 represents a compromise between several pieces of legislation acted upon by the 105th Congress that would have taken varying approaches to Section 110, by extending or eliminating the deadline for system implementation at certain types of ports of entry, or by repealing Section 110 altogether.

The House passed H.R. 2920 on November 10, 1997: this bill would have extended the FY1998 deadline to FY1999 for land border ports, but would have left the FY1998 deadline in place for air and seaports of entry. The Senate Judiciary Committee, in turn, reported S. 1360 (S.Rept. 105-197) on April 23, 1998: this bill would have exempted land border ports and seaports from Section 110's requirements, but would have required that such a system be implemented at all airports of entry by 2 years of enactment.

In the meantime, the Senate passed the FY1999 Commerce, Justice, State and the Judiciary (CJS) appropriations bill (S. 2260) on July 23, 1998, which included a provision to repeal Section 110 in its entirety. Then, on July 30, 1998, the Senate considered the House-passed H.R. 2920, amended it in the nature of a substitute with a slightly revised version of S. 1360, and passed the measure. To give negotiators additional time to work out a compromise, the House and Senate passed stopgap legislation (H.R. 4658/S. 2540) on October 1, 1998 to extend the Section 110 deadline to October 15, 1998. Neither measure was presented to the President; however, the 15-day extension on the deadline for airports of entry was included in P.L. 105-277.

Concerning Border Crossing Cards, both S. 2260 and S. 1360 included provisions to amend Section 104 of the Illegal Immigration Reform and Immigrant Responsibility Act (Division C of P.L. 104-208). The provision included in P.L. 105-27 that amends Section 104 is a variation of these provisions. P.L. 105-277 amends Section 104 to extend the deadline for the replacement of the old border crossing cards with the laser visa from

September 30, 1999 to September 30, 2001. Additionally, P.L. 105-277 amended Section 104 to limit the fee to recover the cost of manufacturing the documents to $13 for minors under 15 years of age. This provision also requires the Secretary of State to process claims for the new Border Crossing Card (the "laser" visa) in the Mexican border cities of Nogales, Nuevo Laredo, Ciudad Acuna, Piedras Negras, Agua Prieta, and Reynosa through the end of FY2001.

Regarding funding for the development of an automated entry/exit control system, conference report language accompanying the FY1999 CJS appropriations (also included in P.L. 105-277) earmarks $20 million to continue the development of a Section 110 system, matching the House-passed CJS Appropriations Act (H.R. 4276) and the Administration's request. The Senate-passed FY1999 CJS Appropriations Act (S. 2260) had included no similar earmark, since this bill included a provision to repeal Section 110. For FY1998, P.L. 105-119 provided INS with $13 million for the continued development of a Section 110 system.

Chapter 7

IMMIGRATION: VISA WAIVER PERMANENT PROGRAM ACT (P.L. 106-396)

William J. Krouse

ABSTRACT

On October 30, 2000, the Visa Waiver Permanent Program Act was signed into law (P.L. 106-396). Besides making this program's authorization permanent, this measure includes other provisions designed to strengthen documentary and reporting requirements. The visa waiver program allows nationals from certain countries to enter the United States as temporary visitors for business or pleasure without first obtaining a visa from a U.S. consulate abroad. By eliminating the visa requirement, this program facilitates international travel and commerce and eases consular office workloads abroad, but it also bypasses the first step by which foreign visitors are screened for admissibility when seeking to enter the United States. The statutory authority for the Visa Waiver Pilot Program had expired on April 30, 2000. In the interim, the INS Commissioner exercised the Attorney General's parole authority to extend the program temporarily.[1] This report reflects final legislative action and will not be updated.

BACKGROUND

The Visa Waiver Pilot Program (VWPP) was established as a temporary program by the Immigration Reform and Control Act of 1986 (P.L. 99-603). Congress periodically enacted legislation to extend the program's authorization, and program participation grew to include 29 countries.[2] In FY1998, there were over 17 million arrivals under this

---

[1] Parole is a temporary authorization to enter the United States and is normally granted when the alien's entry is determined to be in the public interest (Immigration and Nationality Act §212(d)(5)(A)).

[2] Countries designated to participate in the VWPP at the end of 1999 were Andorra, Argentina, Australia, Austria, Belgium, Brunei, Denmark, Finland, France, Germany, Iceland, Ireland, Italy, Japan, Liechtenstein, Luxembourg, Monaco, Netherlands, New Zealand, Norway, Portugal, San Marino, Singapore, Slovenia, Spain, Sweden, Switzerland, United Kingdom, and Uruguay.

program. During the same year, consular officers considered nearly 7.4 million nonimmigrant visa applications and issued 5.8 million nonimmigrant visas.

The VWPP was strongly supported by the U.S. travel and tourism industry, the business community, and the Department of State. The travel and tourism industry pointed to the benefits of increased economic growth generated by foreign tourism and commerce. The State Department, meanwhile, stressed that by waiving the visa requirement for high volume/low risk countries, consular workloads were significantly reduced, allowing for streamlined operations and cost savings. Other contended that the relaxed documentary requirements of the VWPP increase illegal immigration and degrade border security. On February 10, 2000, the House Judiciary Committee's Immigration and Claims Subcommittee held a hearing on the VWPP. Testimony by the Inspectors General of the Departments of Justice and State pointed out several shortcomings in the current program. Of particular concern were stolen passports from VWPP countries, slow implementation of machine-readable passports by participating countries, and INS's inability to account for nonimmigrant overstays.

COUNTRY SELECTION, OVERSTAYS, FRAUD, AND OTHER ISSUES

Under the visa waiver program, the Attorney General, in consultation with the Secretary of State, may waive the *"B' nonimmigrant visa requirement* for foreign nationals of program countries who visit the United States for business or pleasure. This constitutes one of a few exceptions under the Immigration and Nationality Act (INA) where foreign nationals are admitted into the United States without a valid visa. To qualify to participate, countries must: have a low nonimmigrant visa refusal rate; extend reciprocal visa waiver privileges to U.S. citizens; have or be in the process of developing a machine-readable passport program; and not compromise U.S. law enforcement interests, as determined by the Attorney General.

While visa waiver program entrants are admitted under the same conditions as other nonimmigrant visitors for business or pleasure under the B nonimmigrant visa category, there are strict limitations placed on these entrants as a trade-off for dropping the visa requirement. For example, while they are admitted for up to 90 days, they cannot extend their stay or change their status to another nonimmigrant visa category – an option often extended to other visaed nonimmigrants. In the case of an emergency, they are allowed to stay for an additional 30 days, but no longer.[3] Although they may engage in business, they cannot accept employment/earnings from a U.S. employer. Also, visa waiver program entrants, except for immediate relatives of U.S. citizens, are not allowed to adjust their status to legal permanent residency (immigrant status). In addition, visa waiver program entrants waive any right to administrative or judicial review or appeal regarding any determination of inadmissibility, or contest any action for removal. The only exception to this limitation is for persons applying for asylum. In addition, persons

---

[3] This provision was amended by P.L. 106-406 to provide extended voluntary departure to nonimmigrants who enter under the VWPP and require medical treatment.

who are admitted under the visa waiver program and overstay their admission by either six months or one year are subject to the three and ten year bars to admission, as are other persons who violate the terms of their nonimmigrant admission.

In 1998, Congress enacted legislation (P.L. 105-173) that not only extended the program through April 30, 2000, but made other changes to the standard by which countries are selected (designated) to participate in the VWPP.[4] This act revised the average nonimmigrant visa refusal rate standard to no more than 2% over the past 2 fiscal years with neither year going above 2.5%, or a refusal rate during the previous fiscal year of less than 3%. This new standard allowed Portugal and Uruguay to qualify for the program. Some maintain that the nonimmigrant visa refusal rate is an unobjective and arbitrary standard, because it is based on decisions made by consular officers rather than the actual behavior of nonimmigrants. Indeed, when the program was conceived, it was expected that the number of nonimmigrants who overstay the terms of their entry under this program would be a better standard for future program participation. Over the years, Members of Congress have entreated INS to produce better overstay data, not only in regard to the visa waiver program, but in regard to all nonimmigrants in general.[5] Most recently, P.L. 105-173 required the Attorney General to collect data by fiscal year on the number of aliens who overstay their nonimmigrant visas. Presumably, such data would also include VWPP entrants who had stayed longer than 90 days. The Act also required that such nonimmigrant overstay data were to be reported to Congress within 180 days of enactment, and annually thereafter. INS, however, is unable to account for nonimmigrant overstays, because departure control is nearly nonexistent.

Under current law, all visa waiver program applicants are issued nonimmigrant visa waiver arrival/departure forms (Form I-94W). The arrival portion of this document is collected by an INS inspector at the port of entry, and the departure portion is collected by the carrier/airline when the VWPP entrant leaves the United States. These I-94W data are entered into the Nonimmigrant Information System (NIIS. In 1996, INS invested in upgrades to NIIS, but reportedly I-94W data in NIIS are more unreliable today than prior to FY1996.[6] Consequently, INS is unable to account for VWPP entrants who overstay the terms of their entry, i.e., remaining in the United States past 90 days. On the other hand, since 1996, INS has been developing an Arrival Departure Information System (ADIS) as required by Section110 of the Illegal Immigrant Reform and Immigrant Responsibility Act of 1996 (P.L. 104-208).[7] According to the Department of Justice, this system was operational at 4 airports of entry at the end of FY1999, and another 32 airports of entry have received the necessary equipment to implement the system in FY2000. Full implementation of the system is anticipated in FY2001. It is likely that when fully

[4] For further information, see CRS Report 97-309, *Immigration: Visa Waiver Pilot Program*, by Ruth Ellen Wasem.

[5] According to INS estimates, 40% of the approximately 6 million resident undocumented immigrants in the United States are nonimmigrant overstays, some of whom might have entered under the VWPP.

[6] Problems that INS has in meeting VWPP data requirements were discussed in the following report: U.S. Department of Justice, Office of Inspector General Report No. 1-97-08, *Immigration and Naturalization Service Monitoring of Nonimmigrant Overstays*, September 1997.

[7] For further information, see CRS Report 98-89, *Immigration: Visa Entry/Exit Control System*, by William J. Krouse and Ruth Ellen Wasem.

implemented this system will yield reliable data on VWPP entrants for whom no departure records exist.

Regarding stolen passports, the Department of State reported that these documents are in high demand on the black market. INS reported than an estimated 100,000 blank passports were stolen from visa waiver program participant countries in the last few years. Of that number, approximately 80% were not machine-readable. Coupled with the fact that Justice's Inspector General reported that INS inspectors, who have less than a minute to complete most inspections, were not entering non-machine-readable VWPP passport numbers into lookout systems, it is likely that an inadmissible person with such a fraudulent VWPP country passport could easily slip into the country. Indeed, the Department of Justice documented that a terrorist associated with the World Trade Center bombing conspiracy entered into the United States as a VWPP applicant using a photo-substituted Swedish passport.[8]

LEGISLATION TO AMEND THE VWPP

On April 11, 2000, the House passed the Visa Waiver Permanent Program Act (H.R. 3767), which included provisions designed to strengthen the program's documentary and reporting requirements and to improve program performance. This bill was reported by the House Judiciary Committee on April 6 (H.Rept. 106-564). The Senate Judiciary Committee reported a similar measure, the Travel, Tourism, and Jobs Preservation Act (S. 2367) on April 13, without a written report. Senate action of this issue was delayed until October 3, when the Senate amended and passed H.R. 3767. The House passed the Senate version of the bill on October 10. the bill was signed into law on October 30, 2000 (P.L. 106-396), making the visa waiver program permanent. It also allows for the extension of reciprocal visa waiver privileges to designated countries that establish common areas for the purpose of immigration. House report language cited as an example the European Community, which is in the process of establishing uniform standards for entry and duration of stay for foreign visitors to its 15 member states.[9]

To address shortcomings in the program, as identified by the Inspectors General of both the Departments of Justice and State, P.L. 106-396 includes provisions that: 1) strengthen machine-readable passport requirements; 2) require that all visa waiver program applicants be checked against lookout systems; 3) require ongoing evaluations of participating countries (not less than once every 5 years); 4) require the collection of visa waiver program arrival/departure data at air and sea ports of entry; and 5) prohibit the count of visa refusals based on certain discriminatory criteria for determining program country eligibility.

---

[8] For further information, see: U.S. Department of Justice, Office of Inspector General Report I-99-10, *The Potential for Fraud and INS's Efforts to Reduce Risks of the Visa Waiver Pilot Program*, March 1999.
[9] The 15 member states of the European Community (Union) are Austria, Belgium, Denmark, Finland, France, Germany, Greece, Iceland, Italy, Luxembourg, Netherlands, Portugal, Spain, Sweden, and the United Kingdom.

Machine-Readable Passports and Lookout Systems

For those countries designated to participate before May 1, 2000, H.R. 3767 as passed by the House would have required, as a condition of visa waiver program participation, that the governments of those program countries certify not later than October 1, 2000, that a machine-readable passport program that will issue such passports to its citizens will be implemented by October 1, 2003. For those countries designated after May 1, 2000, machine-readable passports would have been a mandatory requirement. It would have also required that, beginning on October 1, 2006, all foreign nationals applying for admission under the visa waiver program must present a valid, machine-readable passport. The Senate bill (s. 2367) included similar deadlines for certifying and implementing a machine-readable program, but would have required that such passports be presented by all applicants for admission under this program by October 1, 2008, 2 years later than in the House bill. P.L. 106-396 establishes an October 1, 2007 deadline. The House bill would have required that all foreign nationals applying for admission under the visa waiver program be checked against lookout systems that are used to screen persons known to be inadmissible (by either manually entering their passport number into lookout systems or by machine-reading the passport number into those systems). It also stipulated that the sole recourse of foreign nationals denied entry on the basis of being found in a lookout system would be to apply for a visa and/or waiver at a U.S. consulate abroad. And, it would have prohibited the Attorney General from exercising her parole authority in order to admit such foreign nationals except for "compelling reasons in the public interests, or compelling health considerations." While S. 2367 did not include provisions related to lookouts, waivers, or parole, P.L. 106-396 includes these provisions, but not the provision limiting the Attorney General's parole authority.

Evaluation of Program Country Participation

H.R. 3767, as passed by the House, would have required the Attorney General, in consultation with the Secretary of State, to evaluate the effect a country's initial designation to participate in the visa waiver program would have on the law enforcement and security interests of the United States, including the enforcement of immigration law. Such a report would have been required to include a determination on this matter, and be submitted in writing to the House and Senate Judiciary Committees with an explanation of that determination. Furthermore, similar reports to evaluate the effect of a country's continue designation would have been required not less than once every 5 years. Termination dates would have become effective 30 days after publication in the *Federal Register*. The Senate bill, S. 2367, included similar reporting requirements related to both a country's initial designation to participate and evaluations of their continued participation. P.L. 106-396 requires that these reports also include evaluations of procedures to extradite to the United States individuals who had committed crimes that violate U.S. law and who are residing in participating countries, and that these reports be submitted to the House Committee on International Relations and the Senate Committee on Foreign Relations, as well as to the Judiciary Committees.

The House-passed bill would have required the automatic termination of any country for which a report evaluating that country's continued participation (described above) was not submitted to the House and Senate Judiciary Committees in the preceding 5 years, beginning in FY2005. This section would have also given the Attorney General, in consultation with the Secretary of State, the authority to terminate a program country's designation in the eventuality of certain emergencies, e.g., the overthrow of a democratically elected government; war (including undeclared war, civil war, and other military activity); disruptive social unrest; a severe economic or financial crisis; or other extraordinary events that threaten the law enforcement and security interests of the United States. S. 2367 did not include provisions related to program terminations. The Senate amendment to H.R. 3767, as reflected in P.L. 106-396, deleted the House language on the automatic termination of any country based upon the absence of an evaluative report, and modified the reasons for the emergency termination of a country's participation.

Visa Waiver Program Arrival/Departure Data Collection

Section 205 of H.R. 3767, as passed by the House, would have required the Attorney General to develop and implement, by October 1, 2001, a fully automated entry and exit control system that would have collected a record of arrival and departure for every alien admitted into the United States under the visa waiver program at sea and air ports of entry. As would have been required by the House bill, this system would have: 1) to the maximum extent possible, consisted of passenger arrival/departure data electronically transmitted by carriers (presumably to INS); 2) prohibited the admission of any visa waiver program entrant unless such data had been transmitted; 3) and required that such data be sufficient to calculate the number of nationals for each program country and fiscal year for whom departure records do not exist. H.R. 3767 would have also required the Attorney General to submit written reports, by January 30, 2003, and every year thereafter, to the House and Senate Judiciary Committees reporting overstay data. This section would have required the Attorney General to submit a report, by October 1, 2004, on the effectiveness of the arrival/departure control system, with recommendations regarding the possible terminations of program country participation based on overstay rates. In addition, H.R. 3767 would have required the Attorney General to establish an automated data sharing system so that overstay data, including a photograph of inadmissible aliens, would be transferred to other record/lookout systems maintained by the State Department and the INS inspections branch. S. 2367 did not include similar provisions related to entry/exit control. P.L. 106-396, however, stipulates that reports on overstays and related recommendations be included in reports required by section 110(e) of the Illegal Immigration Reform and Immigrant Responsibility Act (IIRIRA; Division C of P.L. 104-208). (For further information, see CRS Report RS20627, *Immigration: Integrated Entry and Exit Data System.*)

Visa Refusal Counts, Discrimination, and Miscellaneous Provisions

For the purposes of determining program country eligibility, H.R. 3767 would have prohibited the count of visa refusals based on race, sex, sexual orientation, or disability. Report language stressed that it would be a violation of "deep-seated American principles of equality of treatment and fair play" to deny visas based on discriminatory criteria, but this provision was not to be construed as prohibiting a consular officer from considering an applicant's "economic situation, income level, family situation, and general life circumstances or other factors" when determining a nonimmigrant visa application. The Senate substituted this provision with language to prohibit any consular officer from intentionally classifying the refusal of a visa under a category not included in those categories used to calculate visa refusal rates so that a country's refusal rate would be lower that it would be otherwise. This language, included in P.L. 106-396, also requires the Secretary of State to submit reports to the House and Senate Judiciary Committees and to the House International Relations Committee and the Senate Foreign Relations Committee on consular visa refusal rates. P.L. 106-396 also includes a number of miscellaneous provisions related to 1) conferring special nonimmigrant and immigrant status to employees of INTELSAT, 2) extending the authorization for the immigrant investor pilot program to 2002, 3) allowing business aircraft to participate in the visa waiver program, and 4) modifying the international student information system provision of IIRIRA (section 641; Division C of P.L. 104-208).

Chapter 8

IMMIGRATION: NONIMMIGRANT PROFESSIONAL AND SPECIALTY WORKER (H-1B) ISSUES

Ruth Ellen Wasem

ABSTRACT

Although Congress enacted legislation in 1998 to increase the number of nonimmigrant professional workers, commonly known as H-1B visas, the new ceiling was reached months before FY1999 ended. Many in the business community, notably in the information technology area, again urged that the ceiling be raised, and bills to do so have been introduced. S. 2045 would increase H-1B visas by 297,500 over 3 years and would exclude from the ceiling all H-1B nonimmigrants who have at least a masters degree or who work for universities and nonprofit research facilities. S. 1440/H.R. 2698 would raise the ceiling of H-1B admissions to 200,000 annually for FY2000-FY2002 and would exclude from the ceiling all H-1B nonimmigrants who have at least a masters degree and earn at least $60,000 or who have at least a bachelors degree and are employed by an institution or higher education. S. 1804 would eliminate the ceiling through FY2006. H.R. 3508 would increase the ceiling by 65,000 annually through 2002 for those with masters of PhD degrees if the employers give scholarship funds. Other related bills include H.R. 2687 and S. 1645. This report tracks the legislation and will be updated as needed.

IMMIGRATION POLICY FOR PROFESSIONAL WORKERS

Temporarily Foreign Workers

A nonimmigrant is an alien legally in the United States for a **specific purpose** and a **temporary period of time**. There are over 20 major nonimmigrant visa categories specified in the Immigration and Nationality Act, and they are commonly referred to by the letter that denotes their section in the statute. The major nonimmigrant category for temporary workers is the H visa. The larges classification of H visas is the H-1B workers in specialty occupations. In 1998, the American Competitiveness and Workforce Improvement Act (Title IV of P.L. 105-277) increased the number of H-1B workers and addressed perceived abuses of the H-1B visa.

Any employer wishing to bring in an H-1B nonimmigrant must attest in an application to the Department of Labor (DOL) that: the employer will pay the nonimmigrant the greater of the actual compensation paid other employees in the same job or the prevailing compensation for that occupation; the employer will provide working conditions for the nonimmigrant that do not cause the working conditions of the other employees to be adversely affected; and, there is no strike or lockout. The employer also must post at the workplace the application to hire nonimmigrants. Firms categorized as H-1B dependent (generally if at least 15% of the workforce are H-1B workers) must also attest that they have attempted to recruit U.S. workers and that they have not laid off U.S. workers 90 days prior to or after hiring any H-1B nonimmigrants.

DOL reviews the application for completeness and obvious inaccuracies. Only if a complaint subsequently is raised challenging the employer's application will DOL investigate. If DOL finds the employer failed to comply, the employer may be fined, denied the right to apply for additional H-1Bs, and may be subject to other penalties. The prospective H-1B nonimmigrants must demonstrate that they have the requisite education and work experience for the posted positions.[1] The Immigration and Naturalization Service (INS) then approves the petition for the H-1B nonimmigrant (assuming other immigration requirements are satisfied) for periods up to 3 years, and an alien can stay a maximum of 6 years on an H-1B visa.

Permanent Employment-Based Immigration

Many people confuse H-1B nonimmigrants with permanent immigration that is employment-based.[2] If an employer wishes to hire an alien to work on a permanent basis in the United States, the alien may petition to immigrate to the United States through one of the employment-based categories. The employer "sponsors" the prospective immigrant, and if the petition is successful, the alien becomes a legal permanent resident.[3] Many H-1B nonimmigrants may have education, skills, and experience that are similar to the requirements for three of the five preference categories for employment-based immigration: priority workers – i.e., persons of extraordinary ability in the arts, sciences, education, business, or athletics, outstanding professors and researchers; and,

---

[1] The regulation define "specialty occupation" as requiring theoretical and practical application of a body of highly specialized knowledge in fields of human endeavor including, but not limited to, architecture, engineering, mathematics, physical sciences, social sciences, medicine and health, education, law, accounting, business specialties, theology and the arts, and requiring the attainment of a bachelor's degree or its equivalent as a minimum. Law and regulations also specify that fashion models deemed "prominent" may enter on H-1B visas.

[2] The other potentially confusing category is the "O" nonimmigrant visa for persons who have extraordinary ability in the sciences, arts, education, business or athletics demonstrated by sustained national or international acclaim.

[3] There are also per-country numerical limits. For more information, see: CRS Report 94-146, Numerical Limits on Permanent Admissions, by Joyce C. Vialet and Molly Forman.

certain multinational executives and managers (first preference); members of the profession holding advanced degrees or persons of exceptional ability (second preference); and, skilled workers with at least 2 years training and professionals with baccalaureate degrees (third preference).[4]

Employment-based immigrants applying through the second and third preferences must have job offers for positions in which the employers have obtained labor certification. The labor certification is intended to demonstrate that the immigrant is not taking jobs away from qualified U.S. workers, and many consider the labor certification process far more arduous than the attestation process used for H-1B nonimmigrants.[5] More specifically, the employer who seeks to hire a prospective immigrant worker petitions with the INS and the Department of Labor (DOL) on behalf of the alien. The prospective immigrant must demonstrate that he or she meets the qualifications for the particular job as well as the preference category. If the DOL determines that a labor shortage exists in the occupation for which the petition is filed, labor certification will be issued. If there is not a labor shortage in the given occupation, the employer must submit evidence of extensive recruitment efforts in order to obtain certification.

While the demand for H-1B workers has been exceeding the limit, the number of immigrants who were admitted or adjusted under one of the employment-based preferences – 77,517 in FY1998 – remains considerably less than the statutory limit of 140,000. The first and second preferences fell far short of the almost 40,040 available to each category, with 21,408 and 14,384 respectively. The third preference is at its lowest point in recent years, dropping to 34,317 in FY1998 from a high of 62,756 in FY1996.

TRENDS IN H-1B APPROVALS

As **Figure 1** depicts, demand for H-1B workers has been increasing over the past 5 years. Both the number of attestations that firms have filed – often for more than one job opening – and the number of positions approved is growing, with the exception of a downturn in openings approved in FY1996. Since it is not uncommon for some firms to obtain approval to employ more nonimmigrants than they actually hire, the DOL data greatly overstate prospective H-1B admissions. In addition to these "anticipatory" filings, firms usually file attestations for each work site the H-1B may be assigned to, especially if these work sites are in different labor markets. Such multiple attestations are reportedly common for firms that are subcontractors – referred to by some as "out sourcers" and by others as "body shops." In addition to the multiple counts of potential H-1Bs in the DOL data, DOL data are not linked to the INS admissions data so we do not know which of the 398,324 job openings in FY1997 were filled by H-1B nonimmigrants. Nor has INS issued reports of the occupations of the H-1Bs nonimmigrants that it admits.

---

[4] Third preference also includes 10,000 "other workers," i.e., unskilled workers with occupations in which U.S. workers are in short supply.

[5] Certain second preference immigrants who are deemed to be "in the national interest" are exempt from labor certification.

Figure 1. Attestations Filed and Approved

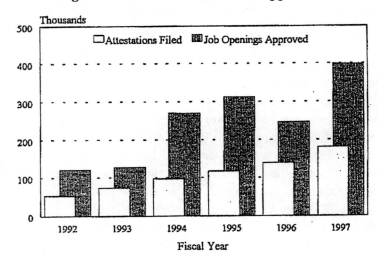

Note: Attestations often include multiple job openings.
Source: CRS presentation of DOL data.

In FY1996 computer-related occupations became the largest category and continue to lead in job openings approved for H-1Bs, going from 25.6% in FY1995, to 41.5% in FY1996, to 44.4% of the openings approved in FY1997. As **Figure 2** presents, therapists – mostly physical therapists, but also some occupational therapists, speech therapists and related occupations – fell from over half (53.5 %) of those approved in FY1995 to one-quarter (25.9%) in FY1997. Since these visas may be approved for periods up to 3 years, employers of H-1Bs approved in prior years may be seeking to renew them now. Anecdotal reports indicate a growing number of elementary and secondary school districts are not seeking H-1B nonimmigrants to work as teachers, particularly for bilingual instruction.

Foreign nationals from India constituted the largest percentage of H-1Bs – 42% in FY1998 and 46% in FY1999. Those from China are at a distant second place, with 11% of the H-1Bs in FY1998 and 10% in FY1999.

INS data confirm that the demand for H-1B visas continues to press against the statutory ceiling, even after Congress increased it (Figure 3). The 65,000 numerical limit on H-1B visas was reached for the first time prior to the end of FY1997, with numbers running out by September 1997. The 65,000 ceiling for FY1998 was reached in May of that year, and – despite the statutory increase – the 115,000 ceiling for FY1999 was reached in June of this year. Pent up demand is also emerging as a factor, as about 5,000 cases approved in FY1997 after the ceiling was hit were rolled over into FY1998. Over 19,000 cases approved in FY1998 after the ceiling was hit rolled over to FY1999.

Figure 2. Occupations of Approved Attestations

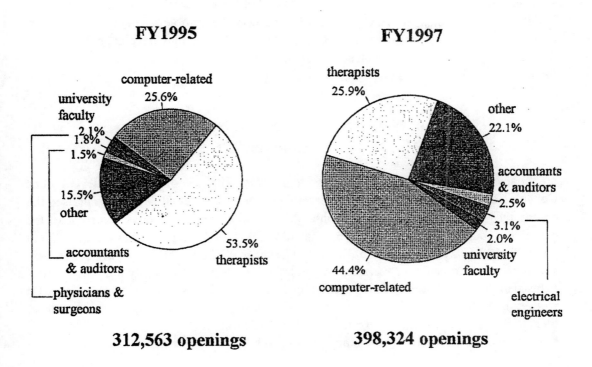

FY1995

computer-related 25.6%
university faculty 2.1%
1.8%
1.5%
15.5% other
accountants & auditors
physicians & surgeons
53.5% therapists

312,563 openings

FY1997

therapists 25.9%
other 22.1%
accountants & auditors 2.5%
3.1%
2.0%
university faculty
44.4% computer-related
electrical engineers

398,324 openings

Source: CRS presentation of DOL data.

Figure 3. H-1B Admissions by Fiscal Year

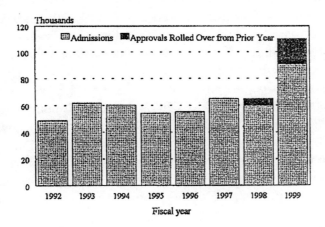

Thousands

Admissions   Approvals Rolled Over from Prior Year

Fiscal year

Source: CRS analysis of INS data.

INS recently admitted that thresholds of H-1B visas beyond the 115,000 were approved in FY1999, allegedly as a result of problems with the automated reporting system. INS now has an auditor investigating how the problems occurred and how pervasive it may be. As many as 10,000 to 20,000 H-1B visas may have been issued over the ceiling in FY1999. It is unclear at this time how these excess cases can and will be treated, especially in terms of the statutory ceiling.

AMERICAN COMPETITIVENESS AND WORKFORCE IMPROVEMENT ACT[6]

Enacted as the 105th Congress drew to a close, Title IV of the FY1999 Omnibus Consolidated and Emergency Supplemental Appropriations Act (P.L. 105-277) raised the ceiling by 142,500 over 3 years and contained provisions aimed at correcting some of the perceived abuses. The ceiling set by the new law was 115,000 in both FY1999 and FY2000, 107,500 in FY2001, and back to 65,000 in FY2002. The new law added new attestation requirements for recruitment and lay-off protections, but only requires them of firms that are "H-1B dependent" (generally if at least 15% of the workforce are H-1B workers). All firms now have to offer H-1Bs *benefits* as well as wages comparable to their U.S. workers. Education for U.S. students and training for U.S. workers are being funded by a $500 fee paid by the employer for each H-1B worker that is hired.

LEGISLATION IN 106TH CONGRESS

Senate Judiciary Committee Chair Orrin Hatch has introduced the "American Competitiveness in the Twenty-first Century Act of 2000" (S. 2045), which would raise the number of H-1B visas by 297,500 over three years, FY2000-FY2002. In addition, S. 2045 would exclude from the new ceiling all H-1B nonimmigrants who have at least a masters degree or who work for universities and nonprofit research facilities. The bill also has provisions that would facilitate the portability of H-1B status for those already here lawfully, would ease the per-country ceilings for employment-based immigrants, and would require a study of the "digital divide" on access to information technology.

The "New Workers for Economic Growth Act" (S. 1440/H.R. 2698) introduced by Senator Phil Gramm and Congressman Dave Dreier would raise the ceiling of H-1B admissions to 200,000 annually FY2000-FY2002. Those H-1B nonimmigrants who have at least a master's degree and earn at least $60,000 would not count toward the ceiling. Those who have at least a bachelor's degree and are employed by an institution of higher education would be exempted from the attestation requirements as well as the ceiling. Senator John McCain has introduced S. 1804, which, among other initiatives, would eliminate the H-1B ceiling through FY2006. Congressman David Wu introduced H.R.

---

[6] For a full account, see: CRS Report 98-531, Immigration: Nonimmigrant H-1B Specialty Worker Issues and Legislation, by Ruth Ellen Wasem, November 2, 1998.

3508, which would increase the ceiling by 65,000 annually through 2002 for those with masters or PhD degrees, provided the employers establish scholarship funds.

The "Bringing Resources from Academia to the Industry of Our Nation Act" (H.R. 2687), introduced by Congresswoman Zoe Lofgren, would create a new nonimmigrant visa category, referred to as "T" visas, for foreign students who have graduated from U.S. institutions with bachelor's degrees in mathematics, science or engineering and who are obtaining jobs earning at least $60,000. The "Helping Improve Technology Education and Competitiveness Act" (S. 1645), introduced by Senator Charles Robb, also would create a "T" nonimmigrant visa category for foreign students who have graduated from U.S. institutions with bachelor's degrees in mathematics, science or engineering and who are obtaining jobs paying at least $60,000. More stringent than H.R. 2687, S. 1645 would include provisions aimed at protecting U.S. workers that are comparable to the provisions governing the H-1B visas.

Now Congress is once again striving to balance the needs of U.S. employers with opportunities for U.S. residents. Proponents argue that increases in the admission of H-1B workers are essential if the United States is to remain globally competitive and that employers should be free to hire the best people for the jobs. They say that the education of students and retraining of the current workforce is a long-term approach, and they cannot wait to fill today's openings. Some point out that many mathematics, computer science, and engineering graduates of U.S. colleges and universities are foreign students and that we should keep that talent here. Others assert that H-1B workers create jobs, either by ultimately starting their own information technology firms or by providing a workforce sufficient for firms to remain in the United States.

Those opposing any further increases assert that there is no compelling evidence of a labor shortage in these professional areas that cannot be met by newly graduating students and re-training the existing U.S. workforce. They argue that the education of U.S. students and training of U.S. workers should be prioritized. Opponents also maintain that salaries and compensation would be rising if there is a labor shortage and if employers wanted to attract qualified U.S. workers. Some allege that employers prefer H-1B workers because they are less demanding in terms of wages and working conditions and that an industry's dependence on temporary foreign workers may inadvertently lead the brightest U.S. students to seek positions in fields offering more stable careers.[7]

Alternatively, some maintain that the H-1B ceiling is arbitrary and would not be necessary if more stringent protections for U.S. workers were enacted. They argue the question is not "how many" but "under what conditions." Some would broaden the recruitment requirements and layoff protections enacted last year for "H-1B dependent" employers to all employers hiring H-1B workers. Others would make the labor market

---

[7] CRS Report RL30140, An Information Technology Labor Shortage? Legislation in the 106th Congress, by Linda Levine; and CRS Report for Congress 98-462, Immigration and Information Technology Jobs: The Issue of Temporary Foreign Workers, by Ruth Ellen Wasem and Linda Levine.

tests for nonimmigrant temporary workers comparable to those for immigrants applying for one of the permanent employment-based admissions categories.

Chapter 9

IMMIGRATION: A GUIDE TO INTERNET SOURCES

Barbara A. Salazar

ABSTRACT

This report identifies selected World Wide Web (WWW) sites from the Internet on immigration topics in the United States. Selected government, legal, and organizational Web site addresses are provided. This report will be updated periodically as new information becomes available and to ensure the currency of the Web addresses.

SELECTED WEB SITES ON IMMIGRATION ISSUES

Listed below are selected WWW sites examining immigration issues in three categories: federal government, legal sites, and organizations. A brief description accompanies each entry with details on related links.

U.S. GOVERNMENT WEB SITES

- **Immigration and Naturalization Service (INS)** Web site at: [http://www.ins.usdoj. gov/graphics/index.htm]. This main page of the INS Web site is the gateway to the latest news from the INS and to links for specific topics, such as:

  - **Case Work – Resources for Immigration Case Workers** at:
    [http://www.ins.usdoj.gov/graphics/aboutins/congress/resources.htm].
    Information for congressional offices on assisting constituents with a variety of immigration questions is provided. It also links to the Web page **Information for Congressional Offices** at [http://www.ins.usdoj.gov/graphics/aboutins/congess/index.htm].

- **CIPRIS – Coordinated Interagency Partnership Regulating International Students** at: [http://www.ins.usdoj.gov/graphics/services/cipris/index.htm]. This Web site has information on the CIPRIS program, which will allow electronic data collection and reporting on nonimmigrant students/visitors and exchange student/visitors (F, M, & J visa categories) and will help the INS better monitor school and exchange programs.
- **Fees and Forms** at: [http://www.ins.usdoj.gov/graphics/formsfee/index.htm]. This Web site has electronic copies of numerous INS forms along with instructions.
- **How Do I...? (Frequently Asked Questions [FAQs] on Immigration)** at: [http://www.ins.usdoj.gov/graphics/howdoi.htm]. Answers to frequently asked questions ranging from "What's a green card?" to "What type of a visa do I need?" are listed alphabetically by subject.
- **Law Enforcement and Border Management** at: [http://www.ins.usdoj.gov/graphics/lawenfor/index.htm]. Information is provided on border security, inspections, detention, deportations, and career opportunities with the Border Patrol.
- **Public Affairs Information** (backgrounders, fact sheets, FAQs, press releases) at: [http://www.ins.usdoj.gov/graphics/publicaffaris/presinfo.htm]. Information is listed alphabetically by subject (admissions, citizenship, benefits eligibility, enforcement, 245i, LIFE, etc.) or chronologically.
- **Statistics for Immigration to the United States, 1994-2000** at: [http://www.ins.usdoj.gov/graphics/aboutins/statistics/index.htm]. Access to INS statistical data from the publication, *Statistical Yearbook of the Immigration and Naturalization Service*, and from other data systems is provided.

• **Library of Congress, American Memory** at: [http://www.lcweb2.loc.gov/ammem/ndlpedu/features/immig/immig.html]. This Web site is maintained by the Library of Congress and contains historical information on immigration to the United States from the Library's collections. In the section "Immigration Today," there is a link to THOMAS, the Library's legislative Web site, to search on current immigration legislation at: [http://thomas.loc.gov/bss/d105/hot-subj.html].

• **U.S. Census Bureau, Foreign-Born Population Statistics** at: [http://www.census.gov/population/www/socdemo/foreign.html]. It has data on the characteristics of the foreign-born population, including legal immigrants, undocumented immigrants, and temporary residents, such as students and workers on business visas.

• **U.S. Commission on Immigration Reform** at: [http://www.utexas.edu/1bj/uscir]. The Commission was created by the Immigration Act of 1990 and dissolved in December 1997. Its reports are available at this Web site maintained by the Lyndon B. Johnson School of Public Affairs.

• **U.S. Department of Justice (DOJ) Immigration Information Page** at: [http://www.usdoj.gov/immigrationinfo.htm]. This Web site links to the main INS

Web site, INS services and benefits, the latest INS news, and to the Executive Office for Immigration Review (EOIR) at: [http://www.usdoj.gov/eoir]. The EOIR was created on January 9, 1983, through an internal DOJ reorganization which combined the Board of Immigration Appeals (BIA) with the Immigration Judge function previously performed by the Immigration and Naturalization Service (INS). It also links directly to the BIA at [http://www.usdoj.gov/eoir/biainfo/htm].

- **U.S. Department of State** at [http://www.state.gov]. This Web site has information on some immigration topics such as visas, refugees, and cultural and educational exchanges.

  - **Bureau of Population, Refugees, and Migration (PRM)** at: [http://www.state.gov/www/global/prm/index.html]. This Web site provides information on the refugee population worldwide and policies regarding assistance and admission to the United States. The PRM has primary responsibility for formulating policies on population, refugees, and migration.
  - **Bureau of Consular Affairs** at: [http://travel.state.gov/vvisas/index.html]. This Web site has information on the new K and V visas, the categories of nonimmigrant visas created by the LIFE Act. Included is information on where to apply and application forms.
  - **Bureau of Educational and Cultural Affairs** at: [http://exhcnages.state.gov/jvisa/J%20Exchange%20Visitor%20Program/index.h tm]. This site has information on the Au Pair program and cultural and educational exchanges like the J Visa Exchange Program.
  - **Visa Services** at: [http://travel.state.gov/visa_services.html]. This Web site provides information on the Diversity Visa (DV) – 2002 Lottery and various other types of visas (employment-based like H-1B, H2-A; family-based, students, etc.).

LEGAL WEB SITES

- **American Immigration Lawyers Association** at: [http://www.aila.org]. This is the Web site of the national bar association of attorneys practicing immigration law.
- **Cornell University Immigration Law** at: [http://www.law.cornell.edu/ topics/immigration.html]. This Web site provides an overview of immigration law and offers access to federal and international legal materials as well as links to "Key Internet Sources."
- **Immigration Web Portal** at [http://www.ilw.com]. This Web site has information for immigration lawyers and those seeking assistance with immigration casework. It also has access to Immigration Daily news at [http://www.ilw.com/lawyers /immigdaily].

ORGANIZATIONS' WEB SITES

- **American Immigration Resources on the Internet** at: [http://www.theodora.com/resouce.html#LISTS]. This Web site has links to immigration reference materials including texts of laws, immigration attorneys, advocacy groups, research, organizations such as the Federation for American Immigration Reform (FAIR) and Minority Affairs Forum, etc., and other useful information.

- **Center for Immigration Studies (CIS)** at [http://www.cis.org]. Founded in 1985, the CIS is an independent, nonpartisan, nonprofit research organization devoted exclusively to analyzing the "economic, social, demographic, fiscal, and other impacts of immigration on the United States." Included are texts of CIS publications, current news articles, and current information on common immigration topics such as citizenship, legal and illegal immigration, refugee and asylum issues, wages, and poverty.

- **Georgetown University, Institute for the Study of International Migration** at: [http://www.georgetown.edu/sfs/programs/isim/publications.htm]. The Institute for the Study of International Migration (ISIM) is part of the Edmund A. Walsh School of Foreign Service and is affiliated with the Law Center at Georgetown University. The ISIM studies issues raised by international migration, including immigration to the United States and its social and legal impact. A list of ISIM publications on immigration is provided.

- **Immigration Superhighway** at: [http://www.immigration-usa.com/i_suphwy.html]. This Web site has information on the links to the Immigration Nationality Act, immigration forms, advocacy groups, and recent new articles on immigration topics.

- **National Visa Services** at: [http://www.nationalvisaservice.com/index.asp]. Founded in 1994, this self-proclaimed "Gateway to America" provides information on applying for the latest diversity lottery to obtain a green card.

- **RAND's Center for Research on Immigration Policy (CRIP)** at: [http://www.rand.org/education/crip.html]. Established in 1988 by RAND, one of the first "Think Tanks" in the United States, CRIP conducts analytical research and policy analysis on the integration of immigrants in the United States, access to public services by immigrants, the education of immigrants and their children, and links between immigration and national security issues. A link to a bibliography of CRIP publications is provided.

- **Urban Institute's Population Studies** at: [http://www.urban.org/centers/psissue. html]. The Urban Institute is a nonpartisan economic and social policy research organization. Its Population Studies Research Center analyzes issues related to immigration such as immigrant health, economic status, undocumented aliens in the criminal justice system, and other topics. A listing of current Population Studies publications on various immigration issues can be accessed by clicking on "Reports/Books" or by going directly to: [http://www.urban.org/centers/pspubs. html].

Chapter 10

TEMPORARY PROTECTED STATUS: CURRENT IMMIGRATION POLICY AND ISSUES

Ruth Ellen Wasem and Shirin Kaleel

ABSTRACT

When civil unrest, violence, or natural disasters erupt in spots around the world, concerns arise over the safety of nationals from these troubled places who are in the United States. Provisions exist in the Immigration and Nationality Act (INA) to offer temporary relief from removal under certain circumstances. The United States currently provides some type of blanket relief from deportation or forced departure to nationals from 10 countries: Angola, Burundi, El Salvador, Honduras, Liberia, Montserrat, Nicaragua, Sierra Leone, Somalia, and Sudan. All but Liberians (who have deferred enforced departure) have Temporary Protected Status (TPS). Under INA, the Attorney General, in consultation with the Secretary of State, grants TPC. Congress, however, has also granted TPS legislatively, and legislation that would grant TPS to nationals of specified countries has been introduced in the last several Congresses, including the 107th Congress.

BACKGROUND

The Immigration and Nationality Act (INA) provides that all aliens (i.e., persons who are not citizens or nationals of the United States) must enter pursuant to the INA and be authorized by the Immigration and Naturalization Service (INS). The major categories of aliens are immigrants, refugees and Asylees (all admitted for or adjusted to legal permanent residence), and nonimmigrants (admitted for temporary reasons, e.g., students, tourists, or business travelers). Aliens who lack proper authorization are generally of two kinds: those who entered the United States without inspection according to immigration procedures, or those who entered the United States on a temporary visa and have stayed beyond the expiration date of the visa. Unauthorized aliens of both kinds are subject to removal.

As a signatory to the United Nations Protocol Relating to the Status of Refugees (hereafter U.N. Protocol), the United States agrees to the principle of *nonrefoulement*, which means that it will not return an alien to a country where his life or freedom would be threatened. *Nonrefoulement* is embodied in several provisions of U.S. immigration law. Most notably, it is reflected in the provisions requiring the Attorney General to withhold the deportation or removal of aliens to a country in which the alien's life or freedom would be threatened on the basis of race, religion, nationality, membership in a particular social group, or political opinion.[1] Provisions in the INA for withholding removal can be traced back to the 1950s.

The legal definition of asylum in the INA is consistent with the U.N. Protocol, which specifies that a refugee is a person who is unwilling or unable to return to his country of nationality or habitual residence because of a well-founded fear of persecution on account of race, religion, nationality, and membership in a particular social group, or political opinion. The definitions of refugee and asylee are essentially the same in the INA, with the notable difference being the physical location of the persons seeking the status. Those who are in the United States or at a U.S. port of entry apply for asylum, while those who are displaced abroad apply for refugee status. The standards of proof and minimum thresholds are similar, but the procedures and priorities for refugee admissions are quite different. The current procedures and guidelines for admitting refugees and for protecting aliens already within the country (i.e., asylum or withholding deportation) were enacted as part of the Refugee Act of 1980.

If the motivation of the migrant is determined to be economic improvement rather than the political reasons that underpin the legal definition, the person is not considered eligible for asylum. This distinction is sometimes difficult to discern, because persecution as well as war may lead to economic hardships, and economic deprivation may trigger persecution or insurrection. Since factors such as extreme poverty, deprivation, violence, and the dislocation brought on by famines or natural disasters may evoke a humanitarian response, the term "humanitarian migrants" encompasses all those who immigrate to the United States for such reasons, including those who receive asylum.[2]

The concept of "safe haven" embraces humanitarian migrants. It covers those who may not meet the legal definition of refugee but are nonetheless fleeing potentially dangerous situations. Safe haven also assumes that the host country, in this instance the United States, is the first country in which the fleeing alien arrives safely, or is the country where the alien is temporarily residing when the unsafe conditions occur. Safe haven is implicitly temporary in nature because it is given prior to any decision on the long-term resolution of the alien's status. It is also a form of blanket relief because it is premised on more generalized conditions of turmoil or deprivation in the country of origin, in contrast to the individual circumstances weighed in the case-by-case asylum process.

---

[1] §208 of INA [8 U.S.C. 1158]; §241(b)(3) of INA [8 U.S.C. 1231]; and §101(a) of INA [8 U.S.C. 1101(a)(42)].

[2] The term "humanitarian migrant" is not defined in the INA, nor, in this context, is it meant to imply that a sympathetic policy response is warranted. Rather, it refers to factors underlying the alien's justification for immigration.

In terms of permanent residence over the long term, the United States endorses the internationally held position that voluntary repatriation is the best outcome for refugees. The international community ranks resettlement in the country of first asylum as the second desirable option, and resettlement in a third country as the last positive alternative.

TEMPORARY PROTECTED STATUS

Temporary Protected Status is the statutory embodiment of safe have for those aliens who may not meet the legal definition of refugee but are nonetheless fleeing – or reluctant to return to – potentially dangerous situations. TPS is blanket relief that may be granted under the following conditions: there is ongoing armed conflict posing serious threat to personal safety; a foreign state requests TPS because if temporarily cannot handle the return of nationals due to environmental disaster; or there are extraordinary and temporary conditions in a foreign state that prevent aliens from returning, provided that granting TPS is consistent with U.S. national interests.[3]

The Attorney General, in consultation with the Secretary of State, can issue TPS for periods of 6 to 18 months and can extend these periods if conditions do not change in the designated country. To obtain TPS, eligible aliens report to INS, pay a processing fee, and receive registration documents and a work authorization. The major requirements for aliens seeking TPS are proof of eligibility, e.g., a passport issued by the designated country, continuous physical presence in the United States since the date TPS went into effect, timely registration, and being otherwise admissible as an immigrant. The regulation specifies grounds of inadmissibility that cannot be waived, including those relating to criminal convictions and the persecution of others.[4]

Aliens who receive TPS are not on an immigration track that leads to permanent residence or citizenship. The "temporary" nature of TPS is apparent in the regulation. INS has made clear that information it collects when an alien registers for TPS may be used to institute exclusion or deportation proceedings upon the denial, withdrawal or expiration of TPS.[5] Moreover, the TPS provision in the INA states that a bill or amendment that provides for the adjustment of lawful temporary or legal permanent resident (LPR) status for any alien receiving TPS requires a supermajority vote in the Senate, i.e., three-fifths of all Senators voting affirmatively.[6]

---

[3] §244 of INA [8 U.S.C. 1254a].
[4] 8 U.S.C. 240.
[5] *Ibid.*
[6] §244(h) of INA [8 U.S.C. 1254a].

OTHER BLANKET FORMS OF RELIEF

In addition to TPS, the Attorney General has provided, under certain conditions, discretionary relief from deportation so that aliens who have not been legally admitted to the United States may remain in this country either temporarily or permanently. The statutory authority cited by the agency for these discretionary procedures is generally that portion of immigration law that confers on the Attorney General the authority for general enforcement and the section of the law covering the authority for voluntary departure.[7] Such blanket relief is an exercise of the discretion of the Attorney General, and thus, the Secretary of State need not be consulted.

Prior to the enactment of TPS, the INS provided relief by means of the suspension of enforcement of the immigration laws against a particular group of individuals. The two most common discretionary procedures to provide relief from deportation have been deferred departure or deferred enforced departure (DED) and extended voluntary departure (EVD). The discretionary procedures of DED and EVD continue to be used to provide relief the Administration feels is appropriate, and the executive branch's position is that all blanket relief decisions require a balance of judgment regarding foreign policy, humanitarian, and immigration concerns. Unlike TPS, aliens who benefit from EVD or DED do not necessarily register for the status with INS, but they trigger the protection when they are identified for deportation. If, however, they wish to be employed in the United States, they must apply for a work authorization from the INS.

NATIONALITIES RECEIVING TEMPORARY PROTECTIONS

Aliens from 10 countries currently have temporary protection from deportation. Aliens from Montserrat were the first granted TPS on the basis of a natural disaster, in this case a volcanic eruption. The estimated number of aliens currently protected range from 300 Montserratians to 150,000 Salvadorans. All have TPS except the Liberians who have DED status. Of those who currently have TPS, aliens from Somalia have had TPS for the longest period – since September 1991. Liberians who now have DED, however, first received TPS in March 1991.

In 1990, when Congress enacted the TPS statute, it also granted TPS for 1 year to nationals from El Salvador who were residing in the United States. Subsequently, the Attorney General, in consultation with the State Department, granted TPS to aliens in the United States from the following countries: Kuwait from March 1991 to March 1992; Rwanda from June 1995 to December 1997; Lebanon from March 1991 to March 1993; the Kosovo Province of Serbia from June 1998 to December 2000; and Bosnia-Herzegovina from August 1992 to February 2001.

Rather than extending Salvadoran TPS when it expired in 1992, the Bush Administration granted DED to what was then estimated as 190,000 Salvadorans through December 1994. The Bush Administration also granted DED to about 80,000 Chinese

---

[7] §240 of INA [8 U.S.C. 1229a]; §240B [8 U.S.C. 1229c].

following the Tiananmen Square massacre in June 1989, and the Chinese retained DED through January 1994. On December 23, 1997, President Clinton instructed the Attorney General to grant DED to the Haitians for 1 year. When the Liberian TPS expired on September 28, 1999, they were also granted DED.

In prior years, various Administrations have given EVD status to Poles (July 1984 to March 1989), Nicaraguans (July 1979 to September 1980), Iranians (April to December 1979), and Ugandans (June 1978 to September 1986). Lebanese had been handled sympathetically as a group, getting EVD on a case-by-case basis since 1976, prior to receiving TPS from 1991 to 1993. Other countries whose nationals have benefited in the past from a status similar to EVD include: Cambodia, Cuba, Chile, Czechoslovakia, Dominican Republic, Hungary, Laos, Rumania, and Vietnam.[8]

Countries Whose Nationals in the United States Benefit from Temporary Relief from Deportation

Country	Status	Dates	Estimated number[a]
Angola	TPS	03/29/00 to 03/29/02	6,672
Burundi	TPS	11/4/97 to 11/02/01	1,000
El Salvador	TPS	03/02/01 to 09/02/02	150,000
Honduras	TPS	12/30/98 to 07/05/02	105,000
Liberia	DED	09/28/99 to 09/29/01[b]	10,000
Montserrat	TPS	08/22/98 to 08/27/01	300
Nicaragua	TPS	12/30/98 to 07/05/02	5,300
Sierra Leone	TPS	11/04/97 to 11/02/01	5,000
Somalia	TPS	09/16/91 to 09/17/01	350
Sudan	TPS	11/04/97 to 11/02/01	1,500

[a] Estimates based upon INS data for designated status or work authorizations. These approximate numbers do not necessarily include all aliens from the countries who are in the United States and might be eligible for the status. INS updates these numbers when it renews TPS for nationals from a given country.

[b] Dates for DED are not as firmly established as those for TPS because registration is not required.

ISSUES

Central Americans

The Bush Administration recently decided to grant TPS to Salvadorans following two earthquakes that rocked El Salvador in January and February. Prior to leaving office in January, the Clinton Administration said it would temporarily halt deportations to El Salvador. A bill to legislatively grant TPS to Salvadorans (H.R. 531) was introduced February 8, 2001. Whether to grant blanket relief to nationals from neighboring Central

---

[8] To the best of our knowledge, this list includes all countries that have benefited from some form of blanket relief since the 1950s.

American countries has perplexed policymakers long before these recent earthquakes. Proponents of granting TPS to the Central Americans maintain it is an appropriate humanitarian response because people should not be forced to return to countries devastated by the natural disaster. Opponents fear TPS for those Central Americans in the United States would serve as a magnet to the millions of people displaced by natural disaster, prompting many of them to seek entry to the United States. In the aftermath of Hurricane Mitch, then-Attorney General Janet Reno announced on November 5, 1998, that she would temporarily suspend the deportation of aliens from El Salvador, Guatemala, Honduras, and Nicaragua. On December 30, 1998, the Attorney General designated TPS for undocumented Hondurans and Nicaraguans in the United States as of that date. The Administration maintained that Honduras and Nicaragua had such extraordinary displacement and damage from Hurricane Mitch as to warrant TPS. For both Nicaraguans and Hondurans, TPS was extended and is now scheduled to expire on July 5, 2002. After Hurricane Mitch, Guatemalans and Salvadorans had their stays of removal extended for 60 days – until March 8, 1999.

Liberians

Approximately 10,000 Liberians in the United States were given DED after their TPS expired September 28, 1999. Their DED status is presently extended to September 29, 2001. These Liberians have had protections for the longest period, of those who currently have TPS or other forms of blanket relief from deportation, having first received TPS in March 1991. Former Attorney General Reno had indicated that she did not wish to keep extending TPS or DED for Liberians. Some assert that it is not safe for the Liberians to return home and that they should do so. Others maintain that those Liberians who have lived in the United States for almost a decade have firm roots in the community and should be permitted to adjust to LPR status.

Peruvians and Colombians

Violence growing out of the drug war and insurgencies have prompted some to request TPS for nationals in the United States from Peru and Colombia. The proponents are not asserting that the governments of these countries are repressing people or violating human rights; rather, they maintain that illegal forces within the country are creating dangerous conditions that the governments have not been successful in remedying. Others maintain that many countries around the world are dangerous and that conditions in Peru and Colombia do not warrant TPS.

Adjustment of Status

Since aliens granted TPS, EVD, and DED are not eligible to become legal permanent residents (LPRs) in the United States, a special act of Congress is required for such aliens to adjust their immigration status. For example, a law enacted in 1987 contained a special extension of the legalization program established by the Immigration Reform and Control Act (IRCA) to include otherwise eligible aliens who had been granted EVD status during the 5-year period following the IRCA legalization cut-off date, i.e., through November 1, 1987. As a result, Afghans, Ethiopians, Poles, and Ugandans were among those who became eligible to legalize as temporary and subsequently permanent resident aliens. Congress also enacted legislation in 1992 that allowed Chinese who had deferred enforced departure following the Tiananmen Square massacre to adjust to LPT status (P.L. 102-404). Legislation enabling Haitians to adjust their status passed on the close of the 105th Congress (P.L. 105-277).[9] Legislation to allow Guatemalans, Hondurans, Liberians, and Salvadorans (among others) to adjust to LPR status received considerable attention in the 106th Congress, but was not enacted. Bills providing legal permanent resident status to those groups have been introduced in the 107th Congress.[10]

---

[9] See: CRS Report 98-270, *Immigration: Haitian Relief Issues and Legislation*, by Ruth Ellen Wasem.
[10] See: CRS Report RL30780, *Immigration Legalization and Status Adjustment Legislation*, by Ruth Ellen Wasem.

Chapter 11

IMMIGRATION: FOREIGN STUDENTS IN THE UNITED STATES

Ruth Ellen Wasem

ABSTRACT

Since the Immigration Act of 1924, the United States has expressly permitted foreign students to study in U.S. institutions. Most foreign students are at least 18 years old and are enrolled in higher education programs. The enrollment of foreign students in institutions of higher education has steadily risen over the past 40 years, from 34,232 in the 1954/55 school year to 453,787 in 1995/96. In terms of doctoral students, the number of foreign students obtaining PhD's grew by 242% from 1970 to 1995. In addition, the percentage that foreign students in institutions of higher education comprise of total enrollment has doubled in the past four decades, and now hovers at 3.1%.

Foreign students enrich the cultural diversity of the educational experience for U.S. residents as well as enhance the reputation of U.S. universities as world-class institutions. While their presence is generally viewed as a positive one, concerns have arisen in recent years that have caused Congress to take a new look at the Immigration and Nationality Act (INA) provisions that govern their admission.

Generally, foreign students are likely to major in business, engineering, and the sciences. The National Research Council Survey of Earned Doctorates, in particular reveals the dominance of foreign students in science and engineering. Indeed, during 1995 there were more foreign PhD recipients in engineering than U.S. citizen recipients – 2.523 and 2,382 respectively. In 1970, however, there were 2,514 U.S. citizens and only 471 foreign students who received PhDs in engineering.

While foreign students are barred from receiving federal financial assistance and from working off-campus (with limited exceptions), they are successful at gaining financial assistance from colleges and universities. The Survey of Earned Doctorates reveals that foreign students are more likely to report the university as their primary source of financial support, including federally-funded research grants, than are U.S. citizens. Only one-third of foreign PhD recipients report that they had educational debts, while over half of U.S. citizen doctoral recipients report educational debts.

The 104th Congress opted not to continue off-campus work programs for foreign students and not to act on a proposal that would have required foreign students to return home upon completion of their program. The questions of financial aid to foreign students and displacement of U.S. students prompted interest in further study, but no action to change policies.

At the close of the last session, however, Congress passed provisions in the Illegal Immigration Reform and Immigrant Responsibility Act (IIRIRA) of 1996, enacted as Division C of P.L. 104-208, aimed at the question of U.S. taxpayers subsidizing the education of foreign elementary and secondary students. IIRIRA now requires certain foreign students to pay tuition if they attend public high schools in the United States and bars certain foreign students from attending public elementary schools. Some educational institutions and groups representing foreign students are seeking the repeal of this provision as well as one strengthening the reporting requirements of educational institutions with foreign students.

INTRODUCTION

Since the Immigration Act of 1924, the United States has expressly permitted foreign students to study in U.S. institutions.[1] Foreign students enrich the cultural diversity of the educational experience for U.S. residents as well as enhance the reputation of U.S. universities as work class institutions. Some foreign students opt to remain in the United States and those who qualify under U.S. immigration laws ultimately adjust their immigration status to that of legal permanent resident.

While their presence is generally viewed as a positive one, concerns have arisen in recent years that have caused Congress to take a new look at the Immigration and Nationality Act (INA) provisions that govern their admission. The 104th Congress notably the Senate, raised several questions about foreign students.

- Are U.S. taxpayers subsidizing the education of foreign students in public elementary and secondary schools?
- Are foreign students receiving a disproportionate amount of financial aid from colleges and universities?
- Are foreign students displacing U.S. students in certain areas of study, and subsequently certain fields of employment?[2]
- Should foreign students be permitted to work off campus?
- Should the foreign students be required to return home when they have completed their program?

The 104th Congress opted not to continue off-campus work programs for foreign students and not to act on a proposal that would have expanded the foreign residency requirements. The questions of financial aid and displacement of U.S. students prompted interest in further study, but no action to change policies.

---

[1] This report is limited to foreign students that are international students legally admitted to the United States to pursue their education. Unless otherwise noted, it does not include foreign-born students residing in the United States as either legal permanent residents or undocumented aliens.

[2] For analysis and discussion of this question, see: CRS Report 92-469, *Foreign-Born Science and Engineering Doctorate Students in U.S. Institutions*, by Christine M. Matthews.

At the close of the last session, however, Congress passed provisions in the Illegal Immigration Reform and Immigrant Responsibility Act (IIRIRA) of 1996, enacted as Division C of P.L. 104-208, aimed at the question of U.S. taxpayers subsidizing the education of foreign students. IIRIRA now requires certain foreign students to pay tuition if they attend public high schools in the United States and bars them from attending public elementary schools. This provision, as well as one strengthening the reporting requirements of educational institutions with foreign students, have led some educational institutions and groups representing foreign students to seek their repeal. Thus far, no action pertaining to these issues has been introduced in the 105th Congress.

TYPES OF FOREIGN STUDENTS

There are three main avenues for students from other countries to temporarily come to the United States to study, and each involves admission as a nonimmigrant. A nonimmigrant is an alien legally in the United States for a specific purpose and a temporary period of time. There are over 20 major nonimmigrant visa categories specified in the INA< and they are commonly referred to by the letter that denotes their section of the statute. The three visa categories used by foreign students are: F visas for academic study; M visas for vocational study; and J visas for cultural exchange. Most foreign students in higher education hold F-1 visas – 85% during the 1996/96 school year. Those with J-1 visas made up about 8% of foreign students in 1995/96.

F Visa

The most common visa for foreign students is the F-1 visa. It is tailored for international students pursuing a full-time academic education. According to the Immigration and Naturalization Service (INS), 93% of F-1 issuances in 1995 were to students at least 18 years old. The F-1 student is generally admitted as a nonimmigrant for the period of the program of study, referred to as the duration of status.[3] The law requires that the student have a foreign residence that they have no intention of abandoning. Their spouses and children may accompany them as F-2 nonimmigrants.

To obtain an F-1 visa, prospective students also must demonstrate they have met several criteria:

- They must be accepted by a school that has been approved by the Attorney General.[4]
- They must document that they have sufficient funds or have made other arrangements to cover all their expenses for 12 months.[5]

---

[3] Those entering as secondary school students are only admitted for 1 year.
[4] Schools that wish to receive F students must file a petition with the INS district director. The particular supporting documents for the petition depend on the nature of the petitioning school. Once a school is

- They must demonstrate that they have the scholastic preparation to pursue a full course of study for the academic level to which they wish to be admitted and must have a sufficient knowledge of English (or have made arrangements with the school for special tutoring, or study in a language the student knows).

Once in the United States on an F visa, the nonimmigrants are generally barred from off-campus employment. Exceptions are for extreme financial hardship that arises after arriving in the United States and for employment with an international organization.[6] F students are permitted to engage in on-campus employment if the employment does not displace a U.S. resident. In addition, F students are permitted to work in practically training that relates to their degree program, such as paid research and teaching assistantships. An alien on an F visa who otherwise accepts employment violates the terms of the visa and is subject to removal and other penalties discussed later in this report.

J Visa

Foreign students are just one of many types of aliens who may enter the United States on a J-1 visa, sometimes referred to as the Fulbright program. Others admitted under this cultural exchange visa include scholars, professors, teachers, trainees, specialists, foreign medical graduates, international visitors, au pairs, and participants in student travel/work programs. Those seeking admission as a J-1 nonimmigrant must be participating in a cultural exchange program that the United States Information Agency (USIA) has designated. They are admitted for the period of the program.[7] Their spouses and children may accompany as J-2 nonimmigrants.

Responsible officers of the sponsoring organizations must be U.S. citizens. The programs that wish to sponsor J visas also must satisfy the following criteria:

- Be a bona fide educational and cultural exchange program, with clearly defined purposes and objectives;
- Have at least five exchange visitors annually;
- Provide cross-cultural activities;
- Be reciprocal whenever possible;
- If not sponsored by the government, the minimum stay for participants must be at least 3 weeks (except those designated as "short term" scholars);

approved it can continue to receive F students without any time limits; however, the approval may be withdrawn if the INS discovers that the school has failed to comply with the law or regulations.

[5] F, J, and M students are barred from federal financial aid. See Section 484(a)(5) of the Higher Education Act of 1965, as amended.

[6] The Immigration Act of 1990 created an F-1 pilot employment program, but authority for this pilot off-campus work program expired Sept. 30, 1996.

[7] As with secondary students entering with F-1 visas, J-1 students in secondary school programs are only admitted for up to 1 year.

- Provide information verifying the sponsoring program's legal status, citizenship, accreditation, and licensing;
- Show that they are financially stable, able to meet the financial commitments of the program, and have funds for J nonimmigrant's return airfare;
- Ensure that the program is not to fill staff vacancies or adversely affect U.S. workers;
- Assure that participants have accident insurance, including insurance for medical evacuations; and
- Provide full details of the selection process, placement, evaluation, and supervision of participants.[8]

As with F visas, those seeking J visas must have a foreign residence they have no intention of abandoning. However, many of those with J visas have an additional foreign residency requirement in that they must return abroad for 2 years if they wish to adjust to any other nonimmigrant status or to become a legal permanent resident in the United States. This foreign residency requirement applies to J nonimmigrants who meet any of the three following conditions:

- An agency of the U.S. government or their home government financed in whole or in part – directly or indirectly – their participation in the program.
- The BECA designates their home country as clearly requiring the services or skills in the field they are pursuing.
- They are coming to the United States to receive graduate medical training.

There are very few exceptions to the foreign residency requirement for those J visa holders who meet any of these criteria – even J visa holders who marry U.S. citizens are required to return home for 2 years.[9]

Although many aliens with J-1 visas are permitted to work in the programs in which they are participating, the work restrictions for foreign students with a J-1 visa are similar to those for the F visa.

M Visa

Foreign students who wish to pursue a non-academic, e.g., vocational course of study apply for an M visa. This visa is the least used of the foreign student visas. Much of the F students, those seeking an M visa must show that they have been accepted by an approved school, have the financial means to pay for tuition, expenses, and otherwise support themselves for 1 year, and have the scholastic preparation and language skills

---

[8] 22 CFR §514.

[9] INA §212(e) provides only a few exceptions, including cases of exceptional hardship to the spouse or child of a J-1 if that spouse or child is a U.S. citizen or permanent resident alien and in cases of persecution on the basis of race, religion, or political opinion if the alien returned home, and if it is in the national interest not to require the return.

appropriate for the course of study. Their spouses and children may accompany them as M-2 nonimmigrants. As with all of the student visa categories, they must have a foreign residence they have no intention of abandoning. Those with M visas are also barred from working in the United States, including on-campus employment.

TRENDS IN ADMISSIONS

Foreign students have been coming to study in the United States for most of this century, and in recent years, the numbers admitted have slowly risen. According to the INS nonimmigrant database, 364,220 students were admitted with either F-1 or M-1 visas in FY1995, up from 257,069 in FY1985. Another 31,260 people came as the spouse or child (F-2, M-2) of a foreign student in FY1995, comparable to 31,056 in FY1985. The INS nonimmigrant database does not identify which J-1 exchange visitors are students, so they are not depicted in **Figure 1**, *Annual Admissions of Foreign Students, 1985-95*. The INS data count "entries" during the fiscal year and, thus, include each time a student returned from going home during a semester break, but exclude students admitted in previous years who did not reenter the United States during that fiscal year.

This increase in the number of foreign higher education students is evident in data collected by the Institute of International Education (IIE) in an annual survey.[10] As **Figure 2** presents, the enrollment of foreign students has steadily risen over the past 40 years. The IIE data, published annually in a volume known as *Open Doors*, is based upon a survey of campus officials at several thousand institutions of higher education (2,715 in the 1995-96 school year). In addition, the percentage that foreign students comprise of total enrollment has doubled in the past four decades, and now hovers at 3.1%.

Over the past 25 years, foreign students in particular have fueled the increase in doctoral recipients. The latest results (from academic year 1995) of the Survey of Earned Doctorates that the National Research Council (NRC) conducts annually indicate that, while the number of PhDs earned by U.S. citizens has remained relatively steady, the number earned by foreign students has risen dramatically. Specifically, the number of citizens receiving PhDs rose by 11% from 1970 to 1995, and the number of foreign students obtaining PhDs grew by 242% during the same period. Foreign students represented 21% of all doctoral recipients in 1995.

---

[10] Since the IIE surveys institutions of higher education, it does not include foreign students at the elementary and secondary level. However, INS nonimmigrant admissions data (which do not record the academic level of the student) imply that the number of elementary and secondary students is small in contrast to postsecondary and graduate students.

Figure 1. Annual Admissions of Foreign Students, 1985-95

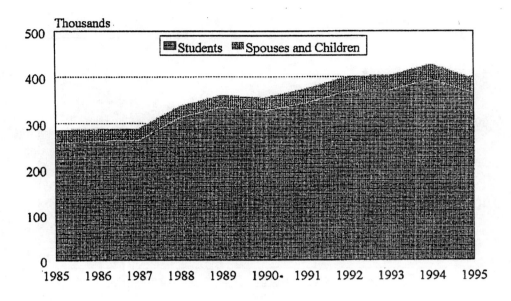

Source: INS data for F-1, F-2, M-1, and M-2 nonimmigrant visa admissions.

Figure 2. Enrollment Trends of Foreign Students in Higher Education

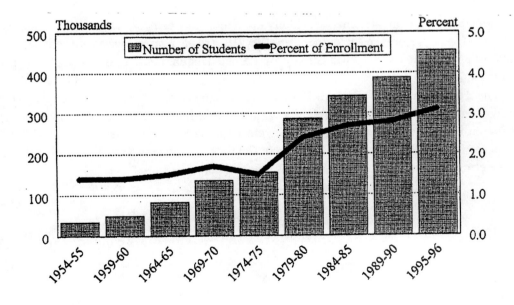

Source: Open Doors, Institute of International Education (1996)

Figure 3. Doctoral Recipient Trends by Immigration Status

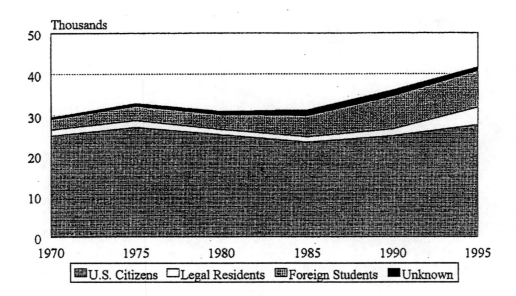

Source: Survey of Earned Doctorates, National Research Council (1996)

FIELDS OF STUDY

Generally, foreign students are likely to major in business, engineering, and the sciences. This preference is evident in the IIE *Open Doors* survey of educational institutions as well as the NRC Survey of Earned Doctorates. **Figures 4** and **5** depict these findings.

The NRC Survey of Earned Doctorates, in particular reveals the dominance of foreign students in science and engineering. Indeed, during 1995 there were more foreign PhD recipients in engineering than there were U.S. citizen recipients – 2,523 and 2,382 respectively. In 1970, however, there were 2,514 U.S. citizens who received PhDs in engineering and only 471 foreign students who did so.[11]

---

[11] For further discussion, see: Matthews, *Foreign-Born Science and Engineering Doctorate Students.*

Figure 4. Most Popular Courses of Study for Foreign Students in Higher Education

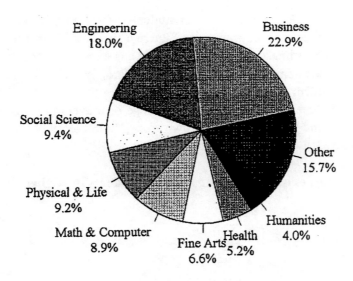

452,635 students in 1995-96 school year
Source: *Open Doors*, Institute of International Education (1996).

Figure 5. Doctoral Recipients' Fields of Study, 1995

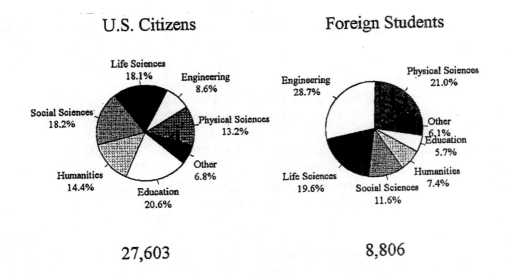

Source: Survey of Earned Doctorates, National Research Council (1996)

SOURCES OF FINANCIAL SUPPORT

According to IIE *Open Doors*, most foreign students rely primarily on their family and personal finances to fund their education, as **Figure 6** depicts.[12] The proportion who report employment as their primary source is small (2%) as expected since most foreign students are barred from off-campus employment. While foreign students are also barred from receiving federal student aid, a notable portion – 17% in the 1995-96 school year – obtained their primary source of funding from the college or university. This percentage relying on U.S. colleges and universities has grown from 9% in the 1979-80 school year (earliest year reported by IIE *Open Doors*).

Figure 6. Primary Sources of Funding for Foreign Students in Higher Education

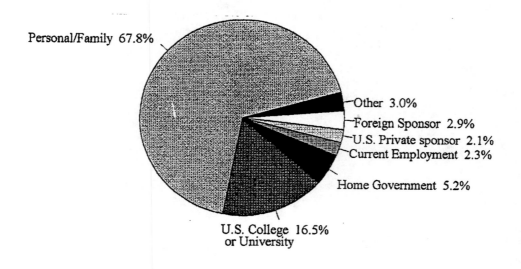

Personal/Family 67.8%

Other 3.0%
Foreign Sponsor 2.9%
U.S. Private sponsor 2.1%
Current Employment 2.3%
Home Government 5.2%

U.S. College 16.5%
or University

452,635 students in 1995-96 school year
Source: Open Doors, Institute of International Education (1996)

The importance of university financial support for foreign doctoral students is clearly illustrated in **Figure 7**, which indicates that 69% of all foreign PhD recipients in 1995 primarily relied on university support. The NRC Survey of Earned Doctorates reports that foreign students were the least likely to draw on personal or family resources. Moreover,

---

[12] Since this question asks for **"primary"** source of funding, it understates the other sources of financial support for students. Experts in educational financial aid observe that most students receive some funding from the college or university, but only a minority get most of their funding from the college or university. Also, this question overlooks the many indirect subsidies that support all students at American institutions, none of whom pay the full costs of their education. Tuition and fees cover, on average, about one-third of the costs. For further analysis, see: CRS Report 97-40, *State Roles on Postsecondary Education and the Higher Education Act (HEA): Options for HEA Reauthorization*, by Wayne C. Riddle.

while over half (55%) of U.S. citizens who earned PhDs in 1995 reported that they had educational debts, only one-third (33%) of foreign students reported educational debts.

Figure 7. Primary Sources of Support for Doctoral Recipients, 1995

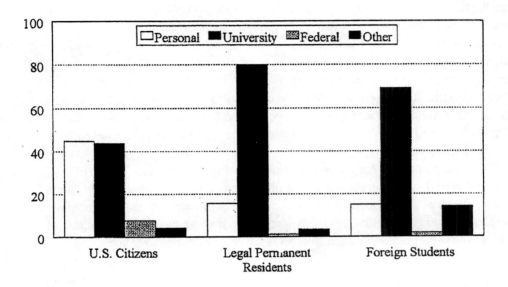

Note: "University" includes federally-funded research grants. "Personal" includes student loans. CRS presentation of data from Survey of Earned Doctorates, National Research Council (1996)

ISSUES

Financial Aid

Concern over the amount of financial aid that foreign higher education students obtain – particularly since F-1 students must demonstrate that they have the resources or support to pay for their education in order to receive a visa and are barred from federal financial aid – has grown in recent years. That foreign students earning PhDs were much more likely to have had university support than U.S. students came up during hearings that the Senate Committee on the Judiciary's Subcommittee on Immigration held in the 104th Congress. In response to former Senator Alan Simpson's questioning whether this funding pattern was in the national interest, David Auston, provost at Rice University and spokesman for the Association of American Universities replied: "We don't' deny that it is a trend that is alarming and one that deserves attention and we are giving it that attention."[13]

Other college and university officials have observed that since foreign students generally cannot work off campus and are barred from federal assistance, it often falls on the university to provide financial support. U.S. students, they maintain, have more options available to fund their education. Moreover, it is reportedly not unusual for foreign students from countries that have unstable currencies to turn to the college or university for help if their own resources unexpectedly dwindle.

Many academic researchers maintain that research assistantships should be granted exclusively on the basis of merit, regardless of alien status, and that it is in the national interest to support the highest caliber of research in the world. Others argue that this federal investment in research should be targeted to developing the skills and talents of U.S. residents and that it does not serve the national interest to subsidize temporary residents who will take skills in these new research technologies abroad to later compete with the United States.

IIRIRA contained a provision (Section 506) that requires the Comptroller General to study and report to Congress the extent that aliens *not lawfully admitted for permanent residence* are receiving postsecondary federal student financial assistance. The issues of federally-funded university research projects subsidizing the education of foreign students and whether the national interest is served by doing so remain.

New Public School Requirements

The question of foreign students being educated at the expense of U.S. taxpayers also came up in the context of elementary and secondary students. The 104th Congress passed a provision in IIRIRA (Section 625) that now requires F-1 foreign students to pay tuition if they attend public high schools in the United States.[14] The public school must assess the tuition (defined as the full unsubsidized per capita cost of educating the pupil for 1 year) and the prospective students must provide evidence that they have paid the tuition before the State Department issues the F visa. F-1 visas to attend public high school are only valid for 1 year and cannot be extended. F-1 students attending private or parochial schools are not affected, but they are not allowed to transfer to a public school. This new rule also prohibits F-1 students from attending public elementary schools and publicly funded adult education programs.[15]

Impetus for this provision came from media accounts of "parachute kids" – a phrase used to describe foreign youth "dropped" in the United States to attend elementary and secondary school while their parents remain in their homes abroad. Early accounts,

---

[13] U.S. Senate Committee on the Judiciary. *Examining Nonimmigrant Immigration Issues.* S. Hearing 104-814, Serial No. J-104-48. Washington, Sept. 28, 1995.

[14] This provision became the newly created Section 214(1) of the INA.

[15] Public schools that offer "English as a second language" (ESL) programs fear that they will be adversely affected by the implementation of the new provision since the law now bars F-1 admission for courses of study at publicly-funded adult education programs and many of these ESL programs are part of publicly-funded adult education programs.

notably a *Los Angeles Times* article published June 24, 1993, depicted the problem as children being left in the United States with inadequate supervision and cited a 1990 UCLA study estimating there were 40,000 "parachute kids" mostly from Taiwan.[16] Other anecdotal stories of foreign students admitted as F-1 students to attend private elementary and secondary schools who then transferred to public schools sparked further concern. Subsequently, many began to view this phenomenon as an immigration problem because the foreign children were attending public schools while their parents who remained abroad were not contributing to the tax base or to the cost of education.[17]

Once the provision went into effect on November 30, 1996, a new round of controversies arose because youth who come to the United States as high school exchange students are now required to pay tuition if they are entering with F-1 visas. While the J visa is generally the option used by exchange programs, many individual schools who set up their own programs have not gone through the USIA approval process. Local high schools who relied on the F-1 visa reportedly are upset by the new provision for several reasons. Foremost, many of these schools consider determining the "unsubsidized per pupil costs" a hassle and the requirement that they charge the foreign students tuition an unwarranted federal intrusion. They also are uncertain about who should be expected to pay the tuition (the youth, the sponsor, or the program), and express discomfort over reciprocity if the U.S. exchange youth are not expected to pay tuition at the "sister" school abroad.

Additionally, many U.S families who have relatives living abroad are voicing their dismay over the new provision. These families who planned to have their nieces, nephews, or other young relatives spend some time studying and living with them in the United States consider this new policy a barrier. They oppose the bar on elementary students entering on the F-1 visa to attend public schools because they assert that the elementary school years in a child's development is a good time for such an experience. Moreover, many argue that the tuition requirement for high school students places a burden on the local schools that, in turn, leads the schools to be uncooperative.

Repercussions of Visa Status Violations

While most nonimmigrants are admitted with visas that have a precise expiration date, foreign postsecondary students are admitted for "duration of status" which lasts as long as they are a full-time student or participating according to the terms of their exchange program. New provisions in IIRIRA that tighten up on aliens staying beyond the expiration of their visa, typically referred to as "visa overstays," have changed the situation of foreign students.

---

[16] INS data on F-1 visa admissions by age suggest a much smaller number.

[17] During the 104th Congress, the House rejected an amendment to H.R. 2202 that would have required the children of illegal immigrants to pay tuition if they attended public schools. The F-1 tuition requirement originated in the Senate, and the two proposals were not debated in tandem publicly. The F-1 issue was narrowly debated as an abuse of the nonimmigrant student visa. The public education for children of illegal immigrants was broadly cast in terms of access to education, control of illegal immigration, punishing children for the actions of their parents, and turning local schools into an immigration enforcement arm.

Specifically, Section 301 of IIRIRA makes aliens who are unlawfully present in the U.S. for at least 6 months but less than 1 year (after April 1, 1997) inadmissible to the U.S. for 3 years after they depart. Aliens unlawfully present for 1 year or more are inadmissible for 10 years. Section 632 of IIRIRA makes the nonimmigrant visa void as soon as the alien overstays the period of authorized stay.[18] INS is interpreting "beyond the period of authorized stay" to be whenever the nonimmigrant "completes, concludes, terminates, ceases, or otherwise interrupts the activity, employment, course of study, or program participation."[19]

In the past, INS generally had the reputation of responding sympathetically to foreign students who violated the terms of their visa by not being enrolled full-time, dropping out for a semester, transferring to another school without obtaining the proper approval, or other infractions of the law. Moreover, it has always been difficult for INS to know when foreign students had overstayed because the duration of status lacks a fixed termination date and schools, although required to report students who stop attending, were not required to systematically report data on the progress of the foreign student (see below). The new law, however, gives INS very little discretion to grant exceptions for illegal presence. Although the lack of a definitive expiration date on the visa may make it more onerous to determine when a foreign student has violated the "duration of stay," the new penalties should induce foreign students to be very conscientious about their status, especially if they hope to return to the United States or to become a legal permanent resident.

New Reporting Requirements

In 1995, INS began a review of the admission and monitoring of foreign students. Impetus for the review came in part from Federal Bureau of Investigation Director Louis Freeh who expressed concern that possible terrorists could use foreign student status as a way of entering the United States.[20] The INS has not been maintaining the addresses of foreign students, and reviews of the existing reporting system found the accuracy of the data questionable. INS Commissioner Doris Meisner emphasized plans to automate a foreign student reporting and monitoring system when she testified before the Senate Committee on the Judiciary's Subcommittee on Immigration.[21]

When Congress enacted IIRIRA, it added statutory language mandating that the Attorney General, in consultation with the Secretaries of State and Education, develop by January 1, 1998, a program to collect data on F, J, and M nonimmigrants from at least five countries. By 2003, the data collection must include all countries. This provision, Section 641 of IIRIRA, requires that INS collect the following data elements:

---

[18] For discussion of these new provisions, see: CRS Report 97-295, *Immigration: New Consequences of Illegal Presence*, by Larry M. Eig.

[19] INS will give F visa holders a grace period of 60 days and J visa holders a grace period of 30 days beyond the date their program or status ends. *Interpreter Releases*, v. 74, Jan. 6, 1997.

[20] For a discussion of Mr. Freeh's memorandum, see: *Interpreter Releases*, v. 71, Dec. 19, 1994.

[21] Senate Committee on the Judiciary, Hearings.

- identity and address of the alien;
- nonimmigrant classification of the alien, date of visa issuance, and any change or extension;
- academic status of the alien (e.g., full-time enrollment); and
- any disciplinary action taken by the school, college, or university as a result of a crime committed by the alien.

INS is to collect the information electronically "where practical." The provision requires the educational institutions to report this information to INS as a condition of continued approval in the program.

The new law also required, as of April 1, 1997, that the educational institutions collect a fee (not to exceed $100) form each of the foreign students to remit to the Attorney General to carry out the program. INS, however, does not plan to implement the fee until the full program is in place. INS promises to have the full program operating several years before the 2003 deadline because of groundwork laid prior to the passage of IIRIRA.

Many educational institutions across the country are expressing their unhappiness over these new reporting requirements. They fear the data collection system will be burdensome and unnecessarily consume staff time. Many argue they are being turned into an enforcement agent of the INS and worry that the confidentiality of their student records may be compromised.[22]

Off Campus Employment

During the late 1980s, some in the business community lobbied to end the bar on off-campus employment for foreign students. This business-led effort – sparked by a perceived labor shortage – was part of a larger drive to increase the pool of immigrant workers. Section 221(b) of the Immigration Act of 1990 established a pilot program allowing foreign students holding F-1 visas to have off-campus work authorization in the United States.

As required by the statute, the INS and Department of Labor conducted a joint evaluation of the F-1 visa pilot program for work authorization. This evaluation stated:

Creating such close linkages between foreign students and the U.S. labor market may promote employment relations that create the expectation of long-term residency on the part of foreign students, and diminish employers' incentives to upgrade job conditions for U.S. workers.

---

[22] *Interpreter Releases*, v. 74, Mar. 17, 1997.

The Administration recommended that the off-campus work authorization for foreign students not be continued.[23]

In a letter dated August 10, 1994, to the President of the Senate and the Speaker of the House, Labor Secretary Robert Reich wrote:

> The Administration welcomes foreign students and recognizes their contribution to U.S. excellence in higher education. However, the pilot program expands upon employment opportunities already available to foreign students, and its design is inconsistent with the statutory intent of the F-1 nonimmigrant visa. Further, the pilot program's mechanisms run counter to this Administration's commitment to an affirmative policy of U.S. labor force development and there is some concern, from existing research, that the program may have adverse consequences for some U.S. workers.

Initially, the pilot F-1 off-campus work program was to sunset at the end of 1994.

The Immigration and Nationality Technical Corrections Act of 1994 (P.L. 103-416) extended the program through 1996. Few students actually participated in the pilot program, reportedly because most prospective employers found the regulatory procedures cumbersome. Although the 104th Congress allowed the pilot program to lapse, there has been discussion that some wish to revive the program in some form or to establish new procedures under which foreign students can work off campus. If there continues to be pressure on colleges and universities to shift financial support away from foreign students, then a new push to ease the work restrictions may emerge.

Foreign Residency Requirements

Although the INA states that foreign students must have a residence in a foreign country that he or she has no intention of abandoning, some foreign students who qualify under the INA ultimately remain in the Unites States and change their immigration status to that of a legal permanent resident.[24] A growing number of foreign students who complete their PhDs report that they have definite plans to remain in the United States. In 1973, 31% of temporary residents who completed their PhDs reported plans to stay, but by 1993, 55% reported that they have definite plans to remain.[25]

It is reportedly common for F-1 students in fields that require practical training to change their nonimmigrant status to that of an H temporary worker, provided they qualify under the INA and have a U.S. employer who will hire them. Some of these former students who succeed on the job may later be sponsored by the employer to become a legal permanent resident. According to FY1995 INS admissions data, 14,471 of the

---

[23] U.S. Department of Labor and Immigration and Naturalization Service. *Report to Congress: An Evaluation of the Pilot Program of Off-Campus Work Authorization for Foreign Students (F-1 Nonimmigrants).* Washington, 1994.

[24] For information on the qualifications for and numerical restrictions on legal permanent residents, see: CRS Report 94-146, *Immigration: Numerical Limits on Permanent Admissions,* by Joyce C. Vialet and Molly R. Forman.

[25] Thurgood, D.H., and J.E. Clarke. *Summary Report 1993: Doctoral Recipients from United States Universities.* National Research Council, National Academy Press, 1995.

716,194 aliens who became legal permanent residents had originally come to the United States on an F-1 visa. Well over half of these F-1 nonimmigrants who adjusted status did so as a spouse of a U.S. citizen, and many others adjusted status as an employment-based immigrant with a job offer from a U.S. firm.

During the 104th Congress and earlier, some immigration observers maintained that many foreign students are violating the intent of the provision that requires they have a foreign residence that they have no intention of abandoning. Specifically, the practice of a foreign student petitioning to adjust to legal permanent resident status or petitioning to change status to nonimmigrant H-1B professional and specialty workers has raised concerns.[26] Fear that foreign students, as well as nonimmigrants on temporary work visas, are "leap frogging" the laws and procedures that protect U.S. workers from being displaced by immigrants prompt some to suggest that all foreign students return home for 2 years to establish residency if they wish to return to the United States.

While most nonimmigrants on a J visa are required to return home for 2 years prior to adjusting to permanent residence status in the United States, there is no foreign residency requirement for F or M visa holders. A proposal circulated in the Senate during the 104th Congress would have expanded the foreign residency requirement to F and M visa holders as well as certain other nonimmigrants, notably temporary workers.

This proposal met with strong and varied opposition from the educational community and business interests. Many argued it would just lead to abuses and increase incentives to manipulate the nonimmigrant visa process. INS Commissioner Doris Meisner, in testimony before the Senate Judiciary's Subcommittee on Immigration, expressed the following position:

> For example, in the case of foreign students, rather than an arbitrary 2-year home residency requirement, a better approach might be to reform the current provisions for practical training. Practical training is that period of a year after graduation in which a former foreign student actually works in the United States. It is during that period that a foreign student is most likely to establish the link with an employer that would then lead to an adjustment of status applicati0on for permanent residency. If this employment linkage is the problem, it would be better to reform that link than to impose on everyone a standard, counterproductive home residency requirement.[27]

The proposal never reached the Senate floor. The 105th Congress, however, is considering proposals that address the practical training element, notably in the context of reforming the H-1B nonimmigrant visa category for specialty and professional workers. Since the H-1B visa is the typical conduit from F-1 to legal permanent residence, reforms of the H-

---

[26] For more information on H-1B issues, see: CRS Report 96-333, *Immigration: Nonimmigrant H-1B Specialty Worker Facts and Issues*, by Ruth Ellen Wasem.
[27] Senate Committee on the Judiciary, Hearings.

1B program may have an impact on foreign students who wish to remain in the United States.[28]

---

[28] Wasem, *Immigration: Nonimmigrant H-1B Specialty Worker Facts and Issues.*

Chapter 12

IMMIGRATION: NUMERICAL LIMITS ON PERMANENT ADMISSIONS

Joyce Vialet

KEY DEFINITIONS

The basic U.S. law governing immigration and naturalization is contained in the Immigration and Nationality Act (INA) of 1952, as amended (8 U.S.C. 1101 *et seq.*). The most significant recent revision of the legal immigration provisions of the INA were made by the Immigration Act of 1990 (P.L. 101-649). The INA defines an *alien* as "any person not a citizen or a national of the United States" and sets forth the conditions under which aliens may enter this country. While both immigrants and nonimmigrants are aliens, a basic distinction is made between them. *Immigrants* are those aliens who are lawfully admitted for permanent residence. *Nonimmigrants* are aliens granted temporary admission for a specific purpose such as tourism or a business trip. Fewer immigrants than nonimmigrants are admitted, and the conditions of their admission are more stringent. However, once admitted, immigrants are subject to fewer restrictions. They may accept and change employment, and may apply for U.S. citizenship through the naturalization process, generally after 5 years. The numerical limits discussed below apply to immigrants rather than nonimmigrants.

WORLDWIDE AND PER-COUNTRY LEVELS

The INA establishes a flexible level of permanent admissions. The law provides for a permanent annual *worldwide level* of 675,000 immigrants. The worldwide level is flexible in that it may be exceeded in certain circumstances as described below. The permanent immigrant level consists of the following components: (a) family-sponsored immigrants, including *immediate relatives* of U.S. citizens and *family-sponsored preference immigrants* (480,000); (b) *employment-based preference immigrants* (140,000 plus certain unused family preference numbers); and (c) *diversity immigrants* (55,000).

Immediate relatives[1] are exempt from direct numerical limits, but family-sponsored *preference* and employment-based preference immigrants are not. The annual level of family-sponsored *preference* immigrants is determined by subtracting the number of immediate relative visas issued in the previous year from 480,000, the total family-sponsored level, and adding employment preference immigrant numbers unused during the previous year. By law, the family-sponsored preference level may not fall below 226,000. If necessary, the 480,000 level will be exceeded to maintain the 226,000 floor on family-sponsored preference visas after subtraction of the immediate relative visas. For FY1997, the family preference ceiling has been set at 226,000.

The INA establishes *per-country levels* that are applicable to family-sponsored and employment-based preference immigrants only. For an independent foreign state, the level is 7% of the total of the family-sponsored and employment-based preference limits. The 7% per-country limit also applies to Hong Kong. The per-country level is **not** a "quota" set aside for individual countries. According to the State Department, the per-country level "is not an entitlement but a barrier against monopolization." The per-country level for FY1997 was 25,620. Each country, of course, could not receive 25,620 visas within the FY1997 overall limit of 366,000 on family-preference and employment-based visas. The FY1999 per-country level is also 25,620.'

REFUGEES AND LEGALIZED ALIENS

Refugees are the only major group of aliens admitted for permanent residence whose admission is unrelated to the worldwide ceiling. They have their own numerical limits and regional allocations that are set annually by the President following consultation with the Congress. Refugees adjust to immigrant status after 1 year's residence in the United States and are counted as immigrants at the time of their adjustment rather than at the time of their admission. Similarly, aliens who legalized their status under the two temporary programs established by the Immigration Reform and Control Act (IRCA) of 1986 are counted as immigrants at the time of their adjustment to permanent resident status. Since most legalized aliens eligible to adjust to permanent status did so in 1991 or earlier, the IRCA legalization adjustments are almost complete.

---

[1] "Immediate relatives" are defined by the INA to include the spouses and unmarried minor children of U.S. citizens, and the parents of adult U.S. citizens. Children born to resident aliens during a temporary visit abroad are also classified as numerically exempt immediate relatives.

Table 1. Immigrant Categories, FY1997 Admissions, and Numerical Limits for FY1997 and FY1999

Classes	Definition	Admission/adjust. FY1997	Numerical limit/allocation FY1997	Numerical limit/allocation FY1999
Immediate relatives		**322,440**	No numerical limit	No numerical limits
Spouses	Spouses of U.S. citizens	170,263		
Parents	Parents of U.S. citizens 21 and over	74,114		
Children[a]	Children of U.S. citizens[b]	76,631		
Children born abroad to alien residents	Children born to legal alien residents during a temporary visit abroad	1,432		
Family-sponsored *preference* immigrants		**213,331**	Worldwide level 226,000	Worldwide level 226,000
1st preference	Unmarried sons and daughters of citizens	22,536	23,400 plus visas not required for 4th preference	23,400 plus visas not required for 4th preference
2nd preference	Spouses, children, & unmarried sons and daughters of permanent residents	113,681	114,200 plus visas not required for 1st preference- 77% to spouses & children under 21, 23% to unmarried sons & daughters 21 & over	114,200 plus visas not required for 1st preference- 77% to spouses & children under 21, 23% to unmarried sons & daughters 21 & over
3rd preference	Married sons & daughters of citizens	21,943[c]	23,400 plus visas not required for 1st or 2nd preference	23,400 plus visas not required for 1st or 2nd preference
4th preference	Siblings of citizens 21 & over	55,171[d]	65,000 plus visas not required for 1st, 2nd, or 3rd preference	65,000 plus visas not required for 1st, 2nd, or 3rd preference
Subtotal – Family-sponsored immigrants		**535,771**		

See footnotes at end of table.

Table 1. Immigrant Categories, FY1997 Admissions, and Numerical Limits for FY1997 and FY1999 - Continued

Classes	Definition	Admission/adjust. FY1997	Numerical limit/allocation FY1997 Worldwide level 140,000	Numerical limit/allocation FY1999 Worldwide level 140,000
Employment-based preference immigrants		90,607		
1st preference	Priority workers: persons of extraordinary ability in the arts, science, education, business, or athletics; outstanding professors & researchers; & certain multi-national executives & managers	21,810[c]	28.6% (40,040) of worldwide limit plus unused 4th & 5th preference visas	28.6% (40,040) of worldwide limit plus unused 4th & 5th preference visas
2nd preference	Members of the professions holding advanced degrees or persons of exceptional abilities in the sciences, art, or business	17,059[c]	28.6% (40,040) of worldwide limit plus unused 1st preference visas	28.6% (40,040) of worldwide limit plus unused 1st preference visas
3rd preference – Skilled	Skilled shortage workers with at least 2 years training or experience, professionals with baccalaureate degrees	33,894[c,d]	28.6% (40,040) of worldwide limit plus unused 1st and 2nd preference visas	28.6% (40,040) of worldwide limit plus unused 1st and 2nd preference visas
3rd preference – "Other"	Unskilled shortage workers	8,702[c]	10,000 (taken from the total available for 3rd preference- see above)	10,000 (taken from the total available for 3rd preference- see above)
4th preference	"Special immigrants," including ministers of religion, religious workers other than ministers, certain employees of the U.S. Government abroad, & others[e]	7,781[c]	7.1% (9,940) of worldwide limit; religious workers limited to 5,000	7.1% (9,940) of worldwide limit; religious workers limited to 5,000
5th preference	Employment creation investors who invest at least $1 million (amount may vary in rural areas or areas of high unemployment) which will create at least 10 new jobs	1,361[c]	7.1% (9,940) of worldwide limit; 3000 *minimum* reserved for investors in rural or high unemployment areas	7.1% (9,940) of worldwide limit; 3000 *minimum* reserved for investors in rural or high unemployment areas

See footnotes at end of table.

Table 1. Immigrant Categories, FY1997 Admissions, and Numerical Limits for FY1997 and FY1999 - Continued

Classes	Definition	Admission/adjust. FY1997	Numerical limit/allocation FY1997	Numerical limit/allocation FY1999
Diversity		**49,374**[c]		
Diversity Immigrants	Immigrants from foreign states with low admission levels; must have high school education or equivalent or minimum 2 years work experience in a profession requiring 2 years training or experience	49,360[c]	55,000	55,000
Diversity transition[f]	Natives of countries "adversely affected" by INA amendments of 1965	14[c]	None-program ended in FY1994	None-program ended in FY1994
Refugees & asylee adjustments				
Refugees	Persons outside of native country unable to unwilling to return because of persecution or fear of persecution, who have resided in the U.S. for 1 year	102,052[c]	No numerical restrictions[h]	No numerical restrictions[h]
Asylees	Persons physically present in the U.S. meeting refugee definition and granted asylum, after residence in U.S. for 1 year	10,106[c]	10,000	10,000
Legalization dependents[g]	Spouses & children of permanent residents legalized under IRCA programs (see below)	64	None-program ended in FY1994	None-program ended in FY1994
Other immigrant categories	Various classes of immigrants such as Amerasians, parolees adjusting status & others	7,856[i]	**Various**	**Various**

See footnotes at end of table.

Table 1. Immigrant Categories, FY1997 Admissions, and Numerical Limits for FY1997 and FY1999 - Continued

Classes	Definition	Admission/adjust. FY1997	Numerical limit/allocation FY1997	Numerical limit/allocation FY1999
IRCA legalization *Resident before 1982*	Unauthorized aliens residing continuously in the U.S. since before January 1, 1982	**2,548** 1,439	**Limited to pending cases** Limited to pending cases	**Limited to pending cases**
Special Agricultural Workers (SAWs)	Unauthorized agricultural workers who worked on perishable crops in 1986	1,109		
Total		798,378		

[a] Children are defined by INA as under 21 and unmarried.

[b] Includes children of fiancés (ées) and orphans.

[c] Numbers include spouses and children.

[d] Includes 142 adjustments under the Chinese Student Adjustment Act.

[e] Others include Panama Canal employees, retired employees of international organizations, certain aliens who served in the U.S. armed forces, and their families and certain aliens declared dependent on a Juvenile Court in the U.S.

[f] AA-1 lottery, temporary program for FY1992-1994 to serve as bridge between the former NP-5 lottery established by IRCA and the diversity immigrant category that became effective in FY1995.

[g] Provided for in the 1990 Immigration Act's family unity provisions for FY1992-1994.

[h] There is no numerical limit on refugees adjusting to immigrant status after a year in the United States. However, there is an annual ceiling on refugee admissions. The worldwide ceiling for both FY1997 and FY1999 is 78,000.

[i] Other classes include, e.g., children born after the issuance of an accompanying parent's visa, American Indians born in Canada, beneficiaries of suspension of deportation or cancellation of removal, Cuban/Haitian entrants (P.L. 90-603), individuals born under diplomatic status in the U.S., beneficiaries of the registry provision (INA, sec. 249).

Source: Table prepared by the Congressional Research Service (CRS) based on data from the INS and State Department documents.

Chapter 13

BASIC QUESTIONS ON U.S. CITIZENSHIP AND NATURALIZATION

Larry M. Eig

1. WHO IS A UNITED STATES CITIZEN AT BIRTH?

United States citizenship is conferred at birth both under the principle of *jus soli* (nationality of place of birth) and the principle of *jus sanguinis* (nationality of parents). The United States Constitution states as a fundamental rule of jus soli citizenship that "[a] persons born or naturalized in the United States and of the State wherein they reside."[1] The exceptions to universal citizenship comprehended by the requirement that a person be born "subject to the jurisdiction thereof" include: (1) children born to a foreign sovereign or accredited diplomatic official; (2) children born on a foreign public vessel, such as a warship; (3) children born to an alien enemy in hostile occupation; and (4) native Indians.[2]

Federal statutes repeat and expand the constitutional grant of citizenship at birth. Respecting *jus soli*, the Immigration and Nationality Act of 1952 (INA), as amended, grants citizenship at birth to a person born in the United States to a member of an Indian, Eskimo, Aleutian, or other aboriginal tribe.[3] The INA also confers citizenship at birth to persons born in various offshore territories who are subject to the jurisdiction of the United States.[4] Respecting *jus sanguinis*, the INA grants citizenship at birth to any person born outside the United States if (1) both parents are United States citizens and at least

---

[1] U.S. CONST. Amend. XIV, §1.
[2] 4 C. GORDON & S. MAILMAN, IMMIGRATION LAW AND PROCEDURE §92.03[3].
[3] INA, §301(b); 8 U.S.C. §1401(a).
[4] Among the territories in which children are born citizens under the INA are Puerto Rico, the United States Virgin Islands, and Guam. By virtue of separate legal authority children born in the Commonwealth of the Northern Mariana Islands are born citizens. Under the INA, children born in American Samoa are nationals of the United States but not citizens. *See* INA, §§302, 306, 307, 308, 101(a)(29), 8 U.S.C. §§1401(a) [persons born in U.S. citizens], 1101(a)(38) [defining "United States" as including Puerto Rico, Virgin Islands, and Guam].

one resided in the United States prior to the person's birth; (2) one parent is a national of the United States and the other parent is a United States citizen who resided in the United States prior to the person's birth; or (3) one parent is an alien and the other parent is a United States citizen who, prior to the person's birth, was physically present in the United States for period totaling at least five years, two or more years of which were after the parent attained age 14.[5]

2. HOW DOES ONE BECOME A NATURALIZED CITIZEN?

The vast majority of individuals who become United States citizens after birth, or naturalized citizens, so do on their own initiative through an administrative naturalization process set forth in the INA.[6] At the same time, minor children become naturalized citizens automatically under the INA on the naturalization of their parents.[7] On occasion Congress has collectively naturalized the population of a territory upon its acquisition by the United States, though in these instances individuals have at times been given the option of retaining their former nationality.[8]

The Constitution empowers Congress to establish a uniform rule of naturalization.[9] Under this authority, Congress has set forth substantive standards and procedures in the INA. The primary substantive requirements for naturalization, while waived or relaxed for aliens within certain classes, are that the applicant (1) have resided continuously in the United States for at least five years as a lawfully admitted permanent resident, (2) be of good moral character, (3) be attached to the principles of the United States Constitution, (4) be literate in English,[10] and (5) have a knowledge and understanding of the history and government of the United States.[11] Subversives and deserters expressly are precluded from becoming naturalized citizens.[12]

To initiate the naturalization process, an applicant must file an application with the Immigration and the Naturalization Service (INS). The applicant must be at least 18 years old to apply. Subsequent to filing, the INS conducts a police check and other pertinent investigations. Before becoming a citizen, the applicant must pass tests on English literacy and a basic knowledge of the history and government of the United States. The applicant also is examined in person. An attorney may be present at this examination but has no right to actively participate. Successful applicants are eligible to take the oath of allegiance, the final step in the naturalization process. An unsuccessful applicant may appeal the adverse decision to administrative authorities and the federal courts.

---

[5] INA, §301 et seq., 8 U.S.C. §§1401 et seq.
[6] INA, §§310 et seq., 8 U.S.C. §§1421 et seq.
[7] INA, §§320-321, 8 U.S.C. §§1431-1432.
[8] E.g., INA, §§306(a)(1), 307(a), 8 U.S.C. §§1406(a)(1), 1407(a).
[9] U.S. CONST. Art. 1, §8, cl. 4.
[10] INA, §312; 8 U.S.C. §1423. The literacy requirement is waived for an applicant who (1) is physically unable to comply, (2) is over 50 years old and has lived in the United States for at least 20 years as a lawfully admitted permanent resident, or (3) is over 55 years old and has lived in the United States for at least 15 years as a lawfully admitted permanent resident.
[11] INA, §§311, 312, 316, 8 U.S.C. §§1422, 1423, 1427.
[12] INA, §§313, 314 8 U.S.C. §§1424, 1425.

Administrative authorities may rely on the original record or conduct their own investigations. On judicial review, the federal courts conduct their own inquiry and come to their own findings of fact and conclusions of law.[13]

3. MUST CITIZENS TAKE LOYALTY OATHS?

No citizen must take a loyalty oath in order to retain citizenship. At the same time, an alien seeking to become a citizen through the naturalization process must take the following oath before citizenship can be granted:

> I hereby declare, on oath, that I absolutely and entirely renounce and abjure all allegiance and fidelity to any foreign prince, potentate, state, or sovereignty, of whom or which I have heretofore been a subject or citizen; that I will support and defend the Constitution and laws of the United States of America against all enemies, foreign and domestic; that I will bear true faith and allegiance to the same; that I will bear arms on behalf of the United States when required by law; that I will perform noncombatant service in the Armed Forces of the United States when required by law; that I will perform work of national importance under civilian direction when required by the law; and that I take this obligation freely, without any mental reservation or purpose of evasion; so help me God.

In addition to taking this oath, any applicant holding a hereditary title or order of nobility in a foreign state must renounce the title or order. The oath of allegiance may be modified for conscientious objectors to military service or for individuals preferring to affirm (to swearing to) the substance of the oath.[14]

4. WHAT IS THE REQUIRED PERIOD OF RESIDENCY PRIOR TO BEING ELIGIBLE FOR CITIZENSHIP?

In order to be eligible for naturalization, an alien generally must reside continuously in the United States for at least five years *as a lawfully admitted permanent resident alien*.[15] A period of continuous residence is broken by an absence of over a year unless the alien is employed abroad by the government, an international organization, a research institute, or an American company engaged in foreign trade. An absence of between six months and one year presumptively breaks continuous residence.[16]

Certain classes of aliens either are exempt from the residency requirement or are subject to shorter residency periods. Unmarried children under 18 living with a citizen parent are exempt from any residency requirement.[17] Aliens who served in the armed

---

[13] Current naturalization procedures are set forth in interim regulations published October 17, 1991. 8 C.F.R. parts 334-337 *published at* 56 Fed. Reg. 50475, 50495-50501 (Oct. 7, 1991).

[14] INA, §337, 8 U.S.C. §337. See also 8 C.F.R. §337.1 *published at* 56 Fed. Reg. 50499 (Oct. 7, 1991).

[15] INA, §316(a), 8 U.S.C. §1427(a).

[16] INA, §316(b), 8 U.S.C. §1427(b).

[17] INA, §322, 8 U.S.C. §1433.

forces for specified periods are also exempt.[18] The residency requirement for spouses of American citizens is three years instead of five years.[19] Residency requirements also are modified for other special classes.

5. IS CITIZENSHIP REVOCABLE?
IF SO, UNDER WHAT CIRCUMSTANCES?

A United States citizen may lose that citizenship through expatriation. Expatriating acts are set forth in the INA. These acts include: (1) voluntary naturalization in a foreign country after the age of 18; (2) making a formal declaration of allegiance to a foreign country after the age of 18; (3) serving in the armed forces of a foreign country that is engaged in hostilities against the United States; (4) serving in the armed forces of a foreign country as a commissioned or non-commissioned officer; (5) holding an office under the government of a foreign country if foreign nationality is acquired or if a declaration of allegiance is required; (6) formal renunciation of citizenship before a U.S. diplomatic or consular officer abroad; (7) formal written renunciation of citizenship during a state of war if the Attorney General approves the renunciation as not contrary to the national defense; (8) conviction of treason, seditious conspiracy, or advocating violent overthrow of the government.[20] The Supreme Court has held that performing an expatriating act alone is an insufficient basis for revoking citizenship. Rather, according to the Court, the Constitution requires that an expatriation act be undertaken with an intent to relinquish U.S. citizenship.[21] This restriction also has been enacted in statute.[22]

All United States citizens potentially are subject to expatriation. Separately, an individual who obtained citizenship through naturalization may have that citizenship revoked through denaturalization. Naturalized citizenship may be revoked on grounds that that citizenship was procured illegally, by concealment of material fact, or by willful misrepresentation.[23] Various acts occurring after naturalization are, by law, evidence of misrepresentation or suppression at time of naturalization. For example, if a naturalized citizen joins a subversive organization within five years of becoming a citizen and membership in that group would have precluded eligibility for naturalization under the INA, then the joining of the organization is held to be a rebuttable presumption that naturalization was obtained by concealing or misrepresenting how attached to the United States the citizen was when naturalized.[24] Similarly, if a naturalized citizen begins to permanently reside abroad within one year of naturalization, taking that residence is deemed a rebuttable presumption that the citizen concealed a lack of requisite attachment to the United States at the time of naturalization.[25]

---

[18] INA, §§326, 329, 8 U.S.C. §§1439, 1440.
[19] INA, §319(a), 8 U.S.C. §1430(a).
[20] INA, §349(a), 8 U.S.C. §1481(a).
[21] *Vance v. Terrazas*, 444 U.S. 252 (1980).
[22] INA, §349(a), 8 U.S.C. §1481(a).
[23] INA, §340, 8 U.S.C. §1451.
[24] *Id.*
[25] *Id.*

Except for acts that bear on the integrity of the naturalization process itself, however, citizenship through naturalization is as secure as citizenship at birth. Also, the United States no longer conditions retention of citizenship at birth abroad on subsequent residence in the United States by a specified age.

6. ARE THERE PROVISIONS FOR DUAL CITIZENSHIP? IF SO, UNDER WHAT CIRCUMSTANCES?

The United States does not categorically forbid its citizens from holding dual nationality nor does it expressly require dual nationals to make an election of citizenship as such at any point. At the same time, Congress has enacted citizenship rules that militate against acquiring dual nationality after birth.

Individuals who acquire United States citizenship under the Constitution by virtue of being born in the United States may lose that citizenship only by committing an act of expatriation. Under the INA, a citizen loses United States citizenship on voluntarily obtaining naturalization in a foreign country with an intent to relinquish United States citizenship.[26] The requisite intent to relinquish need not be expressed. Rather, it may be inferred from the circumstances, including the taking of an oath of allegiance as part of the foreign naturalization process.[27] While a citizen may lose citizenship through voluntary naturalization abroad, the voluntary naturalization of a child's parents abroad no longer results in the child's expatriation even if the child derivatively becomes a foreign national.

Expatriation aside, citizenship acquired at birth abroad under rules set in statue remains subject to congressional regulation. However, Congress no longer conditions retention of United States citizenship at birth abroad on subsequent residence in the United States or otherwise.

Part of the process for becoming a United States citizen is the taking of an oath "absolutely and entirely" renouncing any allegiance or fidelity to any other country. United States naturalization, in combination with the oath of absolute allegiance, may result in loss of foreign nationality under the pertinent foreign laws. Furthermore, United States naturalization may be revoked if illegally or fraudulently obtained. Any exercise of foreign citizenship subsequent to United States naturalization may be evidence of misrepresentation in taking the oath of allegiance and thus potential grounds for denaturalization.

---

[26] INA, §349(a)(1), 8 U.S.C. §1481(a)(1).
[27] *E.g.*, Richards v. Sec'y of State, 752 F.2d 1431 (9th Cir. 1985); *Terrazas v. Haig*, 653 F.2d 285 (7th Cir. 1981).

Chapter 14

U.S. BORDER PATROL OPERATIONS

William J. Krouse

ABSTRACT

In FY1995, the U.S. Border Patrol formally adopted a strategy known as "prevention through deterrence." This strategy calls for deploying Border Patrol agents directly on the border to deter illegal entry outright, rather than attempting to apprehend illegal aliens after they have entered the United States. Congress has supported expanding this strategy by providing the Border Patrol with greater funding and manpower. A key oversight issue for Congress is determining whether this strategy is effective in deterring illegal immigration.

BACKGROUND

The U.S. Border Patrol's primary mission is to secure the 8,000 miles of land and water boundaries of the United States between ports of entry. The Border Patrol's major objectives are to prevent illegal entry into the United States, interdict drug smugglers and other criminals, and compel those persons seeking admission to present themselves legally at ports of entry for inspection. The Border Patrol is an enforcement division of the Immigration and Naturalization Service (INS) — the primary agency in the Department of Justice (DOJ) charged with administering the Immigration and Nationality Act (INA). In contrast to the Border Patrol's mission, INS Inspections and the U.S. Customs Service (a division of the Department of Treasury) share jurisdiction over ports of entry. INS Inspections is responsible for screening travelers seeking admission; the Customs Service is responsible for clearing the entry of goods and merchandise into the country. Under current law, both agencies are cross-designated to enforce each other's respective areas of the law. Further, inspectors from both agencies are cross-designated to enforce federal drug laws. Consequently, INS inspectors, like their Custom's counterparts, interdict inadmissible aliens, contraband, and drugs.

PREVENTION THROUGH DETERRENCE

In the closing weeks of FY1993, the El Paso Border Patrol Chief launched Operation Hold the Line. This operation was a concerted effort to deter illegal entry by significantly increasing line watch operations by deploying 400 of El Paso's 650 Border Patrol agents on a 24-hour-per-day, 7-day-per-week basis, along the 20 miles of border in metropolitan El Paso. As Border Patrol apprehensions and petty crime rates dropped in El Paso, the operation was hailed as a critical success in the popular press. However, initially official reaction to the operation was mixed. Nonetheless, 54 additional agents were redeployed from other sectors to El Paso and the operation was continued, and apprehensions decreased by 72% in FYI 994. In time, Operation Hold the Line became the basis for the comprehensive border control strategy adopted by INS in FY1995 known as "prevention through deterrence." This strategy calls for deploying Border Patrol agents at the border to prevent and deter illegal entry, rather than apprehending undocumented immigrants after they have entered the United States.

The "prevention" strategy was a significant departure from the past. Over the years, the Border Patrol had increased its interior operations, which included activities traditionally assigned to INS Investigations, e.g., employer sanctions enforcement, alien smuggling and immigration fraud investigations, and criminal alien checks in county and local jails. As a result, line watch operations decreased. As undocumented immigrants entered the country more easily, often mingling with legal residents, it became more difficult for Border Patrol agents to differentiate between legal residents and illegal aliens (undocumented immigrants), and the number of allegations of Border Patrol agents violating the civil rights of Hispanics increased. The "prevention" strategy, however, entails focusing Border Patrol efforts at the border, particularly around major ports-of-entry, where the immigration violations are obvious. Moreover, under ideal conditions, preventing illegal entry would eliminate the need to detain and process for arrest apprehended aliens. In the meantime, this strategy — even with technological enhancements, e.g., encrypted radios, motion and seismic sensors, night vision goggles, and infrared scopes — is labor intensive. A key oversight issue for Congress is determining whether this strategy is effective in deterring illegal immigration and, if so, providing the Border Patrol with an adequate level of resources to fully implement it.

BORDER PATROL MANPOWER AND FUNDING

Between FY1993 and FY1997, Congress has substantially increased the Border Patrol's budget, from $362 million to $727 million, and the number of Border Patrol agents has increased from 3,991 to 6,848. Congress funds the Border Patrol in the annual Commerce, Justice, State (CJS) appropriations bill. Although there is no line item for the Border Patrol in the INS account, in recent years, Congress has earmarked specific budget increases for the Border Patrol in terms of both dollars and new positions. For FY1998, both the Senate and House-passed CJS appropriations bills (HR. 2267) include $125 million earmarked to hire an additional 1,000 Border Patrol agents in FY1998 —

double the Administration's request. Such an increase would bring the Border Patrol to over 7,700 agents. In addition, Senate report language directs INS to deploy two-thirds of the newly funded Border Patrol agents to sectors in Texas other than El Paso. House report language directs the agency to deploy the new agents to areas with the highest levels of illegal traffic. Such report language indicates that the regional allocation of Border Patrol assets is an issue in this year's budget process. In FY1997, 92% of Border Patrol agents were deployed on the Southwest border, 42% in the San Diego sector (which accounts for 3% of the Southwest Border). Almost half of new Border Patrol agents hired since FY1993 have been deployed to the San Diego sector.

Table 1. Border Patrol Agents on Duty by Southwest Border Sector, FY1993-FY1997

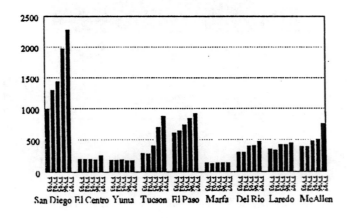

San Diego El Centro Yuma Tucson El Paso Marfa Del Rio Laredo McAllen

CRS presentation of U.S. Border Patrol data as of 9/27/97.

BORDER PATROL APPREHENSIONS

In FY1997, INS apprehended 1.5 million undocumented immigrants. Of this number, the Border Patrol apprehended 1.4 million (a 9% decrease from FY1996); 97% were apprehended on the Southwest Border. Apprehension statistics, however, are an imperfect gauge of illegal immigration for several reasons. One, apprehensions are a measure of events rather than people, and undocumented immigrants are often apprehended more than once. Two, many undocumented immigrants enter the country legally through ports of entry and subsequently violate the terms of their admission by overstaying (up to 40% of the resident illegal alien population, according to recent INS estimates). And, three, apprehension statistics do not capture the number of aliens who elude the Border Patrol. Many factors drive apprehensions. For example, INS and others attributed the FY1994 dip in apprehensions to an economic recession in California, while they attributed the increase in FY1995 to the Mexican peso devaluation. Furthermore, increased Border Patrol strength has led to more apprehensions in some areas and less in others where deterrence has been achieved. However, while apprehension statistics cannot tell the full extent of illegal immigration, they remain a useful indicator of the flow of undocumented immigrants across the Southwest border.

Table 2. INS & Border Patrol Alien Apprehensions Southwest Border in Comparison, FY1981-FY1997

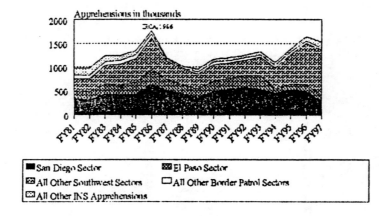

CRS presentation of INS Statistics Division data.

From the Pacific Ocean to the Gulf of Mexico, the Southwest border is 1,952 miles long. The Border Patrol divides coverage of the Southwest border into nine sectors: San Diego and El Centro in California; Yuma and Tucson in Arizona; El Paso sector covering New Mexico and the western most portion of Texas; and Marfa, Del Rio, Laredo, and McAllen sectors covering the remaining border in Texas. For many years, the San Diego and El Paso sectors accounted for the greatest number of alien apprehensions. Prior to Operation Hold the Line, increased apprehensions served as the measure of Border Patrol effectiveness. However, in sectors where Border Patrol strength sufficed to deter illegal entry, decreased apprehensions became the mark of Border Patrol effectiveness. Nevertheless, in FY1994, apprehensions overall continued to rise as the flow of undocumented immigrants shifted from El Paso and San Diego, where Border Patrol strength had been increased, to other sectors on the Southwest border less well manned. As a result, the Tucson and McAllen sectors surpassed El Paso as the sectors with the second and third highest number of apprehensions. Similarly, apprehensions also increased dramatically in the El Centro sector in FY1997 as smuggling networks rerouted aliens from the Tijuana/San Diego corridor.

Entry without inspection is a criminal offense, but it is a misdemeanor for a first-time offense. For subsequent reentries following prosecution, however, it is a felony offense that carries a federal prison sentence ranging from 5 to 20 years. Generally, prosecutions under the misdemeanor provision have not been a priority and the majority of aliens apprehended at the border accept voluntary departure. In addition, identification of unauthorized migrants attempting multiple crossings was until recently nearly impossible since Border Patrol arrest records and fingerprint cards were taken and stored manually. In FY1994, the INS began testing two automated border control systems on a pilot basis. These systems are ENFORCE, a case processing system, and IDENT, a fingerprint-based positive identification system. When fully operational, these programs will allow INS to compile valuable data on identity, rates of recidivism, and nationality of apprehended aliens. Although IDENT is deployed in every sector, to date there is no connectivity between sectors, and often no connectivity between stations within sectors. Nevertheless, 1DENT has already allowed the Border Patrol to identify repeat offenders, criminal aliens, and smugglers for prosecution. The Administration's "Border Czar," U.S. Attorney Alan Bersin, has described IDENT as the "linchpin" to federal efforts on the Southwest border.

**Table 3. Border Patrol Apprehensions on the Southwest Border
FY1993-FY1997 in Comparison, by Sector**

CRS presentation of INS Statistics Division data as of October 1, 1997.

OPERATION GATEKEEPER

Following E1 Paso's Operation Hold the Line, Congress and the public pressured the INS to replicate that operation in the San Diego area. Conditions in San Diego, however, made a "Hold the Line" approach more difficult than in El Paso. First, the San Diego-Tijuana corridor is the busiest border crossing point in the United States: correspondingly, the Border Patrol apprehends more undocumented immigrants in San Diego than in any other sector. Second, the border is not clearly demarcated by the Tijuana river as it is by the Rio Grande in El Paso. Third, sociologists studying illegal immigration have long noted that undocumented immigrants crossing in San Diego have usually traveled long distances from points far in the interior of Mexico. Thus, they are more likely to hire a guide or smuggler, are more determined to cross, and are more likely to attempt multiple crossings. For many years, the western-most portion of the San Diego sector, from the Pacific Ocean to the San Ysidro mountains (14 miles), was a no man's land, where large bands of undocumented immigrants gathered on the U.S. side of the border on a nightly basis. Directed by alien smugglers, these bands routinely overwhelmed Border Patrol agents by rushing their positions en masse. Other criminals preyed on undocumented immigrants, and armed robberies, rapes, and murders were common. Moreover, drug smugglers often drove across open areas of the border, leading Border Patrol agents and other law enforcement officers in high speed vehicular pursuits. To impede this illegal cross-border traffic, INS erected 14 miles of fence constructed of surplus military landing mat and installed permanent stadium style lights, since most crossings are attempted at night.

In FY1995, INS deployed new resources to San Diego, and the Border Patrol launched Operation Gatekeeper in this first 14 miles of the border (covered by the Imperial Beach, Chula Vista, and Brownsfield stations). Gradually, the flow of undocumented immigrants shifted into the mountainous backcountry of East San Diego County, and the cost of crossing increased dramatically. Indeed, there has been significant loss of life on the part immigrants who have perished due to exposure to the elements and other accidents, such as falling off cliffs (one Border Patrol agent has died in such a fall). In addition, undocumented immigrants have become more dependent on smugglers to guide them across the border to highway pickup points. To interdict such traffic, the Border Patrol set up highway checkpoints on major East-West corridors in East San Diego County. As a result, high-speed vehicular pursuits have increased as alien smugglers attempt to evade the Border Patrol. These pursuits have often resulted in crashes in which a number of undocumented aliens have either been severely injured or lost their lives.

Meanwhile, at the San Diego ports of entry (San Ysidro and Otay Mesa), INS inspectors encountered increased numbers of inadmissible aliens, particularly women who would rather take their chances by attempting to cross at a port of entry with either fraudulent or altered documents, or by making a false claim to U.S. citizenship, than by making the trek across East San Diego County. In addition to "mala fide" (bad faith) applicants for admission, inspectors encountered increasing numbers of lane runners and port crashers. Lane running occurs when aliens jump out of a vehicle and rush the inspections booths in an attempt to overwhelm the inspectors on duty. Port crashing occurs when an alien is able to gain enough speed while approaching an inspection booth that he can crash the gate with his vehicle. Hence, as Border Patrol strength is increased, pressure often mounts at ports of entry. Furthermore, detention needs increase as well, since to deter such attempts, mala fide applicants for admission and other criminals need to be detained for prosecution. The Administration's FY1998 request included funding for a 1,000 bed contract detention center near Otay Mesa. In FY1995, the interdiction of aliens committing immigration violations in San Diego prompted the Executive Office of Immigration Reform (EOIR), in conjunction with INS and the U.S. Attorney's Office in Southern California, to establish a port court at the Otay Mesa port of entry. EOIR, a branch of the DOJ, is separate from INS. Among other things, EOIR presides over administrative immigration hearings. At the Otay Mesa port court, Immigration Judges conduct hearings during which persons charged with immigration offenses, if found guilty, are administratively excluded from entry. If they are interdicted again following an administrative sanction, they may face prosecution for felony reentry.

OPERATION SAFEGUARD AND RIO GRANDE

Coinciding with Operation Gatekeeper, the Border Patrol launched Operation Safeguard in the Tucson sector to cope with the increased flow of undocumented immigrants there. More recently, in August 1997, INS launched Operation Rio Grande in the McAllen sector of Texas. In these operations, the Border Patrol adopted measures developed as part of Operations Hold the Line and Gatekeeper, including the installation of landing mat fence and stadium style lighting. Other resources have been committed as well, such as night vision scopes, additional sensors, etc. Apprehension statistics indicate that these operations are developing along lines similar to Operation Gatekeeper. However, every sector presents the Border Patrol with new challenges. For example, in the Tucson sector, the terrain is extremely mountainous with the ranges running in a north-south direction--ideal for smuggling. In FY1997, the focus on border control shifted to the McAllen sector in Texas, where the Rio Grande river twists and turns through farmlands and marshes as it empties into the Gulf of Mexico. Here, the Border Patrol has relied for the most part on highway checkpoints on major north-south routes to interdict undocumented immigrants. Only recently, with the launching of Operation Rio Grande in the area of downtown Brownsville-Matamoros, has the Border Patrol adopted a "prevention" strategy in this sector. It is the Border Patrol's stated objective to expand the "prevention" strategy "up river" in the Laredo, Del Rio and Marfa sectors.

Although it is still too early to declare the "prevention' strategy a success overall, it is clear that a greater Border Patrol presence has slowly ratcheted up the cost of illegal entry. It has also increased tensions in the trans-border region among those who have traditionally profited from a state of lawlessness.

VIOLENCE ON THE SOUTHWEST BORDER

By virtue of their occupations, Border Patrol agents face the threat of violence on the Southwest border. In May and June 1997, there were seven confirmed cases in which snipers fired on Border Patrol agents from the Mexican side of the border in the San Diego/Tijuana area. There have been other shootings in both Sunland Park, NM, and Nogales, AZ. These and other unconfirmed events suggest an upsurge in violence on the Southwest border. Adversaries faced by the Border Patrol on the Southwest border can be categorized into four major groups: drug smugglers, alien smugglers, unauthorized migrants, and border bandits. Clearly drug smugglers pose the greatest threat to both agents and inspectors. Because of the high monetary value of the contraband and inherent risks of their activities, drug smugglers often resort to violence. They have been encountered armed with automatic rifles, body armor, night vision devices, and encrypted radios. In one such encounter, a Border Patrol agent was shot to death by drug smugglers in 1996 near Eagle Pass, TX.

In the past, alien smugglers and their charges posed no serious threat to Border Patrol agents. However, increased border enforcement has driven up fees undocumented immigrants pay smugglers for their services, and alien smuggling has often become more lucrative than drug smuggling. Nevertheless, on the whole, unauthorized migrants by themselves pose little or no threat to the Border Patrol. Most migrants do not resist arrest, once apprehended. Many have relatives in the U.S. and may be eligible for legal immigration benefits in the future; a criminal record would preclude them from such a benefit. "Border bandits", on the other hand, pose a much greater threat to the Border Patrol. These aliens cross the border to commit crimes of opportunity, which range from panhandling and shoplifting to burglary and auto theft. Border Patrol agents and other law enforcement officers have observed that border bandits have become more aggressive in recent years. On the other hand, federal law enforcement statistics show decreases in serious crimes from FY1992 to FY1995. According to the Attorney General, serious crime has decreased by 30% in San Diego; by 5% in Nogales, AZ; by 14% in El Paso; and by 20% in Brownsville, TX.

Chapter 15

REFUGEES IN U.S. FOREIGN POLICY

Lois McHugh

ABSTRACT

Buffeted by the worldwide political changes since the end of the Cold War and a changing focus in U.S. foreign policy, U.S. refugee policy currently faces a series of major challenges. The number of people in need of assistance from the international community has grown from an estimated 8 million in 1984 to over 20 million in 1994. The funds available to help these refugees have not kept pace with the increased needs. The number of people hoping to be admitted to the United States as refugees has also risen in recent years. In addition, the number of people already in the U.S. and applying for asylum has risen dramatically. Although the U.S. continues to accept more refugees than other countries, national sentiment has turned increasingly against the admission of foreigners, whether refuges deserving of compassion and care, or illegal foreign workers taking advantage of the easy entry and availability of work in this country. U.S. budgetary problems and the Clinton Administration's stronger focus on domestic affairs have also made decisions to assist refugees in impoverished countries and to admit refugees to this country increasingly difficult. The end of the Cold War, further, has eliminated the East/West basis for U.S. refugee policy.

United States refugee policy has three major components: humanitarian assistance to refugees in other countries; admission of some refugees of special humanitarian concern to the Unites States; and asylum and protection for people who are physically inside the territory of the U.S. and meet the same "fear of persecution test" as refugees. In all three of these areas, traditional U.S. policy is being questioned and new post Cold War policies are gradually emerging.

The United States has a long tradition of humanitarian assistance to refugees. But the U.S. also helps refugees for political reasons, to promote democratic values and human rights around the world, to maintain stability in regions important to the United States, and to maintain the U.S. leadership role in refugee affairs. The United States responds to refugee emergencies as part of a multilateral effort, whether in giving assistance to refugee populations in other countries or in admitting them to the United States for resettlement. U.S. actions are affected by the actions of other countries, both those countries giving asylum and those offering assistance or resettlement opportunities. In addition, each refugee situation is unique with different needs and limitations.

U.S. refugee policy is an integral part of U.S. foreign policy and decisions on refugee and foreign policy matters affect one another both directly and indirectly. It is also influenced by domestic interests. The United States does not provide emergency assistance to all refugees in equal amounts, and it does not admit all refugees who wish or need to be resettled. There are many reasons for favoring certain refugee groups over others. Among them is a special bilateral relationship with a country experiencing refugee problems, the actions of other governments, international organizations, or domestic interest groups and budgetary concerns. None of these alone explains the differences in policy, but all play a role in that policy.

INTRODUCTION

U.S. refugee policy currently faces a series of major challenges. The refugee population in need of assistance from the international community has grown from an estimated 8 million in 1984 to over 20 million today. Funds available to help these people have risen, but not enough to meet the needs. An additional 24 million are displaced within their own countries, victims either of civil war or natural disaster exacerbated by warfare.[1] The long-term nature of many refugee situations has made the term "temporary" assistance, obsolete, leading to what many believe is an increasing need for longer-term development assistance programs for refugee populations. The number of people hoping to be admitted as refugees to the United States continues to be high. Budgetary problems among other things, have hampered the U.S. ability to finance large numbers of refugee admissions. Finally, governmental changes in the former Soviet Union and Eastern Europe, coupled with growing numbers of people applying for asylum in the United States from all over the world, have blurred the traditional distinction between those who are truly refugees in need of resettlement in the United States and those who are immigrants in search of a short cut to admission.

The unsettled state of U.S. foreign policy also affects refugee policy. From a time when Cold War policy dominated refugee decisions, and refugee admissions and assistance allocations reflected U.S.-Soviet competition and confrontation, we have moved to a period where refugee situations sometimes seem to drive foreign policy decisions. As Phyllis Oakley, Director of the newly created Bureau for Population, Refugees, and Migration within the State Department has stated: "I believe it is fair to conclude that the Department [of State] recognizes, the Congress recognizes, and the President recognizes…that refugee issues and migration have immediate relevance for the major foreign policy crises facing the world today."[2]

With the end of the Cold War, optimists hoped that the new world order would bring peaceful resolution of many refugee situations. In some cases, such as Cambodia, Afghanistan, and Ethiopia, the end of the Cold War did bring repatriation of refugees to their homes. But a rising problem in many countries, including the three cited, is that the

---

[1] Unpublished remarks of Phyllis Oakley to the State of Texas Department of Health and Human Services Refugee Conference, June 2, 1994.

[2] Unpublished remarks of Phyllis Oakley to the State of Texas Department of Health and Human Services Refugee Conference, June 2, 1994.

post-Cold War period has unleashed new or renewed conflicts with local ethnic, religious, and political origins. These changes have prompted the Administration and Congress to pay close attention to refugee programs as they redefine U.S. foreign policy goals.

Domestic concerns also shape U.S. refugee policy, both assistance programs and the admission of some refugees for permanent resettlement in the United States. A complex web of foreign and domestic issues pulls refugee policy different ways. Some express concern that U.S. refugee policy has remained "ad hoc and unfair" despite legislation adopted since 1980 and the end of the Cold War. They argue that traditional American humanitarian goals have been overridden by a foreign policy emphasis in refugee programs. Others believe that special benefits for certain categories of refugees promoted by domestic interest groups have led to serious inequities in U.S. refugee programs favoring domestic priorities over U.S. foreign policy goals. Recently, national sentiment has seemed to turn against admission programs, partly due to anxiety about the economy, partly due to reductions in Federal assistance to State and local governments to help settle refugees, and partly due to anger and concern over apparent misuse of the asylum system by illegal immigrants seeking ways to remain in this country. Discontent about the cost of immigration, regardless of the legal or illegal status of the immigrants, also rose as a major issue during the 1994 election, particularly in California with the debate and passage of Proposition 187.

Today, U.S. refugee policy is at an important crossroads. The pressure of changed circumstances and budget shortfalls has led to calls for rethinking U.S. refugee assistance and admissions policy, some hoping to create a policy that from their perspective is more fair to refugees, others hoping to bring U.S. refugee policy more closely in line with U.S. foreign or domestic interests. This paper discusses the changes in refugee policy and identifies some of the major interests shaping that policy.

THREE COMPONENTS OF U.S. REFUGEE POLICY

Refugees are defined by international convention[3] as persons who are outside their country or traditional homeland and unable to return to that country due to a well founded fear of persecution for reasons of race, religion, nationality, political opinion, or membership in a particular social group. Since early in this century, people identified as refugees have received assistance and protection from the international community. Most of the estimated 20 million refugees in the world have fled across a land border into a neighboring country. Some, however, flee in boats to more distant countries, and others seek asylum in airports or embassies. Admission of an alien to any country is strictly governed by the laws of that country, whether it is for temporary asylum or for permanent resettlement. Identification of any person as a refugee entitled to asylum and protection is also governed by the law of each country.

---

[3] Convention Relating to the Status of Refugees of 28 July 1951 and Protocol Relating to the Status of Refugees of 31 January 1967.

Traditional U.S. refugee policy has three components: (1) relief assistance to people who have fled across borders and taken asylum in countries around the world, (2) the admission as permanent U.S. residents of some of the refugees who have sought asylum in other counties, and (3) asylum and protection for those arriving directly in the United States. Each of these components is currently in flux. Each faces an uncertain future as policies are reconsidered to address changing world conditions and changing U.S. foreign policy.

Refugee Assistance

The first element of U.S. refugee policy – foreign assistance – is described in legislation as the historic bipartisan policy of the United States to respond humanely in cooperation with other governments to the urgent needs of persons subject to persecution in their homelands. According to the FY1995 State Department Congressional Presentation document for Migration and Refugee Assistance, the purpose of this assistance is to share with others in the international community by providing assistance to victims of persecution and civil strife. These programs support:

- the protection of refugees and conflict victims;
- the provision of basic needs to sustain life and health; and
- the resolution of refugee problems through repatriation, local integration, or permanent resettlement opportunities in a third country – including the United States.[4]

This assistance may be provided bilaterally, but usually is channeled through one of the international refugee agencies, primarily the U.N. High Commissioner for Refugees (UNHCR). The United States does not attempt to allocate refugee aid on an equal per capita basis, but contributes to aid programs as one of many donors in response to the particular needs of each group of refugees. According to the State Department, the level of each contribution is determined by such factors as the availability of funds, the nature and urgency of the needs, U.S. foreign policy interest in the particular situation, economic conditions in the asylum countries, and the responses of other donors. Virtually all U.S. refugee assistance is earmarked for particular countries or refugee situations. Refugee assistance provided in recent years, according to the above document, was distributed as shown in table 1.

Other countries allocate their aid based on similar criteria with the result that refugee groups around the world receive varying levels of assistance which is at least partly based on factors other than need.

---

[4] Migration and Refugee Assistance. Emergency Refugee and Migration Assistance. Fiscal Year 1995. United States Department of State. Bureau for Refugee Programs. p. 2.

Table 1. U.S. Refugee Assistance by Region FY1992-1995 (Million of Dollars)

Region	FY1992	FY1993	FY1994	FY1995 (est.)
Africa	111.15	111.21	150.50	--
East Asia	57.75	40.62	36.90	
Europe	22.13	39.46	93.00	--
Latin America	9.32	4.46	8.10	--
N. Africa/Near East	151.17*	74.00	93.15	--
South Asia	--	29.48	27.85	--
Other Activities	17.5	39.82	26.41	--
Total	369.28	339.05	435.91	421.0

* Includes South Asia.

Refugee Admissions

The second component of U.S. refugee policy is admission to the United States for some people who are victims of persecution.[5] The United States endorses the internationally accepted position that the best resolution of a refugee emergency is voluntary repatriation, the second best is resettlement in the country of asylum, and only in cases where neither of these is possible, resettlement in a third country. When third country resettlement is required, the United States has generally insisted that this resettlement is a responsibility shared by all nations and admissions to the United States is provided to those who have no other options and have special ties here.

Resettling refugees in the United States is an important part of U.S. refugee policy. Warren Zimmerman, former Director of the Bureau for Refugee Programs, Department of State, said:

> There is a great American tradition of providing refuge to the persecuted. This tradition goes back to the founding of our nation. It links generations of Americans to one another. It reinforces our democratic values. Indeed, it is part of our national identity.[6]

Prior to a change in the law in 1980, resettlement in the United States was limited to persons living in the Middle East, those fleeing Communism, or to those individuals admitted under the Attorney General's parole authority. The Refugee Act of 1980 replaced the geographical and ideological limitations on the origin of refugees for resettlement in the United States with legislation stating that "admissions under this section shall be allocated among refugees of special humanitarian concern to the United States in accordance with a determination made by the President after appropriate consultation" with Congress. This law instituted a more comprehensive admission

---

[5] For information on U.S. refugee admissions policy see CRS Issue Brief 89025, Refugee Admissions and Resettlement Policy by Joyce Vialet.

[6] U.S. Congress. House. Committee on the Judiciary. Subcommittee on International Law, Immigration, and Refugees. Refugee Admissions Program for Fiscal Year 1994. Hearing. 103rd Cong. 1st. sess. September 23, 1993. p. 16.

procedure to supplant what Congress believed was an ad hoc approach and gave Congress a significant role in deciding who would be admitted. The Refugee Act adopts a "country neutral" definition of refugee, but it does not adopt a standard that gives clear admission priority to the most needy individuals who qualify under the definition. Rather, Congress intended that determining which refugees were to be given admission priority would be "a public policy issue that will be, as it is now, debated and reviewed continuously by Congress, the President, and the American people."[7] Among the factors recognized by Congress to be germane are need, links with family located in the United States, human rights practices in the country of origin, cultural and religious ties, previous contact with the United States, prospects for settlement elsewhere, and other foreign policy interests and treaty obligations. At the time of the 1993 consultation hearing before the House & Senate Judiciary Committees, the countries "of special humanitarian concern" were: Liberia, Somalia, Sudan, Zaire, Vietnam, Laos, Burma, Cuba, Haiti, Iran, Iraq, former Soviet Union, and Bosnia-Herzegovina.[8] Nationals of these countries may be processed at U.S. embassies for refugee admission to the United States without authorization from Washington. Persons of other nationalities may be processed as refugees after authorization from Washington on a case-by-case basis.

Refugee admissions, much like refugee assistance, are not allocated equally to all countries, or even to all designated "of special humanitarian concern." Table 2 (next page) shows the variations from time to time among regions caused by different political conditions and situations.[9] The final column in Table 2, based on anticipated FY1994 admissions, shows how within each region, refugee admissions are limited to certain countries or groups within countries.

Table 2. Refugee Admissions to the United States by Region

Region	1981	1986	1993	1994
Africa	2,119	1,312	6,969	5,856 (mostly Somalia)
Asia	131,139	45,454	49,858	43,581 (mostly Vietnamese)
East Europe	6,704	8,713	2,651	7,368 (Bosnian Muslims)
Soviet Un./FSU	13,444	787	48,627	43,470 (Jews, Evangelicals)
Latin America	2,017	173	4,126	6,437 (Cubans, Haitians)
Near East/Asia	3,829	5,998	7,000	5,861 (Iranians, Iraqis)
Total	159,252	62,440	119,482	112,573

[7] The Refugee Act of 1979. Senate Report 96-256. July 23, 1979. p. 6.
[8] U.S. Department of State. Proposed Refugee Admissions for Fiscal year 1994. Report to the Congress. Department of State Publication 10116. July 1993. p. 7, 10, 12, 13, and 15.
[9] Department of State. Bureau of Refugee Programs. Summary of Refugee Admissions. June 27, 1994. Unpublished document. p. 3.

As with assistance programs, other countries also admit certain groups. Concern that refugees in urgent need of resettlement cannot find havens has led many countries to set aside some admission slots for refugees recommended by the U.N. High Commissioner for Refugees. The United States currently has 3,000 unallocated slots that can be used for this and other purposes.

Asylum

The third component of U.S. refugee policy – asylum – involves admission and protection for people who are physically inside the territory of the United States and meet the same "fear of persecution" test as refugees. Asylum has traditionally been envisaged as protection for small numbers of individuals on a case-by-case basis. In the past, asylum was used primarily for individuals defecting from communist countries. After enactment of the Refugee Act of 1980, eligibility for asylum could be obtained either by applying to the Immigration and Naturalization Service or through the courts. It was expected to be applied on a case-by-case basis to small numbers of individuals. The first problem occurred within a month of enactment with the arrival of large numbers of Cubans and Haitians in 1980 and subsequently, with the arrival of Central Americans who sought asylum along the southern border of the United States. Since then, the number of persons applying for asylum has grown to over 147,600 in FY1994, up from 16,600 in FY1995. In addition, those claiming asylum are from all over the world, rather than being limited primarily to persons from this hemisphere.

As with the assistance and admissions components of U.S. refugee policy, asylum is not granted equally to all nationalities. In addition, the Attorney General has the authority to deny asylum applications when she determines that the conditions in the refugee's country of origin have changed and the refugee would no longer face persecution if returned to this country.

Both the granting of asylum and its termination when circumstances change has been problematic for the United States. Unlike many countries of asylum, the United States has a long history of immigration for economic reasons and is still a magnet for people fleeing economic hardship. The large numbers of persons seeking to immigrate here, the long wait required for immigration from most countries, and the large number of undocumented immigrants already in the United States make it difficult to distinguish between those truly in need of asylum, and those who are merely searching for a shortcut to immigration for economic reasons.

CHANGING GOALS OF U.S. REFUGEE POLICY IN A NEW INTERNATIONAL ENVIRONMENT

Resolving Underlying Causes of Refugee Flows

American policymakers have long emphasized three basic goals of U.S. refugee assistance and admission programs: promoting democratic values and human rights around the world; maintaining stability in regions of interest to the United States; and preserving the U.S. leadership role in refugee affairs. For most of the post war period, including the period when the international refugee instruments and structures were established, Cold War politics governed how these goals were addressed and inequalities in refugee policy reflected this East/West competition. The end of the Cold War has eliminated the East/West underpinning of refugee policy and the evolution of a new foreign policy has muddied the application of these three goals. In addition, the growing U.S. focus on refugee emergencies has elevated refugee policy in U.S. foreign policy to a new level. Increasingly, the underlying cause of refugee emergencies is seen to be other global problems that must be addressed as a whole. And to many concerned with refugee affairs, the complexity and size of these emergencies require a more complex, and expensive, response. Phyllis Oakley, Director of the State Department's Bureau of Migration, Refugees and Population, recently stated:

Refugee flows are triggered by failed political systems, by human rights violations, and by conflict...In what remains of this decade, we must focus our efforts on activities that will ease crises before they boil over, maintain our leadership in the world, reflect the values and compassion of the American people, promote our economic well-being, and secure the health of the planet. —Our work is to defuse the destabilizing and destructive forces of the future which, among other things, lead to refugee flows. We look at refugees and the broader issue of migration as one piece in a global mosaic with links to issues of population growth, the environment, human rights, democracy, and sustainable development.[10]

As a result of this new emphasis on the underlying causes of refugee flows, U.S. refugee programs have taken on an increasingly preventive role. As the Director of the Department of State, Bureau for Refugee Programs stated to Congress:

While we seek to ensure protection for those who are fleeing persecution, we must be resolute in our efforts to make it possible for would-be migrants to remain at home. This Administration's determination to spur world economic growth...with help. So will our assistance on global issues such as population and the environment.[11]

It was with this overlapping of global issues in mind that the Clinton Administration created a new Bureau in the Department of State which will bring together U.S. policies on Population, Refugees and Migration under the direction of a new Under Secretary of

---

[10] Unpublished remarks of Phyllis Oakley, Acting Director, Bureau for Refugee Programs, Department of State to Public Members Association of the Foreign Service International Club, May 5, 1994.
[11] Refugee Admissions Program for FY1994. Hearing. p. 10.

State for Global Issues. Addressing these global issues, however, is expensive and not without consequence for other foreign policy initiatives. Any redirection of funds of a declining foreign aid program to these underlying causes of refugee flight may require resource trade-offs with new priorities established for the foreign aid program by the Clinton Administration and approval by Congress. Changes in the underlying causes of refugee emergencies will also require a very long-term commitment.

Emergency Aid Consuming Larger Portion of Development Resources

Recurring civil wars in poor, less developed countries also create a downward spiral that leads to increasing domestic crises followed by increased social, economic and political unrest. The destruction caused by civil war also creates a need to rehabilitate a country so refugees can repatriate. For many refugees, the return to a country devastated by war, dotted with land mines, and with its infrastructure destroyed is worse than life in the squalid and dangerous refugee camps. But the funds available to pay for rehabilitation have never been large, and now are even more difficult to obtain. According to a recent article by Jessica Mathews, who is a senior fellow at the Council on Foreign Relations, between 1990 and 1992, the cost to the United States of emergency assistance has gone up by 8 percent, while development assistance has dropped 11 percent. The share of U.N. assistance going to refugees and humanitarian emergencies grew from 25 percent in 1988 to 45 percent in 1992.[12] For several years, many Members of both the House and Senate have urged the Administration to focus more assistance on rehabilitating countries recovering form conflict, (which incidentally have produced the majority of the world's refugees). They believe that aid to such countries would also provide an incentive to refugees to return to their homelands. Multilateral refugee assistance now often includes small re-integration programs of a developmental nature (Quick Impact Projects), as well as assistance in reestablishing infrastructure such as medical, school, and other local government facilities. In the FY1995 budget, the Clinton Administration requested, as part of the Foreign Disaster Assistance Account, an appropriation of $20 million to fund a transition initiative, the beginning of a program to assist countries emerging from a civil war or long-term natural disaster.

Even if a consensus can be reached to redirect U.S. foreign policy toward easing the underlying causes of refugee emergencies, the rise of larger, more complicated humanitarian emergencies in the last few years has placed increased pressure on major donors to provide greater amounts of assistance. Between FY1992 and August 1, 1994, the U.S. government spent $728 million on former Yugoslavia. The cost of responding to the post Gulf War refugee crisis between FY1991 and FY1993 totaled $700 million.[13] These emergencies often have their roots in long standing ethnic, religious or political conflict. They require a military presence and national building assistance as well as long-term humanitarian aid. The cost and nature of these new complex emergencies and concern for the long-term effect of population movements on developments have led to

---

[12] Mathews, Jessica. Robbing development to pay for disaster relief. Washington Post. July 5, 1994. A12.

new views on refugee aid. Increasingly, the U.S. and western donors are focusing on quick repatriation of refugees, and emphasize keeping refugees in safe areas within their own countries, rather than providing resettlement in third countries or assistance, for long time periods, in refugee camps in countries of asylum. Both of these options often require a military component to provide security.

Evolving Role of the Military in Refugee Emergencies

The increased need for security had led to another area of changing refugee policy – the growing role of military forces in meeting the needs of refugees and humanitarian aid workers in conflict areas. Both U.S. and other military forces have long been used to provide immediate assistance in both natural and manmade disasters. What has changed in recent years has been, first, increasing reliance on the military to provide assistance in large disasters, and second, increased reliance on military forces to protect humanitarian assistance personnel and supplies in the midst of warfare. Although most observers give the military high marks for its flexibility in responding to rapidly changing and varied humanitarian emergencies, the role of the military in these emergencies is a matter of debate and concern. Some Members of Congress are concerned with Clinton Administration efforts to establish humanitarian assistance as a larger part of the military mission, and to rely heavily on Department of Defense funds to provide humanitarian aid. It is likely that these concerns will be raised in any future decisions to use U.S. military forces in humanitarian aid situations. In addition to Members of Congress and the Department of Defense, the humanitarian assistance agencies themselves are divided over what role, if any, the military should play in humanitarian assistance. While some see the military as a powerful new addition to the agencies anxious to relieve suffering, others fear that the introduction of military personnel, no matter how well meaning, changes the nature of a humanitarian response, creates friction with local military personnel, and endangers, rather than protects the humanitarian workers in civil conflict

Changes in Admission and Asylum Policies

The end of the Cold War is also leading to changes in U.S. refugee admission policy. The dissolution of the Soviet Union and the growth of democratic governments in Eastern Europe are expected to lead to a decline in refugee admission from that region. Similarly, those persons requiring resettlement from Southeast Asia, should all be resettled by FY1996. These two groups currently comprise about 75 percent of U.S. refugee admissions. Some hope that the United States will move to a refugee admission policy based more strictly on application of the international refugee definition. Others hope that refugee admissions will be allowed to fall significantly. During hearings on refugee admissions, Secretary of State Christopher stated:

---

[13] U.S. Agency for International Development Office of Foreign Disaster Assistance. August 17, 1994.

We agree wholeheartedly with the observation that the refugee resettlement program must evolve to meet changing needs. As the Indochinese and Former Soviet Union programs begin to wind down and move toward immigrant visa operations over the next few years, we will be able to divert resources to processing more diverse groups of refugees around the globe. To this end, we already have begun working with UNHCR to assist vulnerable refugees in need of resettlement, especially in Africa, and are working to make our refugee officers and cooperating voluntary agencies more flexible in resettlement operations. Further, an interagency review process already has been initiated within the government to explore changes in refugee policies needed to meet new developments in the world refugee situation.[14]

U.S. asylum policy is also being examined, both by the Congress and by the Administration. This is taking two forms. First, there is a growing interest in improving the procedures for granting asylum. The ability of people to travel great distances in search of asylum, and the existence of organized criminal groups who make money smuggling aliens into countries throughout the world as asylum seekers, have lead to calls for a change in U.S. asylum laws. As Senator Strom Thurmond noted in the 1993 consultation hearing:

> Our nation has a long and proud tradition of accepting refugees from other countries who are fleeing persecution. On the other hand, the American people do not expect their generosity to be abused. It appears that public support is diminishing for current refugee and immigration policies because of severe problems with the asylum process, as well as the large amount of illegal immigration.
> Americans are deeply concerned because of the view that the immigration system encourages fraud by allowing unqualified aliens to circumvent our laws and readily enter our country simply by claiming asylum.[15]

Europe and most of the industrialized world have already tightened asylum controls. Many refugee experts, including the U.N. High Commissioner for Refugees, express concern that these tightened asylum policies are making it much more difficult for true refugees to obtain asylum. They advise that the United States should not be too quick to follow other countries.

The other change in asylum policy is to make it possible for asylum seekers to return to their homelands. The United States has not traditionally offered "temporary asylum", preferring instead to grant permanent status to successful asylum seekers. But the growing numbers of asylum seekers and their diverse origins led to a policy of temporary asylum. The United Sates first offered temporary asylum in 1990 to the Salvadorans and established a permanent legislative mechanism for continuing to offer this status to other groups. Ending the temporary status has not been easy. The Bush Administration hoped to encourage Salvadorans to return to their country with the end of the civil war there. A combination of bilateral foreign policy and domestic pressure have prevented it. The Clinton Administration has announced plans to encourage the Salvadorans to return home

---

[14] U.S. Congress. Senate. Committee on the Judiciary. U.S. Refugee Programs for 1994: Annual Refugee Consultations. Hearing. 103rd Congress. 1st sess. September 23, 1993. p. 69.
[15] Annual Refugee Consultations. Senate. September 23, 1993. p. 4.

beginning in 1995. Similarly, some see the U.S. military intervention in Haiti as a policy driven by interest in enabling the Haitians to return to their homeland. While this policy is still evolving in the United States, for other countries, particularly in Europe, it is operational. Temporary asylum for Yugoslavs in many countries and programs to repatriate Albanians with development assistance, are two recent examples.

OTHER FACTORS IN U.S. REFUGEE POLICY

U.S. refugee policy is not made in a vacuum. As with most U.S. foreign policy decisions, U.S. refugee assistance and admission policy is driven by a mixture of many foreign and domestic interests. A special bilateral relationship with a particular country experiencing refugee problems may be a significant factor. Actions of other countries or the international community, as well as the influence of domestic interest groups or budgetary concerns also affect the policy decision. In many cases, several factors are involved in U.S. support for a particular refugee group. None of them alone explains the differences in policy, but all play a role in its development and implementation.

U.S. Bilateral Relations

A range of bilateral relations between the United States and either the refugee producing country or the country of asylum, and often both countries, play an important role in U.S. refugee policy. These can include security considerations, drug and terrorism policy, and economic issues. These relations can affect both assistance and admissions programs.

The history of U.S. policy concerning Soviet Jews is an example of how complicated these relations can be. Human rights conditions in the former Soviet Union have been an important aspect of bilateral relations since World War II, particularly regarding the treatment of minorities such as Jews and Armenians, and a citizen's right to emigrate. For decades, the United States pressed the Soviet Union to allow free emigration, and most Soviet Jewish émigrés who came to this country entered as refugees. Congressional legislation and U.S. policy over the last several decades stressed these concerns in trade legislation and multilateral security agreements. U.S. admissions policy also reflected this bilateral goal. Despite the fact that they have not fled across borders and face relatively less danger to their lives in comparison to refugees in other regions of the world, Jews and other minorities from the former Soviet Union have been one of the two largest groups admitted to the United States as refugees in the last few years. Currently they arrive directly from Moscow with the approval of the Russian government. More citizens of the former Soviet Union sought admission to the United States than the United States was prepared to admit. Consequently, many thousands of Soviet Jews have settled in Israel. Although this U.S. policy was welcomed by the government of Israel, this has had serious ramifications for the country, which must absorb many new citizens who may have little understanding either of their Jewish heritage or language. This increased migration has also affected the Middle East peace process, and relations within and between the countries of the Middle East, as well as further complicating U.S. relations with the Soviet successor governments.

The admission of several thousand Iraqis after the Gulf War provides another example. Following the Gulf War, the United States encouraged an internal uprising against Saddam Hussein. When that uprising failed, many fled to allied occupied areas of southern Iraq, and when the allied forces withdrew, fled to Saudi Arabia. Saudi Arabia, with no policy of permanently accepting refugees or foreigners, and with other cultural, political, and religious concerns about the Iraqis, accepted them only reluctantly and temporarily. The Gulf War allies agreed to remove these refugees from Saudi Arabia and they have been resettled in many countries. In defending the U.S. admissions decision, including the admission of former Iraqi soldiers, the Director of the Bureau of Refugee Programs stated:

> I think you have to also ask yourself what would be the consequences of our failure to treat these people as refugees and to bring them to our country. We encouraged them to rise up against Saddam Hussein. We promised them that we would take care of them if they did that. From our point of view, they are freedom fighters; they are people who tried to get rid of a tyrant and a dictator. I think we have more than just a legal or a political obligation to them. I think we have a moral obligation to them.[16]

Actions of Other Countries in Refugee Situations

The United States does not act alone in refugee matters, nor can it. Each refugee situation is different, with different variables defining both the problem and the assistance provided. Conditions of international involvement for the care and maintenance of refugees are set by the country of asylum. The United States or other donor countries may use bilateral assistance or political support in other areas to influence the policies of the asylum country. In addition, the United States is only one of several donors, and may not be the one with the strongest historic or political interest in the refugee situation. Finally, local or international private voluntary agencies may be involved in providing care for the refugees. U.S. refugee policy is affected by the conduct of the asylum country, by the actions of other donors, and by activities of the international community itself.

Country of Asylum
U.S. refugee policy responds, both for assistance and resettlement, to the actions taken by the countries giving refugees asylum, while at the same time working to convince governments to deal humanely with refugees. How these countries treat refugees, how sympathetic they are to the refugees' reasons for fleeing, how much assistance the asylum country can afford to provide, and how remote the area to which the refugees have fled all affect how the refugees will be treated and what kind of aid will be provided, including aid from the United States.

---

[16] Refugee Admissions Program for FY1994. Hearing. p. 42.

The refugee flood of Southeast Asia in the late 1970s, for example, was complicated by the absence of any regional support for the long-term stay of refugees in neighboring countries of asylum. These countries offered asylum only if resettlement for all Vietnamese occurred fairly quickly in a country outside of the region. They would tolerate no residual population of refugees and insisted that international funding pay the cost of care and resettlement. Periodically, this attitude has been reinforced in resettlement countries, voluntary agencies, and U.N. refugee agencies by governmental pushbacks of refugees across the border, or pushoffs of boats attempting to land in countries of asylum. As a result of this attitude, the international community emphasized third country resettlement over the other preferred options of repatriation and resettlement in the country of asylum. Nearly two million Southeast Asians have been resettled in other countries, primarily outside the region, an undertaking unprecedented in the history of international refugee activities.

In some countries, any support for refugees, including asylum, is seen as support for antigovernment groups. Ethiopia, Somalia, and Sudan all give asylum to refugees from neighboring countries, for example, and each is accused by that country of supporting antigovernment factions. Private voluntary agencies providing assistance to refugees are also suspected of aiding the enemy, even groups as highly respected and impartial as the International Committee of the Red Cross (ICRC).

Some countries provide generous asylum to refugees, including many in Africa. Because of the artificiality of the colonial borders, some refugees cross borders and are welcomed by members of the same ethnic group. Many refugees from Sudan, Somalia, and Ethiopia, for example, are more closely related to populations in neighboring countries than to the ruling ethnic groups of their own country. Other countries, either because of poverty, or ethnic or other differences with refugees, do not provide asylum, provide asylum reluctantly or only when the cost is borne entirely by donor nations. And some countries, with no working government, provide neither assistance nor permission to refugee aid programs.

Other Refugee Aid Donors

While countries of asylum constitute the first, and often the most serious limitation on refugee assistance, U.S. refugee policy also adjusts to the refugee assistance policies of other donors. In some cases other donor countries have a stronger historical or political commitment either to the country of asylum or to the refugees themselves. Other countries, just as the United States, target their assistance to certain refugee situations or to assist certain countries. Some European countries emphasize assistance to former colonies. In other cases, such as Japan and Australia, donors emphasize assistance to countries within their own region. Moslem countries have broadened their assistance programs from the Middle East and now contribute to refugee programs serving other Moslems, in particular those in Bosnia, and the republics of the former Soviet Union with large Muslim populations such as Azerbaijan.

Countries have domestic reasons of their own for supporting particular refugee assistance programs. Switzerland has long bee the largest financial contributor to the regular or headquarters budget of the International Committee of the Red Cross, a Swiss run international private voluntary agency. Switzerland was second only to the United States in overall contributions to the ICRC in 1992. Similarly, Japanese contributions to the UNHCR increased significantly after a Japanese national was named U.N. High Commission for Refugees. In 1992, the German contribution to the International Organization for Migration (IOM) was larger than the U.S. contribution. The Germans, with by far the largest number of asylum seekers in Europe, were contributing to support an IOM program of repatriation for rejected asylum seekers. Although the United States has traditionally provided the largest share of refugee assistance around the world, in recent years the European Union agreed to increase its contributions in humanitarian emergencies. Consequently, the contribution of the European Union to UNHCR has been nearly equal to that of the United States in several humanitarian emergencies.

U.S. admission policy also takes into account the admissions policies of other countries. Although refugee resettlement is a shared international responsibility, other countries have varying interests in the different refugee situations. For example, in calendar 1992, virtually all of the 638 refugees admitted to Japan came from Indochina, and more than half of the asylum seekers receiving government aid in Austria came from Bosnia. Australia announced in August 1994 that its refugee admission program for the fiscal year just beginning would focus on admitting refugees from Indochina, the Middle East, and former Yugoslavia. Spain has historically provided asylum to Latin American refugees.

A third influence is the role of the international community in refugee emergencies. The way international organizations, such as the United Nations, or regional organizations, such as ASEAN, address a refugee problem affects how much and what kind of assistance can be provided in a refugee situation. For example, in regard to the expulsion and terrorizing of the Muslim population in Bosnia-Herzegovina, the international community and the government of Bosnia-Herzegovina have discouraged the resettlement of Muslim refugees outside of Yugoslavia – in fact, outside of Bosnia. Their expressed concern is that such resettlement would assist the "ethnic cleansing" campaign of the Bosnian Serb authorities. Consequently, relative few of the two million displaced Bosnian Muslims have been permanently resettled outside of the former Yugoslavia.

Domestic Interest Groups

U.S. refugee policy is also affected by the domestic concerns of ethnic and other constituent groups within the country. They lobby Congress and the Administration, and their concerns are weighed in the decisions made by Members of Congress. U.S. ethnic and constituent groups affect both admissions to this country and assistance to refugees abroad. Ethnic groups, such as East Europeans, Cubans, and Southeast Asians support the admission of their countrymen, but other interest groups are also influential. Jewish and various Christian groups supported a special category of admission for Soviet Jews and Evangelical Christians. Opponents of Reagan Administration policy in Central America supported the asylum claims of Salvadorans. African Americans have supported the asylum claims of Haitians. Opponents of the Chinese enforced birth control policy have supported asylum for Chinese.

Some are concerned that U.S. admissions are still largely grounded in Cold War history and lead to the continuing admission of persons who are actually immigrants and to the exclusion of many true refugees. Expressing this concern in the annual refugee consultation hearings held in September 1993, Senator Alan Simpson remarked that "we have allowed our program to turn into an immigration program, while at the same time the U.N. High Commissioner for Refugees have difficulty finding resettlement opportunities for a few thousand refugees who she believes really do meet the test and need to find a new place to live..."[17] Others are concerned that the continued congressional response to domestic interest groups in creating special categories of refugees admissible as groups, rather than on an individual basis, has changed our refugee admissions program into a specialized immigration program. The "Lautenberg amendment", which made it easier for Jews, Evangelical Christians, and other religious groups in the former Soviet Union and Vietnam to receive refugee status, is cited as an example of this.[18] Others claim that those considered of special concern under the "Lautenberg amendment" are treated no differently than other special interest groups have been treated in the past.[19]

At times, domestic interest groups have been in conflict with each other. During the late 1980s, when rising numbers of Soviet Jews were arriving, admission numbers were taken from other areas, such as Eastern Europe and Vietnam. Congress raised the issue vociferously, with the result that overall levels of admission were raised to accommodate all groups. Sometimes a single ethnic group is divided in its position for optimal U.S. policy. One example of this is the conflict among Hmong Americans. Congressman Obey expressed his exasperation during hearings on assistance to the Hmong:

> You have an immense amount of politics going on within the Hmong community, and I have people often at each other's throats on this issue. You have one group which is insisting that virtually all 30,000 Hmong in the camps in Thailand come to the United States. You have other groups who want to support the efforts of a good number of those people to return to their country.[20]

The low approval rate by the United States for Haitians seeking asylum despite decades of human rights abuses, the overthrow of the democratically elected government of President Aristide, and subsequent oppression of his supporters has been contrasted to the nearly automatic acceptance of Cubans, based on pressure from Cuban Americans, the Cuban Adjustment Act of 1966, and other political considerations. Some view this as

---

[17] Annual Refugee Consultations. Senate. September 23, 1993. p. 3.
[18] Sections 599D and 599E of P.L. 101-167 were amended by P.L. 103-236, the Foreign Relations Authorization Act for FY1994-1995, to extend the Lautenberg amendment through September 30, 1996.
[19] Rohde, David. U.S. urged to end bias in policy toward refugees. Christian Science Monitor. August 11, 1994. p. 4.
[20] U.S. Congress. House. Committee on Appropriations. Foreign Operations Appropriations, Export Financing, and Related Programs Appropriations for 1995. Part 4. Hearings. 103rd Cong. 2d sess. April 21, 1994. p. 202.

a sign of racism in U.S. refugee policy. Support for Haitian asylum claims by the Congressional Black Caucus is seen by some as a response to this alleged racism. Others have pointed out that it is not the Haitians who are treated differently, but the Cubans who have been singled out for special treatment based on strong pressure by Cuban Americans in south Florida. This preferential policy changed abruptly in late August 1994 when the Clinton Administration announced that Cuban boat people would be intercepted and detained outside the United States in safe haven camps like the Haitian boat people. Angry at a U.S. policy slowing immigration from Cuba to the United States, the Cuban government had stopped controlling emigration by boat from coastal waters. The U.S. change in policy came in response to a state of emergency declared by the Governor of Florida and heavy pressure by Floridians to prevent another "Mariel boatlift," the rapid arrival of 125,000 Cubans by boat from Mariel harbor, Cuba, to south Florida in 1980 that resulted from similar Castro action. "Mariel boatlift," and the Cubans it brought to this country, arguably played a role in both the defeat of President Carter for reelection and Governor Clinton for reelection in Arkansas. While Cuban Americans used their own boats to bring in friends and relatives in 1980, the Cuban American community was much less supportive of accepting large numbers of Cubans in 1994. Mindful of the severe disruption of schools, social services, and employment after Mariel as well as the crime wave which occurred because many criminals were released from Cuban jails by Castro and forced onto ships leaving Mariel, Cuban Americans tempered their support for the 1994 Cuban boat people. Evidence of the political underpinning of policy on Cuban migration may be suggested by the softening of our stance on those detained in safe haven camps since the November election.[21]

In recent years, interest groups have increasingly sought relief in the courts for asylum policies that they deemed unfair. In a recent discussion of U.S. asylum policy, one observer noted that "a widespread network of civil rights and immigration attorneys has scored repeated successes with lawsuits attacking the handling of asylum cases and the special means used to deal with Haitians."[22] These successes, however, primarily have been restricted to treatment of aliens who have reached the United States. The Supreme Court has upheld the separate interdiction program for Haiti, and stated that our treaty and statutory obligations regarding asylum begin at our shores.

In a much less visible fashion, the interests of domestic groups affect U.S. refugee assistance to particular refugee groups in other countries. Congressional pressure to respond to refugee emergencies reported extensively on television, for example, have driven U.S. humanitarian assistance efforts in northern Iraq, Bosnia-Herzegovina, Somalia, and most recently Rwanda. Lack of press coverage is also seen by some as a reason why equally distressing situations in Liberia, Angola, Afghanistan, and Burma have not received high-level attention. Other examples of domestic pressure include congressional earmarks for specific refugee populations which have been added to refugee assistance appropriations bills. Earmarks for Tibetans who have settled in India, Burmese students, and Jews settling in Israel, as well as hearings on the living conditions

---

[21] Booth, William. Florida declares refugee state of emergency. Washington Post. August 19, 1994. A. 34.
[22] Booth, William. Florida declares Refugee State of Emergency. Washington Post. August 19, 1994. A. 34.

and repatriation of Highland Lao, reflect the strong interest of some constituents or Members of Congress in specific refugee groups. Legislation targeting refugee children, orphans, and refugee women who are victims of rape are other examples of congressional attempts to direct U.S. refugee policy.

U.S. refugee policy also reflects the jurisdictional interests of and conflict between various congressional committees. Conflicts have occurred between the House the Senate Judiciary committees, whose primary interest is refugee admissions, and the foreign aid authorizing committees and regional subcommittees of the House Foreign Affairs and Senate Foreign Relations Committees who are concerned primarily with U.S. foreign policy. In the last few years, the Appropriations committees have played a growing role in refugee concerns over the budgetary impact of refugee programs have broadened the debate over refugee programs to include the domestic refugee budget and efforts to control the Federal budget deficit. As refugee problems have begun to be seen as part of other issues of interest to the United States, they have attracted the attention of other congressional committees, such as the Armed Services and the Agriculture committees.

Type and Availability of Funding

A final determining element affecting U.S. refugee policy is funding.[23] The money appropriated in foreign aid spending measures for both refugee assistance and refugee admissions has grown from $428 million in FY1990 to $670 million in FY1994. During this four-year period, the number of refugees needing assistance from UNHCR grew from 15 to 20 million. In addition, the U.N. humanitarian agencies have increasingly been directed by the western donors to assist in the care and protection of several million internally displaced persons, usually the victims of civil war. The cost of helping refugees has grown even faster than the rising numbers indicate because their location and condition have become more complex and dangerous. Almost all victims today are fleeing warfare and are often located in countries at war. Many of them flee to particularly inaccessible areas and arrive in bad physical shape. Assistance must often be provided by airlift rather than by cheaper land transport and security of relief personnel and assistance must be ensured.

The Migration and Refugee assistance account, which funds refugee assistance in other countries and the initial screening and admission of refugees to this country, falls within the International Affairs Budget Function 150 and is funded as part of the annual Foreign Operations Appropriations. Refugee programs must compete with other foreign assistance programs which have powerful constituencies and with changing international needs and foreign policy goals. For example, after providing no aid to the Soviet Union, the United States has extended over $3.7 billion to Russia and the other successor states since FY1993. Aid to Eastern Europe, population programs, and for environmental initiatives also increased substantially. And, while funding for refugees in other countries may be considered by the United States as an appropriate extension of the U.S. foreign assistance program to a country, most countries do not welcome assistance to refugees if it is extended at the expense of assistance to the local, and often equally impoverished population. In the last few years rising refugee assistance programs in some countries have been accompanied by a decline in the overall level of bilateral economic assistance provided.

Due to greatly increased need for assistance, the money in the Migration and Refugee assistance account is providing a smaller part of the U.S. contribution to refugee emergencies. Depending on the individual circumstances, funding for refugee emergencies comes from the P.L. 480 account of emergency food contributions, the USAID Office of Foreign Disaster Assistance (OFDA) account, and increasingly, from Department of Defense funds. Expenditures by OFDA, established in 1961 to respond to both natural and manmade disasters, have risen substantially in recent years. More significantly, the number of manmade disasters declared by OFDA has doubled since 1992, while the number of natural disasters has declined dramatically.[24] Moreover, the budget, personnel, and equipment of the Department of Defense have increasingly been used to respond to refugee and other humanitarian emergencies. Although the Department of Defense has traditionally responded to natural and manmade disasters, DOD personnel, equipment, and funds have become a primary component of U.S. refugee assistance response in several recent refuge emergencies. This use of DOD funds and personnel has been controversial in Congress, in the Department of Defense, and within the Bush and Clinton Administrations.

The same competition has also affected the refugee admissions budget. Assistance to refugees resettling in the United States is funded by the Department of Health and Human Services budget and the budgets of the States, counties, and urban areas where they reside. Some complain that funds devoted to resettling refugees in the United States come at the expense of needy Americans, especially in this time of tight budget limits. Pressures to reduce the Federal deficit have led to a relatively static budget for assistance to refugees resettling in the United States. Refugee admissions to the United States, however, have increased, jumping 25 percent in FY1989 to over 100,000, after remaining well below that number during most of the 1980s. The numbers since FY1989 have remained well above 100,000.

The failure of funds to keep pace with increasing refugee admissions has resulted in reduced Federal contributions to the cost of resettlement of each refugee in the United States. The FY1992 Department of Health and Human Services, Office of Refugee Resettlement (HHS/ORR) appropriation of $410.6 million to address the resettlement of 132,000 refugees was less half of the FY1981 appropriation of $901.7 million to resettle 159,000 refugees. The appropriation per refugee is considerably lower than it was during the early 1980s. This has left State and local governments, and sometimes private voluntary agencies, paying a greater share of the costs of integrating refugees into American society. Since refugees have tended to settle in relatively few States and urban

---

[23] For additional information on refugee funding issues see CRS Issue Brief 89150, Migration and Refugee Assistance Budget: Problems and Prospects by Lois McHugh.

[24] USAID. Office of Foreign Disaster Assistance. Unpublished document. September 1994.

areas, this shortage has had a significant impact on States such as California, Florida, Texas, and New York, and has led to increased resistance in these States to the admission of refugees and asylum seekers.

Current budgetary problems have forced U.S. policymakers to look closely at both refugee admissions and refugee assistance in a search for ways to more efficiently use the limited funds available. In the admissions area, some Members of Congress and some in the Administration suggested that refugees or private groups pay the costs of resettlement in the United States. Both the Bush and Clinton Administration set aside a few thousand refugee slots which could be used only if the cost was borne by voluntary agencies or other groups, and not by the U.S. Government. These programs have so far been unsuccessful because the cost of resettling refugees, especially providing health care coverage, has been too high without Federal support.

Chapter 16

THE FOREIGN-BORN POPULATION: A PROFILE

Julio C. Teran

ABSTRACT

The foreign born population residing in the United States in 1998 totaled 26.3 million, 9.8% of the total U.S. population. In analyzing the data on these foreign-born, several findings are significant:

- Since the early 1970s, the foreign-born population grew considerably as a percentage of the U.S. population, reflecting the accelerated pace of migration during this period. Nearly two-thirds of the foreign-born population arrived after 1980.
- Of the foreign-born living in the United States, the majority of those who arrived before the 1960s were of European origin, while among those who began arriving in the late 1970s and onward, the majority were from Asia and Latin America.
- The foreign-born population is older on average than the native-born, since the larger percentage of foreign-born persons migrated in their twenties and early thirties. Of the total foreign-born, 43.6% arrived between the ages of 18 and 32, while 31.5% arrived when they were less than 18 years of age.
- While the foreign-born are just as likely as natives to be college-educated, they are less likely to have completed high school. The following groups of persons were found to be the better educated foreign-born: more recent arrivals (after 1991); those who arrived at a younger age (under 18); and those who have become naturalized citizens.
- The labor market characteristics of the foreign-born suggest that persons who have lived in the country for longer periods, as well as those who have become naturalized citizens have higher earnings than the more recent arrivals, and are more similar to natives in their occupational distribution.
- While the percentage of persons living below the poverty line is higher among the foreign-born than among natives (19.9% vs. 12.4%), those who have lived in the country for longer periods and/or have become naturalized citizens are also less likely to live in poverty than more recent arrivals. In the case of naturalized citizens, their poverty rate is slightly lower than that of natives.

INTRODUCTION

Over the last two decades, Congress has become increasingly concerned with issues associated with immigration, as reflected in the enactment of several major immigration law initiatives. In part, the greater interest surrounding this issue has been driven by the growing number of foreign-born persons in the U.S. population. According to Census Bureau data, 26.3 million foreign-born persons lived in the U.S. in 1998, totaling 9.8% of the population. This was up from 7.9% in 1990 and 6.2% in 1980.

As the foreign-born population becomes an increasing part of the U.S. population, the issue of immigration will undoubtedly remain a central issue for policy makers. In the past, much of the debate has been shaped by the current perceptions of the profile of the foreign-born population presently living in the United States. Drawing largely upon the Census Bureau's March 1998 Current Population Survey (CPS), this report profiles the current foreign-born population in order to provide context for more informed discussion on this issue.

Later, the report explores the educational attainment and the labor market characteristics of the foreign-born, focusing on differences based on when they arrived, their age at arrival, and whether they have become naturalized citizens or not. Lastly, it looks at the percentage of foreign-born persons living in poverty and their income distribution, also discerning differences by period of arrival and citizenship status. Where possible, the report discusses reasons that might explain the patterns observed in the data.

Data Sources and Limitations

The data presented here are taken from analysis conducted on the Census Bureau's march 1998 CPS. Each month the Census Bureau conducts the CPS, considered the primary source for national employment and unemployment data. Currently, 47,000 households are interviewed monthly, scientifically selected to provide a representative sample of the nation as a whole. Although the purpose of the CPS is to collect information on employment it also serves as an important source of information on the demographic status of the population (such as age, sex, race, educational attainment, and family income). In addition, the CPS consists of a disproportionately large sample of Hispanics, and is therefore considered the best source of information on the foreign-born population.

It should be noted that the Census Bureau data, like other self-reported survey data pertaining to naturalization of the foreign-born, does not offer precise measures of naturalization rates, nor of the actual number of persons who have become naturalized citizens. On the one hand, the "social desirability" of saying one is a citizen, as well as the confusion that can result from foreign-born people having already completed a variety of applications and verifications, may lead some persons to incorrectly report that they are citizens.[1] On the other hand, the CPS data understate naturalization rates because temporary residents, undocumented aliens, and other persons not eligible for naturalization are included.

The data in the 1998 CPS contain information on foreign-born persons residing in the United States, and not on the actual population of migrants that arrived over time (because, some who came have left or died.) The data available on the period of arrival of the foreign-born are used here for analyzing differences in characteristics based on the period of time when the foreign-born arrived. As such, the estimates derived from the period of arrival should not be interpreted as an approximation of the changing characteristics of persons migrating into the United States.

Key Definitions

CPS defines citizens by birth as those born in the United States, Puerto Rico, or other outlying areas of the United States, as well as persons who were born in a foreign country but had at least one parent who was a U.S. citizen. All others are defined as foreign-born. These include legally admitted immigrants, refugees, temporary residents such as students and temporary workers, and undocumented immigrants. The terms citizens by birth and native-born will be used here synonymously.

Under the Immigration and Naturalization Act (INA), naturalized citizens are persons admitted as legal residents who have lived here for a minimum of 5 years (3 years for spouses of U.S. citizens and veterans), show that they have good moral character, demonstrate the ability to read, write, and speak English, and pass an examination on U.S. history and government. Permanent resident aliens who are at least 50 years old and have lived in the United States at least 20 years, or who are at least 55 years old and have lived in the Untied States at least 15 years, may be waived from the language requirement. Special consideration is also given on the civics requirement to persons who are over 65 and have lived in the United States for at least 20 years.

Basic Profile

The 1998 CPS finds that there are 26.3 million foreign-born persons living in the United States, of which 37% or 9.7 million have become naturalized citizens. This was up from 24.6 million persons in 1996, while the percentage of naturalized persons has increased from 32.2%.[2]

Naturalization of the foreign-born has increased notably in recent years. Based on self-reported data contained in the 1996 and 1998 CPS, the number of foreign-born persons naturalized increased 23% over this period, in comparison to only a 7% increase

---

[1] The number of foreign-born persons who misreport their citizenship status appears to have increased in recent years. For example, the 1998 CPS finds a considerable number of cases of persons who arrived too recently to have been able to complete the naturalization process.

[2] The 1996 figures are taken from a Census Bureau report profiling the foreign-born population in 1996.

in the number of foreign-born persons as a whole, and a 1.8% increase in the U.S. population as a whole.

Figure 1. U.S. Population in 1998

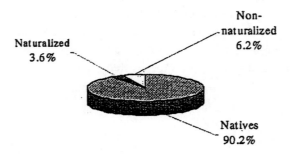

Source: CRS analysis of CPS

The rate of naturalization increases proportionally with length of residence. Of persons arriving since 1990, 9.2% have naturalized. This rate jumps to 32.4% for those who have arrived during the 1980s, and 55.2% among those who arrived during the 1970s.

While overall naturalization rates have increased, significant differences exist in naturalization rates based on the region of origin of the foreign-born. For example, the percentage of Asian-born persons who have naturalized is significantly higher than the percentage of those who arrived from Latin America. Among Latin American born migrants, 26.9% have naturalized, versus 44.6% of Asian-born persons. Among persons originating in Mexico, the largest country of origin, the percentage of naturalized persons is only 18.2%.

GENERAL TRENDS

Period of Entry

In terms of when the current foreign-born entered the country, the data show that their rate of arrival was not uniformly distributed over time. Data in the 1998 CPS, pertaining to the year of arrival of the foreign-born, show that an increasing percentage of persons began arriving after 1980. Of the foreign-born presently living in the United States, 32.8% entered since 1990, while 64.1% entered after 1980.

While 1980 and 1981 were peak years of arrivals of the current foreign-born population, the largest percentage of persons began arriving in the late 1980s. The total number of persons who arrived in the period 1988-1989 surpassed that of the 1980-1981 period and increased steadily thereafter.[3]

Although the data here refer only to the foreign-born residing in the United States in 1998, this finding is consistent with Immigration and Naturalization Service (INS) data on immigration admissions in the late 1980s. Figure 2 shows the total number of immigrants admitted between 1961 and 1995, in the categories of immediate relatives, preference immigration, refugees, and others. Immigrants legalized under the 1986 Immigration Reform and Control Act (IRCA) and under provisions of the 1990 Act are excluded since there are no reliable data available on when they actually entered the United States.[4]

The data show that admissions grew considerably throughout the 1980s and into the early 1990s. The total number of non-IRCA admissions rose from about 2.6 million in the period 1976-1980 to 3.8 million in 1991-1995. This would suggest that the period of arrival reported in the CPS closely parallels the actual data on admissions over that same period, showing that the pace of migration accelerated considerably beginning in the late 1980s.

Figure 2. Immigrant Admissions (excluding IRCA legalizations)

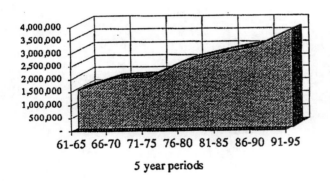

Source: CRS analysis of INS data.

The growth in migration after 1980 is partly attributable to the fact that the total number of admission under the basic system, consisting of preference immigrants and immediate relatives of U.S. citizens, was augmented considerably by legalized aliens and refugees. A 1997 CRS report notes that these latter two categories together accounted for

---

[3] Estimates correspond to the period of arrival data in the 1998 CPS.
[4] The INS admissions data presented here omit those who became residents beginning in 1989 under the Immigration Reform and Control Act and under certain provisions of the 1990 Act. Many of those eligible had to have arrived before 1982. According to INS, such legalizations represented about 36% of all admissions between 1989 and 1995. The cases are omitted from the analysis since the purpose here is to highlight the growth in migration at around this time, as compared with the year of arrival data in the 1998 CPS, and because there are no reliable data on when they entered the country. It is believed that the majority of them entered between 1977 and 1982.

35% of total immigration during the period 1981-1995.[5] The number of refugees admitted increased from 718,000 in the period 1966-1980 to 1.6 million during the period 1981-1995, after the enactment of the refugee act of 1980.

In addition, the Immigration Act of 1990 increased the ceiling on employment-based preference immigration, with the provision that unused employment visas would be made available the following year for family preference immigration.

Region of Origin

The CPS finds that of the total foreign-born population, the largest percentage, 51% arrived from Latin America, which includes Mexico and Central America, South America, and the Caribbean region. Mexico accounted for the largest share with 27% of the foreign-born, followed by the Caribbean region with 10.7%, and Central America with 6.8%. The second largest group of foreign-born persons originated in Asia, which represented 23.6% of the foreign-born, followed by Western Europe with 13.8%.

Figure 3. Foreign-born Population in the United States, 1998

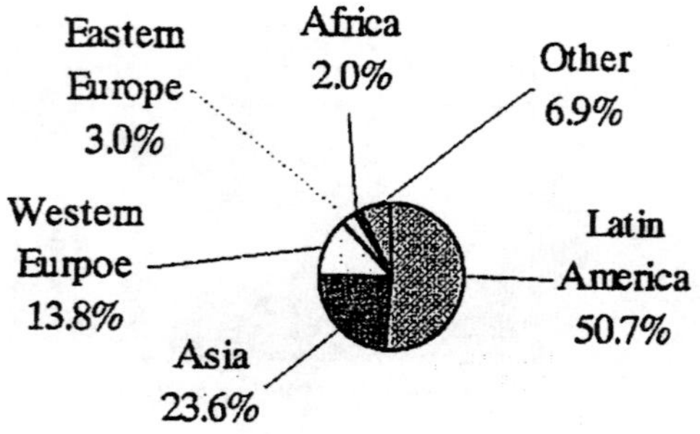

Source: CRS analysis of CPS

Region of Origin and Period of Entry

The relative number of persons arriving from different regions of the world has fluctuated over time. Often it has been determined by particular social and political events, occurring both abroad and domestically. For example, political events in Central America resulted in large inflows of refugees and asylum-seeking migrants in the early 1980s. Likewise, following the enactment of the Refugee Act of 1980, large numbers of refugees were admitted primarily form Southeast Asia and the Soviet Union as a result of the aftermath of the Vietnam War and the Cold War.

---

[5] The data on immigrant categories were taken from CRS Report 97-230, *Immigration: Reasons for Growth, 1981-1995*, by Joyce C. Vialet. February 12, 1997.

According to the Immigration and Naturalization Service (INS), the relative proportion of immigrants admitted from Latin America grew rapidly in the 1980s. Between 1981 and 1985, 35.3% of all immigrants admitted came from Latin America, while in the period 1986-1990, 54.7% originated in Latin America and 49.8% in 1991-1995. The percentage of admissions from Asia reached as high as 45.3% between 1981 and 1985, and later decreased to 32.2% during the period 1986-1990 and 30.1% during 1991-1995.[6]

Based on the 1998 CPS data on the period of arrival of the foreign-born, the percentage of persons arriving from Latin America was highest during the period 1986-1991. Of persons that arrived during this period, 57.4% came from Latin America, while the percentage that arrived from the largest sending country in the region, Mexico, reached 34.4%. In comparison, of those who arrived after 1991, the percentages that did so from Latin America as a whole and from Mexico were 50.4% and 27.9% respectively. Likewise, the percentage of foreign-born persons who arrived from Central America declined from 9.5% in 1986-1991 to 6.2% after 1991, while the Caribbean region increased from 7.5% to 10% over this period.[7]

Similarly, the percentage of current foreign-born persons who arrived from Asia reached its highest point in relative terms in the early 1980s. Among the foreign-born that arrived during the period 1980-1985, 31.3% originated in Asia. This percentage declined to 24.3% among those that arrived between 1986 and 1991 and later increased to 26.6% among those arriving after 1991.

Figure 4. Period of Arrival of Foreign-born Population Living in the United States, 1998

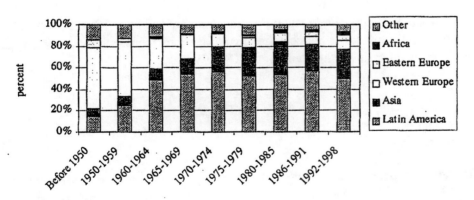

Source: CRS analysis of CPS

---

[6] Unlike the overall admissions data, the INS data presented here on the region of origin and period of admission does include legalizations under the Immigration Reform and Control Act of 1986. As such, they will not reflect the exact period of arrival of immigrants arriving from different regions.

[7] When looking at the CPS data on the period of arrival, the periods of time are divided so as to coincide with key policy changes. For example, the period 1980-1985 begins during the enactment of the 1980 Refugee Act, while the periods 1986-1991 and 1992-1998 correspond to the 1986 Immigration Reform and Control Act and the 1990 Immigration Act respectively.

Table 1. Period of Arrival of Foreign-born Population Living in the U.S., 1998 (% of all arrivals per period)

Region of Origin	Before 1950	1950-1959	1960-1964	1965-1969	1970-1974	1975-1979	1980-1985	1986-1991	1992-1998	Total
Latin America	14.7	25.4	48.8	54.3	55.7	53.1	53.4	57.4	50.4	50.8
Asia	7.1	7.7	10.2	13.6	23.8	25.3	31.3	24.3	26.6	23.6
Western Europe	57	51	28.1	22.3	12.2	9.4	7.8	7.5	8.2	13.8
Eastern Europe	7.3	3.1	n/a	n/a	n/a	1.7	.8	3.9	5.6	3.0
Africa	n/a	n/a	1.4	1.2	1.5	1.3	2.5	2.2	2.8	2.0
Other	13.6	12.9	11.2	8.2	6.8	9.3	4.4	4.6	6.5	6.9
% Total	**3.6**	**4.7**	**4.1**	**5.8**	**7.5**	**10.1**	**17.8**	**21.8**	**24.7**	**100**

Note: The periods of time are divided so as to coincide with key policy changes. For example, the period 1980-1985 begins during the enactment of the 1980 Refugee Act, while the periods 1986-1991 and 1992-1998 correspond to the 1986 Immigration Reform and Control Act and the 1990 Immigration Act respectively.

Source: Table prepared by the Congressional Research Service (CRS) based on analysis of data from Current Population Survey, March 1998.

INS data show that migration from Europe decreased notably in comparison to other regions from the levels reached in the 1950 and 1960s. Of those that arrived during the period 1955-1964, 50.2% came from Europe, while of those arriving during the period 1991-1995, only 14% originated in Europe. Not surprisingly, the CPS data on the year of arrival of the foreign-born show that among those that arrived between 1950 and 1959, 54.2% came from Europe, while among persons that arrived after 1991, only 13.8% were from Europe. Of this latter percentage, many were persons migrating from Eastern European countries following the end of the Cold War.

AGE PATTERNS

Age Distribution

Foreign-born persons are older on average than natives, with a median age of 39.6 years compared to 34.6 years for natives. Not surprisingly, foreign-born persons who have become naturalized are older on average than both natives and the non-naturalized foreign-born. Naturalized citizens have a median age of 47.7, as compared with 34.7% for the non-naturalized.

The data in **Figure 5** show that the foreign-born population has a lower percentage of persons under 18 and a higher percentage between the ages of 25 and 44. This is expected since most persons arrived after the age of 18. The reason the non-naturalized foreign-born are the same age on average as the natives is that despite the former having a lower proportion of persons under the age of 18, they also have a lower percentage of persons over the age of 65. This may reflect the lower numbers of older-aged people who have migrated into the United States in recent years or it may be attributable to a certain percentage of older-aged people returning to their country of origin after they retire. Another possibility is that some groups of immigrants may have a shorter life expectancy than the rest of the population.

Figure 5. Age Distribution of Native and Foreign-born Persons in the United States, 1998

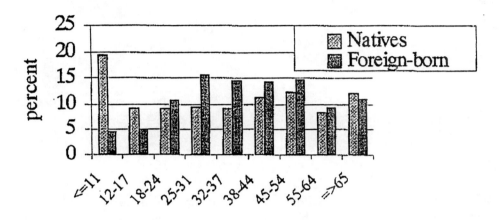

Source: CRS analysis of CPS

Age at Arrival

In terms of the ages at which the foreign-born arrived, the largest group of persons, 43.6%, entered between the ages of 18 and 31. The second largest age range consists of those under 18 years of age (31.5%), followed by those entering between the ages of 32 and 44 (16.6%) and those 45 years of age and over (8.2%).[8]

---

[8] The age at arrival figures are estimated from the CPS data on the period of arrival and age of the person. Since the CPS does not provide the exact year of arrival of the foreign-born, but rather a period of several years within which the person reportedly arrived, the figures are estimated by taking the end-point of each time interval of when persons arrived. As such, the estimates are subject to a certain degree of error in the case of persons who arrived near the cut-off point of two different age groupings. The midpoint of the intervals was not used in order to avoid the possibility of obtaining negative values for the age of arrival. However, there is no significant difference in the age distribution by using the endpoint or the midpoint. The age at arrival data divide ages based on the same categories used in the age distribution analysis, with the exception that in the former, groups are condensed into fewer groups in order to provide a large enough interval for reliable estimates.

**Figure 6. Educational Attainment of
the Native-born Population, 1998**

**Figure 7. Educational Attainment of
the Foreign-born Population, 1998**

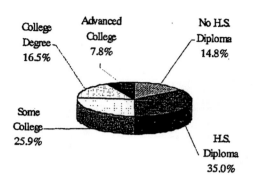

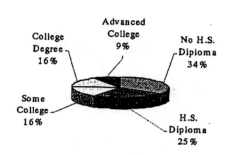

Source: CRS Analysis of CPS

Source: CRS analysis of CPS

EDUCATIONAL ATTAINMENT

While the foreign-born as a whole are just as likely, and in some cases more likely, than natives to be found at the higher end of the educational ladder, they are also more likely to be at the bottom. The percentage of foreign-born persons with a college education is similar to that of natives. However, foreign-born persons are considerably less likely to have graduated form high school than the native-born. While only 14.8% of native-born persons over the age of 25 do not have a high school diploma, 34.5% of foreign-born persons do not.[9]

Several factors appear to be linked to educational attainment. First, the data show the foreign-born persons who arrived in the country at an earlier age (under 18) are more likely to have graduated from high school than other foreign-born persons. While 34.5% of foreign-born persons do not have a high school diploma, among those who arrived before the age of 18, only 26% do not. Foreign-born persons who arrived before the age of 18 are also just as likely as natives to have a college education, although still less likely to have graduated from high school.

Secondly, the foreign-born that entered the country most recently appear to be more college-educated than those who arrived before them. Of the foreign-born who entered after 1991, 32.1% have a college degree or more. This exceeds the rate found among natives and among all naturalized citizens (24.3% and 30.7% respectively). Recent arrivals are also more likely to have graduated from high school than foreign-born persons who entered before them. Among persons who entered the country after 1991, 31.1% do not have a high school degree, in comparison to 34% of all foreign-born persons and 39.1% of those that entered between 1986 and 1991.

---

[9] Sample consists of all persons over the age of 25.

Figure 8. Educational Attainment of Foreign-born Persons by Age at Arrival, 1998

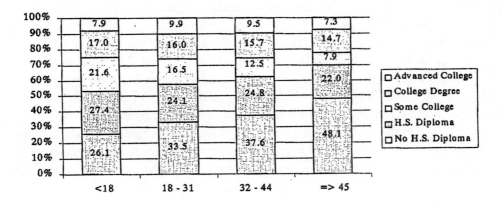

Source: CRS analysis of CPS

Figure 9. Educational Attainment of Foreign-born Population by Period of Arrival, 1998

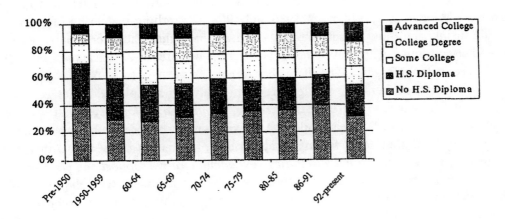

Source: CRS analysis of CPS

Thirdly, citizenship status is strongly correlated with education. Among naturalized citizens, 30.7% have a college degree or more, in comparison to only 24.3% of natives. Also, naturalized foreign-born persons are more likely to have advanced college degrees than native-born persons. While only 23% of naturalized citizens have not completed high school, this percentage remains considerably higher than the percentage found among native-born.

Non-naturalized persons over the age of 25 have the overall lowest educational attainment of all three groups (native, naturalized citizens, non-naturalized). While 43% have not graduated from high school, only 21% have a college degree or more.

Despite the higher educational attainment of some foreign-born groups, it is unclear why such a high percentage are also found at the low end. Although naturalized citizens, recent arrivals, and those entering the country at a young age have the highest proportion of college-educated persons, the percentage of persons in these groups not having completed high school remains above the rate found among the rest of the population.

LABOR FORCE CHARACTERISTICS

Occupation

There are important differences between the foreign-born and the native-born in terms of the occupational distribution of workers. The data in the 1998 CPS indicate that foreign-born workers who have resided in the country for longer periods more closely resemble native-born workers in their occupational distribution. Moreover, foreign-born workers who have been naturalized also tend to more closely resemble the native population.

Table 2 shows the occupational employment distributions in 1998 of native-born workers, foreign-born workers who entered the United Stated before 1986, and foreign-born workers who entered between 1986 and 1998. Controlling for period of entry may provide insight into how closely the jobs held by the earlier and later groups resemble each other and those of the native born. The sample consists of all those over the age of 18 who are participating in the civilian labor force.

Foreign-born workers as a whole were more likely to be employed in the less-skilled occupational categories of *services, farming, fishing, and forestry*, and *operators, fabricators, and laborers*. Meanwhile, the native-born were more likely to be employed in the higher-skilled occupational categories of *executive, administrative, and managerial, sales, professional specialties, and administrative support and clerical*.

The foreign-born who arrived before 1986 were more likely than the later cohort (after 1986) to be employed in the occupational categories of *executive, managerial, and administrative*, and *administrative support and clerical occupations* and less likely to be employed in the categories of *laborer, operator, and fabricator*. In this sense, the occupational distribution of the earlier cohort of foreign-born workers more closely resembles that of native-born workers. Nevertheless, there were still statistically significant differences found between the native-born and the earlier cohort of foreign-born (pre-1986) across most occupational categories.

Table 2. Occupational Employment in 1998 of Adult Native-Born and Foreign-Born Workers by Period of Entry (% distribution)

Occupational category	Native-born	Foreign-born	
		Pre-1986	1986-1998
Executive/adm./managerial	14.3	11.6	6.7
Professional specialties	15	13.1	13.3
Technicians	3.4	2.9	2.9
Precision production/craft/repair	10.9	12.4	11.1
Administrative support/clerical	15.1	10.9	6.7
Sales	12.3	10.3	9.4
Operator/fabricator/laborer	14.1	16.7	22.3
Service (non-household)	12.5	16.6	19
Farming/forestry/fishing	2.1	4.1	6.5
Private household	n/a	1.5	2.1
Percent totals	**100%**	**100%**	**100%**

Note: Adults are defined as all workers, part-time or full-time, and full-year or part-year in the civilian work force who are at least 18 years old. Occupation corresponds to the longest held occupation during the last year.

Source: Table prepared by the Congressional Record Service (CRS) based on analysis of March 1998 Current Population Survey.

The data in **Table 3** look at the occupational distribution of natives and foreign-born workers based on their citizenship status. In addition we analyzed workers in two age groups: those under 36 years of age and those 36 years and over. We control for age to avoid biases resulting from the fact that naturalized citizens tend to be older on average than other groups and that age is an important determinant of labor marker characteristics.[10]

Naturalized foreign-born citizens resemble native workers much more closely than non-citizen foreign-born persons do. In most occupations there is no significant difference between the naturalized foreign-born and the natives in terms of their occupational distribution. A similar pattern occurs when controlling for age group. The only statistically significant difference found between naturalized persons and natives was that among those over the age of 36, native-born persons were more likely to be employed in *executive, managerial, and administrative* occupations than the naturalized citizens.

Non-naturalized foreign-born persons did show significant differences when compared to both naturalized foreign-born persons and natives, regardless of age group.

---

[10] The data in **Table 2** and **Table 3** do not differentiate between those under 36 and those 36 and over. Such analysis was conducted on the CPS, but only the results described in the text are presented here.

While 9.5% of all foreign-born workers are employed in high-skilled *executive, managerial, and administrative* occupations, among naturalized citizens the percentage increases to 13.1%, and among non-naturalized persons is only 7.2%.

Table 3. Occupational Employment in 1998 of Adult Native-Born and Foreign-Born Workers by Citizenship Status (% distribution)

		Foreign-born		
Occupational category	**Native-born**	**Naturalized**	**Non-naturalized**	**Total foreign-born**
Executive/adm./managerial	14.3	13.1	7.2	9.5
Professional specialties	15	15.8	11.5	13.2
Technicians	3.4	4.4	2.0	2.9
Precision production/craft/repair	10.9	10.8	12.4	11.8
Administrative support/clerical	15.1	12.6	6.9	9.1
Sales	12.3	11.4	9.0	9.9
Operator/fabricator/laborer	14.1	14.1	22.3	19.1
Service (non-household)	15.2	15.3	19.1	17.6
Farming/forestry/fishing	2.1	1.7	7.3	5.1
Private household	N/A	N/A	2.4	1.8
Percent totals	**100%**	**100%**	**100%**	**100%**

Note: Adults are defined as all workers, part-time or full-time, and full-year or part-year in the civilian work force who are at least 18 years old. Occupation corresponds to the longest held occupation during the last year.

Source: Table prepared by the Congressional Research Service (CRS) based on analysis of March 1998 Current Population Survey.

The naturalized foreign-born resemble the natives more closely in terms of the occupational distribution than both the earlier cohort (pre-1986) and the later group (after-1986). In part, this may reflect the higher education and skill lever of foreign-born persons who have naturalized. It may be the case that more educated and successful residents in the United States are generally more committed to remaining in the country and are therefore more likely to naturalize. Furthermore, better-educated and skilled persons generally find it less difficult to go through the naturalization process.

Although it is unclear what factors differentiate the naturalized foreign-born from the non-naturalized, it is likely that length of time in the country does play a role in determining their degree of success in the U.S. labor market. Persons who have lived in the country for longer periods have had more time to acquire the labor market characteristics of the native born (language proficiency, skills useful in the united States market, etc), a phenomenon known as labor market assimilation. In general, naturalized foreign-born persons have resided in the country for longer periods for several reasons, including the length of time a person is required to live in the United States before he or she can become naturalized, or as other studies have suggested, naturalized persons tend to represent those who have remained in the United States because of their success, while the less successful migrants are more likely to have left the country.

Wages and Salaries

When comparing the median wages and salaries of the foreign-born and the natives, there are important differences based on period of arrival and citizenship status, as well as by occupation. On the whole, foreign-born persons earn lower median salaries than natives. The median salary for native-born workers is $22,500, in comparison to $18,000 for foreign-born persons.

When dividing the foreign-born based on when they arrived in the country, however, the data show no statistical difference between the median salaries of those who lived in the country longer (since before 1986) and the natives. The CPS also finds no statistical differences in the salaries of the naturalized foreign-born and the natives. Foreign-born persons who arrived more recently or who are not naturalized citizens earned considerably lower salaries than all other groups across most occupational categories.

Table 4. Median Wages and Salaries in 1998 of Adult Native-Born and Foreign-Born Adult Workers by Citizenship Status

Occupational category	Native-born	Foreign-born		Total foreign-born
		Naturalized	Non-naturalized	
Executive/adm./managerial	$36,000	$40,000	$30,774	$36,000
Professional specialties	$34,500	$43,680	$32,000	$35,000
Technicians	$27,000	$30,000	$21,000	$27,000
Precision production/craft/repair	$27,000	$26,000	$18,200	$26,000
Administrative support/clerical	$19,000	$22,000	$15,600	$19,000
Sales	$18,000	$22,000	$14,000	$18,000
Operator/fabricator/laborer	$19,500	$19,000	$14,000	$18,200
Service (non-household)	$11,000	$13,000	$11,700	$11,000
Farming/forestry/fishing	$12,000	$15,000	$10,150	$12,000
Private household	N/A	N/A	$7,000	$5,590
Percent totals	**$22,500**	**$25,000**	**$15,000**	**$22,000**

Note: Adults are defined as all workers, part-time or full-time, and full-year or part-year in the civilian work force who are at least 18 years old. Occupation corresponds to the longest held occupation during the last year.

Source: Table prepared by the Congressional Research Service (CRS) based on analysis of March 1998 Current Population Survey.

Natives earned higher salaries than the foreign-born as a whole in the categories of *precision production, craft, and repair*, and *operators, fabricators, and laborers*. The latter would generally be considered low to medium-skilled blue-collar jobs. In all other occupations, there is no statistically significant difference in the salaries of native-born and foreign-born workers.

On the other hand, naturalized foreign-born citizens earned significantly higher salaries and wages than both natives and non-naturalized foreign-born workers in the categories of *executive, managerial, and administrative* occupations and in *professional specialties*. Only in the case of persons over the age of 36 employed in *executive, managerial, and administrative* occupations was there no significant difference in the median salary of natives and naturalized persons.

Length of residence in the country appears to be an important determinant of success in the U.S. labor market. More recent arrivals are clearly less successful than earlier arrivals and natives. The median salary for those who arrived before 1986 is $21,000, in comparison to $14,500 for the more recent arrivals, and $22,500 for natives.

Table 5. Median Wages and Salaries in 1998 of Adult Native-Born and Foreign-Born Adult Workers by Period of Arrival

Occupational category	All foreign-born		All Foreign-born
	Pre-1986	1986-1998	
Executive/adm./managerial	$37,000	$33,000	$36,000
Professional specialties	$41,000	$34,000	$38,000
Technicians	$30,000	$21,000	$29,000
Precision production/craft/repair	$24,000	$16,000	$20,000
Administrative support/clerical	$20,000	$15,411	$19,500
Sales	$21,000	$12,480	$17,000
Operator/fabricator/laborer	$17,500	$13,000	$15,000
Service (non-household)	$13,000	$10,920	$12,000
Farming/forestry/fishing	$12,000	$10,000	$11,000
Private household	$7,000	$8,000	$8,000
Percent totals	**$21,000**	**$14,500**	**$18,000**

Note: Adults are defined as all workers, part-time or full-time, and full-year or part-year in the civilian work force who are at least 18 years old. Occupation corresponds to the longest held occupation during the last year.

Source: Table prepared by the Congressional Research Service (CRS) based on analysis of March 1998 Current Population Survey.

While age may be a contributing factor for the higher earnings found among the earlier arrivals, it does not alone explain the wage difference between the earlier and later cohort of arrivals. Table 5 shows that when comparing the wages of the earlier (pre-1986) and later (after-1986) cohorts, earlier arrivals earned significantly more than recent arrivals across most age categories. Similarly, naturalized foreign-born persons earned more than the non-naturalized and about the same as natives when controlling for age group.

In general, the non-naturalized foreign-born, as well as the more recent arrivals, earned considerably less than all other groups in most occupations. This may be due to a number of reasons. As mentioned before, naturalization may be a more likely occurrence among the more skilled and educated, as well as among those who have demonstrated a willingness to remain in the country due to professional success. In the case of persons who have lived in the country longer, labor market assimilation may also be a contributing factor for their higher earnings.

Table 6. Median Wages and Salary for Native and Foreign-Born Adults by Age, Period of Arrival and Citizenship Status, 1998

Age Range	Foreign-born Persons					Native-born
	Pre-1986	1986-present	Naturalized	Non-naturalized	Total foreign-born	
18-31	$16,000	$12,480	$17,000	$12,500	$13,250	$15,000
32-44	$22,561	$18,000	$26,000	$17,000	$20,000	$27,000
45-64	$24,000	$15,600	$28,000	$16,000	$21,000	$28,500
=>65	$13,650	$7,600	$13,000	$10,400	$12,000	$9,240
Total	**$21,000**	**$14,500**	**$25,000**	**$15,000**	**$18,000**	**$22,500**

Note: Adults are defined as all workers, part-time or full-time, and full-year or part-year in the civilian work force who are at least 18 years old. Occupation corresponds to the longest held occupation during the last year.

Source: Table prepared by the Congressional Research Service (CRS) based on analysis of 1998 CPS.

As some have suggested, however, it may also be the case that, among those who arrived earlier and have lived longer in the country, the less successful migrants may have left the country, leaving the earlier arrivals with a higher percentage of more successful persons. Similarly, these self-selecting effects may also be present among the naturalized citizens.

Poverty Rates

While the poverty rate among the foreign-born has declined in recent years, it remains considerably higher than the rate found among the native-born population. In 1998, 19.9% of the foreign-born lived below the poverty line, compared to 12.4% of native-born persons. In 1996, the respective percentages were 22.2% and 12.9%.[11]

Poverty rates vary among the foreign-born based on their length of residence in the country, as well as their citizenship status. Among naturalized citizens, 11.4% live below the poverty line, while nearly 25% of the non-naturalized live in poverty. Moreover, of persons that arrived after 1991, 29% live below the poverty line, in comparison to 23.8% of those that arrived between 1986 and 1991, and 18.7% of those arriving between 1980 and 1985. Of the foreign-born that arrived before 1980, only 12.3% live below the poverty line. This would suggest that length of residence in the country is strongly correlated with income.

---

[11] This was taken from a Census Bureau report profiling the foreign-born population in 1996.

As with labor market success, while age may play a factor in the lower incidence of poverty found among the earlier arrivals and naturalized citizens, it alone cannot explain this. It is likely that persons who have lived in the country for longer periods have been better able to approximate the living standards of the rest of the population.

Figure 10. Income Distribution of Native and Foreign-born Persons by Citizenship Status, 1998

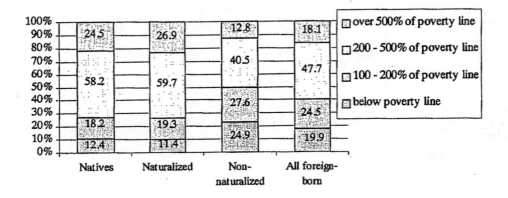

Source: CRS analysis of CPS

Figure 11. Income Distribution of Foreign-born Persons by Period of Arrival, 1998

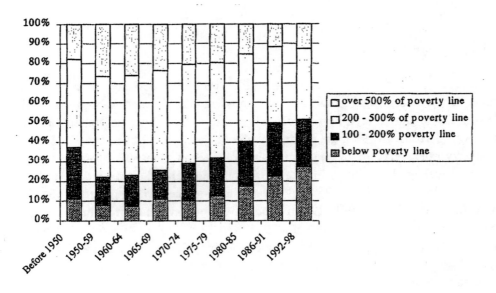

Source: CRS analysis of CPS

INDEX

WEIRD WILDLIFE

MAMMALS

Jen Green

32222000001133

RAINTREE
STECK-VAUGHN
PUBLISHERS

A Harcourt Company

Austin   New York
www.raintreesteckvaughn.com

LOOK FOR THE ELEPHANT

Look for the elephant in boxes like this. Here you will find extra facts, stories, and other interesting information about mammals.

▼ Gorillas live in the tropical forests of Central Africa. Find out more about them on page 24.

Published by Raintree Steck-Vaughn Publishers, an imprint of Steck-Vaughn Company

Designer: Katrina Fiske
Editors: Cathy Grant, Pam Wells
Consultant: Joyce Pope

Library of Congress Cataloging-in-Publication Data
Green, Jen.
  Mammals / Jen Green.
    p. cm.
  Summary: Provides an overview to the variety, distribution, habits, physical characteristics, and more of mammals.

  ISBN 0-7398-4856-9
    1. Mammals—Juvenile literature.
[1. Mammals.] I. Title.

QL706.2 .G74 2002
599—dc21   2001034938

Printed in Hong Kong.
Bound in the United States.
1 2 3 4 5 6 7 8 9 0 LB 05 04 03 02 01

J13Acknowledgments
We wish to thank the following individuals and organizations for their help and assistance and for supplying material in their collections: Bruce Coleman Collection 12 top (Joe McDonald), 17 top (Antonio Manzanares), 22 (Jen & Des Bartlett); Corbis 4 (Kevin Schafer), 5 top (Gallo Images/Nigel J Dennis), 5 (Kevin Schafer), 6 top (Galen Rowell), 8 top (Michael & Patricia Fogden), 9 (Keren Su), 10 bottom Su), 27 (Tom Brakefield), 28 (Tom Brakefield); FLPA 6 bottom (Dembinsky), 7 (Gerard Lacz), 10 top (Gerard Lacz)(Wolfgang Kaehler), 11 (Joe McDonald), 12 bottom (The Purcell Team), 14 (Randy Wells), 15 left (Gallo Images/Nigel J Dennis), 15 Right (Yann Arthus-Bertrand), 17 bottom (Lynda Richardson), 18 bottom (Karl Ammann), 21 (Tom Brakefield), 23 top (Tom Brakefield), 25 (Keren , 13 (Gerard Lacz), 18 top (E Schuiling), 20 top (Minden Pictures), 20 bottom (Silvestris), 26 (Winifried Wisniewski); MPM Images 1, 2, 3, 8 bottom, 16, 23 bottom, 24; NHPA 30 (Roger Tidman), 31 (Gerard Lacz); Oxford Scientific Films 19 (Rudie H Kuiter), 29 (David M Dennis).

CONTENTS

▶ These strange-looking mammals are called manatees. Find out more on page 8.

THE WEIRD WORLD OF MAMMALS

Animals as different as whales, elephants, and mice have one vital thing in common. They are all mammals—members of one of the main groups of animals on Earth.

▲ Some mammals, like this beluga whale, spend their whole lives in water.

The mammal group includes many weird and wonderful creatures. Scaly armadillos, spiky porcupines, long-nosed tapirs, and night-loving bats are all part of this family of animals. There are about 4,000 different kinds of mammals. People are mammals, too.

Mammals vary a lot in size. Blue whales are the largest mammals. A big blue whale weighs 25 times as much as the largest land mammal, the African elephant. The hefty elephant weighs as much as 100 adult people. The world's smallest mammal is Kitti's hog-nosed bat, which has a body the size of a bumblebee!

▶ Apes and monkeys, like proboscis monkeys, belong to a group of mammals called primates. Humans belong to the same group.

LIVE YOUNG

Most mammal mothers give birth to fully formed babies, rather than laying eggs like birds and reptiles. Babies feed on their mother's milk. Adult mammals look after their young and may teach them the skills they need in life.

◀ Many mammal babies stay with their parents for months or even years. Young aardvarks drink their mother's milk for four months.

MAMMALS EVERYWHERE

Mammals can be found all over the world: on dry land, in ponds and streams, and in the oceans. Bats spend part of their lives in the air and monkeys swing through the treetops. Moles live underground.

On land, mammals are found in tropical jungles, pine forests, grasslands, and even high in the mountains. Sheep, cows, and horses are mammals that have been tamed so they can live and work with humans. Dogs and cats share our homes as pets. But most mammals run wild!

▲ Llamas live high in the Andes Mountains in South America. Their thick, fine fur keeps them warm in the icy winds.

◄ The strange-looking star-nosed mole makes its home in an underground burrow. This strong swimmer finds its food in ponds and streams.

▶ **Elephant seals spend most of their lives in the oceans. But they come ashore to breed on rocky beaches. Only the males have swollen snouts that look like elephants' trunks.**

Mammals are warm-blooded. Surprisingly, their body temperature stays about the same even when it is very cold or hot. This means that mammals can survive in harsh places such as icy Arctic wastes and hot, dry deserts. However, keeping an even body temperature uses up lots of energy, so mammals need to eat a lot of food.

INSIDE AND OUT

All mammals have a bony skeleton, though their bodies may be large or small and come in many different shapes. All mammals also have hair covering their bodies, though some don't have very much!

Mammals have similar bodies, however large or small they are. Land mammals all have four limbs, and most have a tail, though humans do not. Dolphins and whales look a lot like fish, but they are also mammals. Their front limbs have developed into flippers, and their back legs have disappeared completely. Their smooth, tapering shape helps them swim through the water easily.

▲ The kinkajou uses its tail as an extra limb to hang onto branches. Other mammals use their tails to flick away flies or to balance when running along tree branches.

◀ Manatees are mammals that dwell in water, like seals, whales, and dolphins. They swim along by beating their powerful tails up and down.

8

The hair on mammals' bodies helps them to keep warm. In cold weather, the hairs stand up to trap a layer of warm air next to the skin. The musk oxen of the Arctic have the longest hair of any mammal. Mammals that live in cold places, such as seals and whales, have an extra layer of fat, called blubber, under their skin. This keeps them warm even in icy water and snow.

▼ All mammals groom or clean their fur to keep it in good condition. Macaque monkeys help one another by removing ticks and fleas.

HIBERNATION

Some mammals survive the winter cold by falling into an amazing deep sleep called hibernation. They hardly breathe, and their hearts beat very slowly. They use little energy. Groundhogs retreat to their burrows to hibernate in autumn. Strangely, all groundhogs wake up on about the same day, usually on February 2.

GETTING A MOVE ON

Mammals move around in many different ways. Some creep along quite slowly. Others swim, fly, hop, or run at great speed.

In African grasslands, cheetahs race along at up to 59 miles per hour (95 kmh). Kangaroos are the fastest mammals on two legs—they are champion hoppers. Killer whales are fastest in the oceans. They swim at speeds of up to 34 miles per hour (55 kmh).

▲ Verreaux's sifaka, a type of lemur, is equally agile in the trees and on the ground.

◀ In the tropical forests of South America, sloths spend long hours sleeping. They move very little. Tiny plants called algae grow in their fur and give it a green color.

▶ Flying squirrels cannot really fly, but they have furry flaps of skin between their front and hind legs that they use for gliding. The outstretched skin acts as a parachute, allowing the squirrel to swoop from tree to tree.

Bats are the only mammals that can truly fly. They glide through the air on skin-covered wings, looking for insects or sweet nectar to eat. Bats are nocturnal—they are awake at night. They spend the daylight hours asleep hanging upside-down.

 ALL KINDS OF FEET

Mammals have differently shaped feet that help them to move around in their surroundings. Elephants have pillarlike legs and feet to support their great weight. A sloth's curved claws are ideal for hooking around branches. Moles have front feet shaped like shovels, which help them burrow through soil.

INCREDIBLE SENSES

Mammals experience the world around them using their senses. The five main senses are sight, hearing, smell, taste, and touch.

▲ A little brown bat swoops among the branches, guided by echolocation.

Humans most often use sight to find out about their surroundings. Dogs, foxes, and wolves rely on their keen senses of hearing and smell instead. A bloodhound can track someone down just by following the smell of his or her footprints.

Bushbabies are small, monkeylike creatures. They live in the forests of Africa. Their huge eyes and large, sensitive ears help them to catch flying insects even in dim light.

◄ Like apes, monkeys, and humans, bushbabies see in color. Most other mammals probably see in black and white.

KEEN HEARING

Many mammals have keen sight and hearing to alert them to the danger of predators. Jackrabbits listen for enemies with large ears that turn a round to pinpoint sounds. Mammals are the only animals to have ears placed on the outside of their heads. Lions can turn their ears in different directions to pick up sounds when they hunt.

Sight is a lot less important to other mammals who hunt in darkness or in murky water. Bats and dolphins use an amazing super-sense called **echolocation** to catch their prey. They make high-pitched sounds when they are hunting. These sounds bounce off animals close by, and the bat or dolphin can hear the returning echo. This helps them to find their prey. Echolocation also helps bats to move around easily in the dark.

In Australia, duck-billed platypuses hunt in muddy streams and rivers. They search for worms, fish, and insects with their extremely sensitive bills, or beaks.

▼ The duck-billed platypus uses its amazing beak to sense tiny electrical charges given off by swimming creatures. This mammal looks so weird that when the first platypuses were brought to Europe, experts thought they were fakes.

A Bite to Eat

Mammals need to eat a lot of food just to keep going. Many, including cows, deer, and rabbits, are plant eaters, or herbivores. Others are fierce meat-eating hunters, or carnivores, and they kill animals for food.

Giraffes, the tallest mammals, are plant eaters. They use their long necks to reach up and pluck tender leaves from tall trees. Leaves, grass, and other plant foods are not very nourishing, so giraffes and other plant-eating mammals have to spend a lot of time feeding just to stay alive.

Most animals eat either plants or animals, but pigs, bears, chimpanzees, and humans can eat both. They are called omnivores.

◀ A few types of mammals are bold and powerful enough to kill a person. The tiger is one such animal.

◀ The aye-aye is a strange lemur from the woods of Madagascar, an island off the southeast coast of Africa. It has an extra-long, thin middle finger that it uses to hook out juicy insects from under tree bark.

▶ Giraffes are extraordinary creatures with incredibly long necks, slender legs, and mottled coloring. The first Europeans to see them in Africa could hardly believe their eyes.

Many meat-eating mammals have special colors and markings on their fur that help them hide in their natural surroundings. This is called camouflage, or disguise, and means the hunting animal can creep up on its prey without being seen. In a zoo, a tiger's black-and-orange coat may stand out and look tigerlike, but the same stripes conceal the big cat in its jungle home.

WHAT'S ON THE MENU?
All kinds of creatures are hunted by mammals. Big cats such as lions and tigers prey on other mammals and birds, too. Shrews and hedgehogs eat worms and insects. Marsh mongooses hunt crabs, fish, frogs, and snakes.

KEEPING SAFE

Many mammals have lots of enemies in the wild—including other mammals. They must be alert to escape possible attackers. Some swim, hop, or run away as quickly as possible. Others have secret weapons or tricks that they use to escape or hide from their enemies.

▼ The porcupine's prickly spines protect it from predators.

Many mammals use camouflage to help them blend in with their surroundings and hide from danger. A zebra's stripes hide it among the grasses of the African plains. A deer's spotted coat helps conceal it in shady woods.

THE EYES HAVE IT

The position of a mammal's eyes can tell you if it is a creature that hunts or one that is hunted. Deer and rabbits, for example, have eyes set on the sides of their heads, so they can spot danger from all around. Predators, such as cats, have eyes that look forward so they can focus and pounce on their prey.

▶ The armadillo is built like a tank, with a covering of tough, bony plates all over its upper body. When threatened, it rolls into a ball to protect its soft belly.

Some mammals have natural armor that protects them when they are threatened. Porcupines and hedgehogs are covered with sharp spines. When cornered, the porcupine turns the sharp spikes on its back toward its enemy and backs away! But a hedgehog in a tight spot rolls itself into a spiny ball. Hedgehogs are found in Europe, Asia, and Africa.

◀ The Virginia opossum has a clever trick to get out of trouble. If a predator spots it, it drops to the ground and lies still, playing dead. Most predators will not touch dead animals, so they move on.

17

PRODUCING BABIES

Like other animals, one of the main goals in a mammal's life is to produce young. Most baby mammals develop inside their mother's body. There are a few strange animals who produce young in other ways.

In the breeding season, male and female mammals meet to mate. Many males create special areas called territories, where they show off to the opposite sex. Some males get into terrible battles with their rivals to find out who is strongest. Only the winners get the chance to mate.

▲ This female tenrec has an unusually large litter, or group of young. She can rear up to 24 young. Tenrecs live on the island of Madagascar.

▶ Male hippos fight for the right to mate and lead the herd of females. Rivals open their jaws wide to frighten one another. Then they lunge forward and attack their opponent with their teeth.

18

▲ The female echidna lays a single leathery egg that develops inside a skin pouch on her belly. The baby hatches after about ten days.

GROWING INTO A BABY

Baby mammals spend different amounts of time in the womb before they are ready to be born. This time is called **gestation**. Mice take less than three weeks to grow; humans take nine months. Asian elephants take over 20 months, the longest time of all.

Most baby mammals develop inside their mother's womb, where they are fed by an organ called the placenta. They are born fully formed. The group of marsupials that includes kangaroos develop in a different way. The baby kangaroo is born early, when it is still tiny and unfinished. It crawls up into the warm pouch on its mother's belly, where it finishes growing.

A third, small group of mammals called monotremes have even more unusual breeding habits. They lay eggs instead of giving birth to live babies like other mammals. Of 4,000 different mammals, only three are monotremes: the platypus and two species of echidnas.

GROWING UP

This baby kangaroo, or joey, is finishing its development in its mother's pouch.

Most animals don't look after their young. They just lay their eggs and leave. When they are born, the new babies can look after themselves. Mammals are different. Many spend weeks or even years raising their young. Parents help them to learn skills they will need in adult life.

Mammals are the only animals that produce food for their babies from their own bodies. All baby mammals feed on their mother's milk. The milk contains all the nourishment that the baby needs.

Mouse opossums are South American marsupials. Females give birth to about ten tiny, helpless babies. They continue to grow in their mother's pouch and later ride around on her back.

▲ These young red fox cubs are play-fighting. This helps them to grow stronger and teaches them hunting skills.

At birth, some mammal babies, such as mice, are bald, blind, and helpless. Others, including newborn lambs and calves, are furry and can stand and walk right away.

Baby mammals are born knowing how to do certain things, such as drink their mother's milk. Other skills have to be learned. The young learn hunting and other skills by watching their parents and by practicing. Playing with brothers and sisters also helps to strengthen muscles and develop hunting skills.

 TIME TO GROW UP

Small mammals, such as mice, produce many babies that grow up very quickly. In just a few weeks, the young are fully grown and able to produce babies themselves. Larger mammals have fewer babies that grow up much more slowly. Human children take the longest time of all to grow up, perhaps because we have so much to learn.

HAPPY FAMILIES

Some mammals live alone, except when the females are raising babies. Others spend most or all of their lives in a group.

Group life provides safety for all kinds of mammals, especially those that are hunted by predators. On the grasslands of Africa, zebras and antelopes live in big herds. While the herd is grazing, each animal looks up from time to time to check for danger. It warns the others if it sees a threat approaching. Then the whole herd gallops off.

▼ Young elephants grow up in a herd. There are about ten closely related females and their babies. Aunts and grown-up cousins help with baby care. Females stay with the herd when they grow up. Males leave to join a small group of males or live on their own.

Dolphins live and hunt in a group called a school. They whistle to one another to organize their movements as they spread out to surround a shoal, or large group, of fish.

Meerkats live in large underground colonies. To watch for danger, they rear right up on their back legs.

WHAT'S IN A NAME?

Mammal groups have different names. A group of lions is called a pride. Killer whales hunt in a pod, dolphins in a school. Monkeys live in troupes. Bats roost in colonies. Can you find out any other names of mammal groups?

Among lions, wolves, and dolphins, the group is also a hunting party. Group members work together to hunt faster or larger prey than they could on their own. It is mainly female lions who do the hunting. African hunting dogs band together to tackle prey as large as zebras and wildebeest.

MAMMALS IN DANGER

Wild mammals face many natural dangers, including storms, droughts, and predators. Today, however, the biggest danger comes from human beings. Some of the weirdest, wildest mammals are now in danger of dying out altogether, mainly because of humans.

For centuries, people have hunted mammals, such as whales, deer, and buffalo, for meat. Cheetahs and other big cats have been shot for their beautiful skins. Wild mammals like rhinos and tigers have been killed because people think they are dangerous. Now many of these amazing creatures are very rare.

▼ A mountain gorilla sleeps in the grass in a forest in Rwanda. Mountain gorillas are in danger of dying out because they are hunted by people.

HABITAT DESTRUCTION

Humans often destroy the homes of other mammals when they clear forests and grasslands to build new towns and roads. As more and more natural places are destroyed there is less and less space for wild mammals to live safely. This is called habitat destruction.

Today, more people are starting to care that beautiful mammals, such as pandas and gorillas, may die out altogether. All over the world, parks and preserves have been set up to help them survive.

Some rare mammals have been bred in zoos and then released into the wild. You can help by sponsoring a rare mammal or joining a conservation group. See page 31.

▶ Giant pandas live in remote mountain forests in China. They are now very scarce in the wild.

FACTS ABOUT WEIRD MAMMALS

The blue whale

This giant whale is the world's largest mammal. A big blue whale weighs 150 tons and may be 105 feet (32 m) long. Female whales grow bigger than the males.

Elephants

These are the largest land mammals, standing up to 11.5 feet (3.5 m) high and weighing up to 6.6 tons. The rhinoceros is the second-largest mammal found on land.

Giraffes

These long-necked animals are the world's tallest mammals, towering up to 19 feet (5.8 m). They strip the tender leaves from the acacias and scrub that grow in Africa.

Kitti's hog-nosed bat

This bat is the world's smallest mammal and comes from Thailand. The tiny creature weighs just 0.07 ounce (2 g) and has a wingspan of 6 inches (15 cm). Its body is the size of a bumblebee.

Polar bears

The skin of the polar bear is actually black. This is because black absorbs heat better than paler colors, and allows the bear to get some heat from the Arctic sun.

▼ Walrus are the heaviest members of the seal family. Big males weigh up to 3,527 pounds (1600 kg). Both sexes have long tusks.

Siberian tigers

These are the world's largest cats, measuring up to 10 feet (3.15 m) long from the nose to the tip of the tail. Unfortunately, these beautiful mammals are now very rare.

Giant primates

Gorillas are the largest primates—members of the ape and monkey group that includes humans. A male lowland gorilla stands up to 6 feet (1.8 m) tall, shorter than the tallest human, but weighs up to 386 pounds (175 kg).

South American capybara

This is the world's largest rodent (the mammal group that includes rats, mice, and squirrels). It grows up to 4.6 feet (1.4 m) long. The northern pygmy mouse from North America is one of the smallest rodents.

► Mandrills are large, heavy monkeys from Africa. Only the male has bright colors on his nose and cheeks.

Speedy cheetah

The cheetah is the fastest short-distance runner. But it tires quite quickly. This large cat puts on a burst of speed to overtake prey.

The three-toed sloth

This odd creature comes from South America and is the world's slowest mammal. It spends four-fifths of its life sleeping.

Humans

Humans live longer than any other mammals, sometimes reaching ages of 105 or more.

Giant anteater

This creature has a very long tongue—up to 24 inches (60 cm) long. It uses it to slurp up ants and termites, and eats up to 30,000 insects a day.

Sperm whales

These whales hold the record as the deepest divers among mammals. These large whales are thought to descend to depths of 9,843 feet (3000 m) when hunting deep-sea prey.

Arctic ground squirrels

These animals spend longer in hibernation than any other mammal. In icy northern lands they spend up to nine months asleep.

WORDS ABOUT WEIRD MAMMALS

blubber (BLUH-bur)
A fatty layer found under the skin of some mammals, such as seals and whales. It keeps them warm in cold water.

camouflage (KAM-uh-flahzh)
The colors and patterns on a mammal's fur that help it to blend in with everything around it. This way it can hide from enemies or sneak up on its prey.

carnivore (KAR-nuh-vor)
An animal that eats the flesh of other animals.

▼ Tasmanian devils are marsupials from the island of Tasmania, south of Australia. They are mainly active at night.

echolocation (ek-oh-loh-KAY-shuhn)
Bats use high-pitched sounds when they hunt. The sounds bounce off animals close by and echo back to the bat. This way the bat can find its prey.

gestation (je-STAY-shuhn)
The carrying of the young.

habitat (HAB-uh-tat)
The particular place where a mammal lives, such as a jungle or a desert.

hatch (hach)
When a fully developed baby animal breaks out of its shell.

herbivore (HUR-bur-vor)
An animal that eats plants.

hibernation (HYE-bur-na-shuhn)
Almost a deathlike state that allows mammals to survive the winter cold. It involves a complete physical change including heartbeat, breathing, and lower body temperature.

litter (LIT-ur)
A group of young all born to a female mammal at once.

mammal (MAM-uhl)
One of the group of animals that have a bony skeleton, fur on their bodies, and glands that produce milk for the young to feed on.

marsupial (mar-SOO-pee-uhl)
One of a group of mammals whose young are born at a very early stage and finish developing in their mother's pouch.

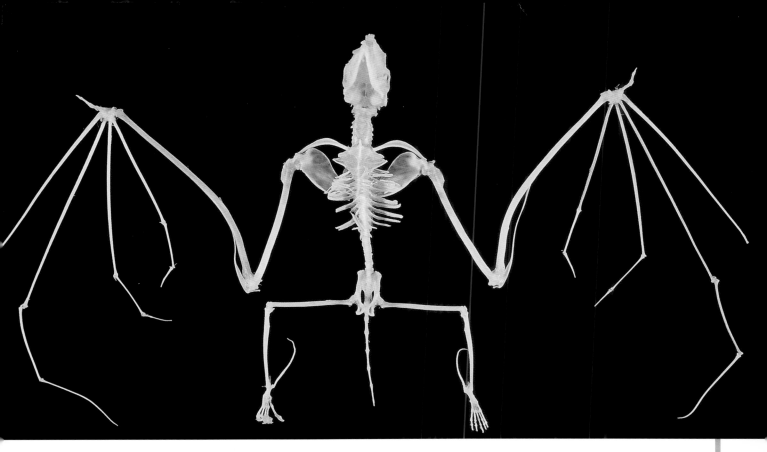

▲ Like all mammals, bats have a bony skeleton to support their bodies.

monotreme (MON-uh-treem)
One of a small group of mammals that lay eggs instead of giving birth to live young.

nocturnal (nok-TUR-nuhl)
An animal that rests by day and is active at night.

predator (PRED-uh-tur)
An animal, such as a tiger or leopard, that catches and kills other animals for food.

prey (pray)
An animal that is hunted for food, such as a rabbit that is hunted by eagles.

primate (PRYE-mate)
A member of the group of mammals that includes apes, monkeys, and humans.

rodent (ROHD-uhnt)
One of the large group of mammals that have chisel-shaped front teeth designed for gnawing plants.

skeleton (SKEL-uh-tuhn)
The bony framework that supports the bodies of animals, such as mammals and birds.

species (SPEE-sheez)
A particular type of animal. The duck-billed platypus is a species of mammal. There are about 4,000 different species of mammals in all.

sponsor (SPON-sur)
To pay for something, usually for a good cause. If you sponsor a rare mammal, you will be helping its species survive.

warm-blooded (WORM-BLUHD-id)
Describes an animal whose body temperature stays about the same, whatever the temperature of its surroundings. Mammals and birds are warm-blooded animals.

How to Spot Weird Mammals

The countryside and even the city where you live is home to all kinds of mammals. Get to know the species in your area by using these hints and tips.

A guidebook of local wildlife will give you details of the mammals that live locally. Some are out and about by day. Others only emerge to look for food at night.

MAMMAL WATCHING
Wear warm, waterproof clothing, in dull colors if possible, when you go mammal watching. Always take an adult with you to keep you safe. Binoculars will help you to study distant mammals. A camping mat will keep you dry on the ground.

▼ These children are mammal watching with an adult.

Wild mammals are naturally shy and will run away if they see you. Approach them downwind (with the wind blowing in your face) so they don't pick up your scent. Move slowly and carefully. The best way to study mammals is to hide behind a tree or bush, and keep very still and quiet!

Find out about local mammals by looking for clues they leave behind them—tufts of hair caught on barbed wire, bones, and droppings. Look out for paw prints in wet soil, by the riverbank, or in fresh snow. Your guidebook will help you to identify the mammals that left them.

Some of the weirdest mammals featured in this book may not live in your local area. The best way to see them may be to visit a zoo.

You can also study how mammals behave by watching your pets, or just look in the mirror!

CONSERVATION GROUPS

World Wildlife Fund Website

www.worldwildlife.org/fun/kids.cfm

Kid's Stuff page gives fun activities to learn more about protecting animals and our planet.

MAMMAL WEBSITES

If you have access to the Internet, there are lots of websites where you can try to find out more about mammals.

Websites change from time to time, so don't worry if you can't find some of these. You can search for sites with

▲ A mother cat carries one of her kittens by holding it gently in her mouth.

your favorite mammals using any search engine. Include the mammal's scientific (Latin) name if you know it, to narrow your search.

WWF's endangered species page for rare mammals: www.worldwildlife.org/endangered species

Animal Planet www.animal.discovery.mammals

Smithsonian National Museum of Natural History, Division of Mammals www.mnh.si.edu/museum/VirtualTour/vttemp.html

Take a Virtual Tour of the mammal exhibitions at the Smithsonian National Museum.

INDEX

© Belitha Press Ltd. 2002